PENGUIN BOOKS

EXILE'S RETURN

Malcolm Cowley grew up in Pittsburgh, Pennsylvania, and interrupted his undergraduate career at Harvard to drive an ambulance during World War I. He moved to New York City in 1919 and worked as an editor of *The New Republic* from 1929 to 1944. He served as president of the National Institute of Arts and Letters from 1956 to 1959 and from 1962 to 1965 and was chancellor of the American Academy of Arts and Letters from 1966 to 1976. He wrote numerous books of literary criticism, essays, and poetry, and edited many collections and anthologies. Among his many awards and honors were the Gold Medal for Belles Lettres and Criticism from the American Academy and Institute of Arts and Letters and the Hubbell Medal of the Modern Language Association for service to the study of American literature. Until his death in March, 1989, Mr. Cowley lived with his wife, Muriel, in Sherman, Connecticut.

Also by Malcolm Cowley

*—And I Worked at the Writer's Trade:
Chapters of Literary History, 1918–1978

Black Cargoes:
The Story of the Atlantic Slave Trade
(with Daniel P. Mannix)

*Blue Juniata:
Collected Poems

Books That Changed Our Minds (with Bernard Smith)

*The Dream of the Golden Mountains:
Remembering the 1930s

Dry Season (poems)

*The Faulkner-Cowley File:
Letters and Memories, 1944–1962

*The Flower and the Leaf

The Literary Situation

A Many-Windowed House:
Collected Essays on American Writers and American Writing

*A Second Flowering:
Works and Days of the Lost Generation

Think Back on Us . . . :
A Contemporary Chronicle of the 1930s

Unshaken Friend:
A Profile of Maxwell Perkins

*The View From 80

Edited by Malcolm Cowley

After the Genteel Tradition:
American Writers 1910–1930 (with others)

The Complete Walt Whitman

Fitzgerald and the Jazz Age (with Robert Cowley)

*Leaves of Grass

*The Portable Faulkner

*The Portable Hawthorne

*The Portable Hemingway

The Stories of F. Scott Fitzgerald

*The Viking Critical Library

*Writers at Work:
The Paris Review Interviews (First Series)

*Available from Penguin Books

Exile's
Return

A Literary Odyssey of the 1920s

by Malcolm Cowley

PENGUIN BOOKS

PENGUIN BOOKS
Published by the Penguin Group
Penguin Books USA Inc.,
375 Hudson Street, New York, New York 10014, U.S.A.
Penguin Books Ltd, 27 Wrights Lane,
London W8 5TZ, England
Penguin Books Australia Ltd, Ringwood,
Victoria, Australia
Penguin Books Canada Ltd, 10 Alcorn Avenue,
Toronto, Ontario, Canada M4V 3B2
Penguin Books (N.Z.) Ltd, 182–190 Wairau Road,
Auckland 10, New Zealand

Penguin Books Ltd, Registered Offices:
Harmondsworth, Middlesex, England

First published in the United States of America by
Viking Penguin Inc. 1951
Viking Compass Edition published 1956
Reprinted 1959, 1961, 1962, 1964, 1965,
1966, 1967, 1968, 1969 (twice), 1970,
1971, 1972, 1973 (twice), 1974, 1975
Published in Penguin Books 1976

9   10

LIBRARY OF CONGRESS CATALOGING IN PUBLICATION DATA
Cowley, Malcolm, 1898–1989.
Exile's return.
Reprint of the 1956 ed. published by
The Viking Press, New York.
Includes index.
1. Authors, American—20th century—Biography.
2. American literature—20th century—History and
criticism. 3. Cowley, Malcolm, 1898–1989—Biography—
Youth. I. Title.
(PS1 29.c6   1976)   811'.5'2 (B)   76-26484
ISBN 0 14 00.4392 6

Printed in the United States of America
Set in Granjon

Contents

Exile's Return

to Muriel

Prologue: The Lost Generation

This book is the story to 1930 of what used to be called the lost generation of American writers. It was Gertrude Stein who first applied the phrase to them. "You are all a lost generation," she said to Ernest Hemingway, and Hemingway used the remark as an inscription for his first novel. It was a good novel and became a craze—young men tried to get as imperturbably drunk as the hero, young women of good families took a succession of lovers in the same heartbroken fashion as the heroine, they all talked like Hemingway characters and the name was fixed. I don't think there was any self-pity in it. Scott Fitzgerald sometimes pitied himself, and with reason. Hart Crane used to say that he was "caught like a rat in a trap"; but neither Crane nor Fitzgerald talked about being part of a lost generation. Most of those who used the phrase about themselves were a little younger and knew they were boasting. They were like Kipling's gentlemen rankers out on a spree and they wanted to have it understood that they truly belonged "To the legion of the lost ones, to the cohort of the damned." Later they learned to speak the phrase apologetically, as if in quotation marks, and still later it was applied to other age groups, each of which was described in turn as being the real lost generation; none genuine without the trademark. In the beginning, however, when the phrase was applied to young writers born in the years around 1900, it was as useful as any half-accurate tag could be.

It was useful to older persons because they had been looking for words to express their uneasy feeling that postwar youth —"flaming youth"—had an outlook on life that was different from their own. Now they didn't have to be uneasy; they could read about the latest affront to social standards or to literary conventions and merely say, "That's the lost generation." But the phrase was also useful to the youngsters. They had grown up and gone to college during a period of rapid change when time in itself seemed more important than the influence of class or locality. Now at last they had a slogan that proclaimed their feeling of separation from older writers and of kinship with one another. In the slogan the noun was more important than the adjective. They might or might not be lost, the future would decide that point; but they had already had the common adventures and formed the common attitude that made it possible to describe them as a generation.

In that respect, as in the attitude itself, they were different from the writers who preceded them. Sectional and local influences were relatively more important during the years before 1900. Two New England writers born fifteen or twenty years apart—Emerson and Thoreau, for example—might bear more resemblance to each other than either bore to a Virginian or a New Yorker of his own age; compare Emerson and Poe, or Thoreau and Whitman. Literature was not yet centered in New York; indeed, it had no center on this side of the ocean. There was a Knickerbocker School, there was a Concord School, there was a Charleston School; later there would be a Hoosier School, a Chicago School. Men of every age belonged to the first three and might have belonged to the others, had these not been founded at a time when writers were drifting to the metropolis.

Publishing, like finance and the theater, was becoming centralized after 1900. Regional traditions were dying out; all regions were being transformed into a great unified market for motorcars and Ivory soap and ready-to-wear clothes. The process continued during the childhood of the new generation of writers. Whether they grew up in New England, the Midwest, the Southwest or on the Pacific Coast, their environment was almost the same; it was a little different in the Old South, which had kept some of its local manners but was losing them. The childhood of these writers was less affected by geography than it was by the financial situation of their parents, yet even that was fairly uniform. A few of the writers came from wealthy families, a very few from the slums. Most of them were the children of doctors, small lawyers, prosperous farmers or struggling businessmen—of families whose incomes in those days of cheaper living were between two thousand and perhaps eight thousand dollars a year. Since their playmates were also middle-class they had the illusion of belonging to a great classless society.

All but a handful were pupils in the public schools, where they studied the same textbooks, sang the same songs and revolted rather tamely against the same restrictions. At the colleges they attended, usually some distance from their homes, they were divested of their local peculiarities, taught to speak a standardized American English and introduced to the world of international learning. Soon they would be leaving for the army in France, where they would be subjected together to a sudden diversity of emotions: boredom, fear, excitement, pride, aloofness and curiosity. During the drab peacemaking at Versailles they would suffer from the same collapse of emotions. They would go back into civilian life almost as if they were soldiers on a long furlough.

Some of them would go to Greenwich Village to begin the long adventure of the 1920s. Only long afterward could the period be described, in Scott Fitzgerald's phrase, as "the greatest, gaudiest spree in history." At first it promised to be something quite different, a period of social and moral reaction. The Prohibition Amendment had gone into effect in January 1920, strikes were being broken all over the country, and meanwhile Greenwich Village was full of plain-clothes dicks from the Vice Squad and the Bomb Squad. I remember that many young women were arrested and charged with prostitution because the dicks had seen them smoking cigarettes in the street, and I remember that innocent tea-rooms were raided because they were thought to harbor dangerous Reds. Then Harding was elected, the Red scare was forgotten and, after a sharp recession in 1921, the country started out to make money; it was the new era of installment buying and universal salesmanship. The young writers couldn't buy luxuries even on the installment plan. They didn't want to advertise or sell them or write stories in which salesmen were the romantic heroes. Feeling like aliens in the commercial world, they sailed for Europe as soon as they had money enough to pay for their steamer tickets.

Nor would this be the end of their adventures in common. Until they were thirty most of them would follow a geographical pattern of life, one that could be suggested briefly by the names of two cities and a state: New York, Paris, Connecticut. After leaving Greenwich Village they would live in Montparnasse (or its suburbs in Normandy and on the Riviera), and some of them would stay there year after year in what promised to be a permanent exile. Others would go back to New York, then settle in a Connecticut farmhouse with their books, a portable typewriter and the best intentions. Whether they were at home or abroad in 1929, most of them would have found a place in the literary world and would be earning a fairly steady income. The depression would be another common experience, almost as shattering as the war.

I am speaking of the young men and women who graduated from college, or might have graduated, between 1915, say, and 1922. They were never united into a single group or school. Instead they included several loosely defined and vaguely hostile groups, in addition to many individuals who differed with every group among their contemporaries; the fact is that all of them differed constantly with all the others. They all felt, however, a sharper sense of difference in regard to writers older than themselves who hadn't shared their adventures. It was as if the others had never undergone the same initiatory rites and had never been admitted to the same broad confraternity. In a strict sense the new writers formed what is known as a literary generation.

Their sense of being different has been expressed time and again in the books they wrote. Take, for example, the second paragraph of a story by Scott Fitzgerald, "The Scandal Detectives," in which he is describing an episode from his boyhood:

Some generations are close to those that succeed them; between others the gulf is infinite and unbridgeable. Mrs. Buckner—a woman of character, a member of Society in a large Middle Western city—carrying a pitcher of fruit lemonade through her own spacious back yard, was progressing across a hundred years. Her own thoughts would have been comprehensible to her great-grandmother; what was happening in a room above the stable would have been entirely unintelligible to them both. In what had once served as the coachman's sleeping apartment, her son and a friend were not behaving in a normal manner, but were, so to speak, experimenting in a void. They were making the first tentative combinations of the ideas and materials they found ready at their hands—ideas destined to become, in future years, first articulate, then startling and finally commonplace. At the moment she called up to them they were sitting with disarming quiet upon the still unhatched eggs of the mid-twentieth century.

Boys like Ripley Buckner and his friend—who was Scott Fitzgerald under another name—were born shortly before 1900. Since they were in their teens when the twentieth century was also in its teens, it is no wonder that they fell into the habit of identifying themselves with the century. They retained the habit until they—and the century—were well along in the thirties. As representatives of a new age they had a sense of being somehow unique; one catches an echo of it in the affectionate fashion in which Fitzgerald often used the phrase "my contemporaries." It seems to me now that the feeling was insufficiently grounded in fact and that Mrs. Buckner, for example, was closer to her son and his friend than the youngsters realized. Edith Wharton was of Mrs. Buckner's age and she could understand Fitzgerald perhaps better than he understood Mrs. Wharton. Going farther back, many young writers of the 1890s had also been in revolt and had tried to introduce European standards of art and conduct into American literature; they too were a lost generation (and more tragically lost than their successors). The postwar writers, in their feeling that their experiences were unique, revealed their ignorance of the American past. On the other hand, the feeling was real in itself, however ill grounded, and it made them regard all other members of their own age group, whether artists or athletes or businessmen, as belonging to a sort of secret order, with songs and passwords, leagued in rebellion against the stuffy people who were misruling the world.

They were not a lost generation in the sense of being unfortunate or thwarted, like the young writers of the 1890s. The truth was that they had an easy time of it, even as compared with the writers who immediately preceded them. Dreiser, Anderson, Robinson, Masters and Sandburg were all in their forties before they were able to devote most of their time to writing; Sinclair Lewis was thirty-five before he made his first success with *Main Street*. It was different with the new group of writers. Largely as a result of what the older group had accomplished, their public was ready for them and they weren't forced to waste years working in a custom house, like Robinson, or writing advertising copy, like Anderson. At the age of twenty-four Fitzgerald was earning eighteen thousand dollars a year with his stories and novels. Hemingway, Wilder, Dos Passos and Louis Bromfield were internationally known novelists before they were thirty. They had a chance which the older men lacked to develop their craftsmanship in book after book; from the very first they were professionals.

Yet in spite of their opportunities and their achievements the generation deserved for a long time the adjective that Gertrude Stein had applied to it. The reasons aren't hard to find. It was lost, first of all, because it was uprooted, schooled away and almost wrenched away from its attachment to any region or tradition. It was lost because its training had prepared it for another world than existed after the war (and because the war prepared it only for travel and excitement). It was lost because it tried to live in exile. It was lost because it accepted no older guides to conduct and because it had formed a false picture of society and the writer's place in it. The generation belonged to a period of transition from values already fixed to values that had to be created. Its members began by writing for magazines with names like *transition, Broom* (to make a clean sweep of it), *1924, This Quarter* (existing in the pure present), *S 4 N, Secession.* They were seceding from the old and yet could adhere to nothing new; they groped their way toward another scheme of life, as yet undefined; in the midst of their doubts and uneasy gestures of defiance they felt homesick for the certainties of childhood. It was not by accident that their early books were almost all nostalgic, full of the wish to recapture some remembered thing. In Paris or Pamplona, writing, drinking, watching bullfights or making love, they continued to desire a Kentucky hill cabin, a farmhouse in Iowa or Wisconsin, the Michigan woods, the blue Juniata, a country they had "lost, ah, lost," as Thomas Wolfe kept saying; a home to which they couldn't go back.

I wrote this book almost twenty years ago. At the time I was trying to set down the story of the lost generation while its adventures were still fresh in my mind. I wanted to tell how it earned its name and tried to live up to it, then how it ceased to be lost, how, in a sense, it found itself. Since I had shared in many of the adventures I planned to tell a little of my own story, but only as illustration of what had happened to others. Essentially what I wanted to write was less a record of events than a narrative of ideas. But the ideas would be of a certain type: they were not the ones that people thought they held at the time or consciously expressed in books and book reviews; they were rather the ideas that half-unconsciously guided their actions, the ideas that they lived and wrote by. In other words I was trying to write something broader in scope than a literary history. Ideas or purposes of this nature are always connected with a general situation that is social and economic before becoming literary. They react on the situation that produced them, they conflict with one another and they end by affecting the lives of many who never regarded themselves as literary or artistic —for example, in the late 1920s there were people all over the country who had never been to New York and yet were acting and talking like Greenwich Villagers. Writers don't exist in a vacuum; they have masters and disciples and casual readers; in periods of change they are more sensitive and barometric than the other professions. So, the story of the lost generation and its return from exile would be something else besides; it would help to suggest the story of the American educated classes, what some of them thought about in the boom days and how they reached the end of an era.

The book that was published in 1934 fell considerably short of those aims, and I am grateful to the Viking Press for giving me this opportunity to revise it. I hate to write and love to revise, and the first edition of *Exile's Return* gave me plenty of scope for practicing my favorite trade of revisionist. When I re-read the book carefully for the first time in years, I realized how many gaps there were in the story. The chapter on Harry Crosby was one example; it had meaning in itself but I had failed to show its connection with the rest of the narrative. The intimate reason for that failure was clear enough, in 1951; I had written at length about the life of Harry Crosby, whom I scarcely knew, in order to avoid discussing the more recent death of Hart Crane, whom I knew so well that I still couldn't bear to write about him.

The whole conclusion of the book was out of scale with the beginning; and there were also the political opinions that intruded into the narrative. I had to explain to myself, before explaining to the reader, that the book was written in the trough of the depression, when there seemed to be an economic or political explanation for everything that happened to human be-ings. "The trough of the depression," I have just said, taking the first phrase that came into my mind; but actually the years 1933 and 1934 were a madly hopeful time when it seemed that great changes in the economic system were already under way. Russia in those days didn't impress us as a despotism or as the great antagonist in a struggle for world power; it was busy within its own boundaries trying to create what promised to be a hap-pier future. "We are changing the world!" the Young Pioneers used to chant as they marched through the streets of Moscow. Here too it seemed that everybody was trying to change the world and create the future; it was the special pride and pre-sumption of the period. We hadn't learned then—nor have most of our statesmen learned today—that human society is neces-sarily imperfect and may disappear from the earth unless it comes to accept what T. S. Eliot calls "the permanent conditions upon which God allows us to live upon this planet."

Opinions about the future of society are political opinions.

There were not many of them in the book I wrote in 1934, but there were too many for a narrative that dealt with the 1920s, when writers were trying to be unconcerned with politics, and I have omitted most of them from the new edition. I have expanded the last part of the book, to bring it into scale with the beginning (besides putting Harry Crosby into the right perspective), and I have written a new epilogue to round out the story. On the other hand, while adding new episodes here and there, I have left most of the narrative untouched, out of a feeling that myself in 1934 had as good a right to be heard as myself today; where he went wrong I would rather have others correct him. It seems to me now that many characters in the story, myself included, did very foolish things—but perhaps the young writers of the present age aren't young or foolish enough and, once out of college and the army, settle down too safely to earning a sensible living. Moreover, there is this to say about the foolishness of writers in the 1920s, that even the worst of it caused no suffering except to the perpetrators of the foolishness and their immediate families. It wasn't like the statesmen's high-principled foolishness of later years, in all countries, which has left them in office while bringing the rest of us to the brink of something we aren't prepared to face.

I: Mansions in the Air

1: Blue Juniata

Somewhere the turn of a dirt road or the unexpected crest of a hill reveals your own childhood, the fields where you once played barefoot, the kindly trees, the landscape by which all others are measured and condemned. Here, under the hemlocks, is a spring. Follow the thread of water as it winds downward, first among moss, then lost in sweetfern or briers, and soon you will see the bottom lands, the scattered comfortable houses, the flat cornfields along the creek, the hillside pastures where the whitetop bends in alternate waves of cream white and leaf green. The Schoharie Valley in August . . . or perhaps what we find is an Appalachian parade of mountains rank on rank: the first ridge is a shadowy green, the second a deep blue; the ridges behind it grow fainter and fainter, till the last is indistinguishable from the long cloud advancing to hide and drench the mountains, flood the parallel creeks, and set the millwheels turning in the hollows and coves. Or perhaps— our childhoods differ—we are on a low bluff overlooking the Cumberland. Northward into Kentucky, south into middle Tennessee, the river lands continue with their bluffs, their bottoms, their red-clay gullies, their cedars dotting the hillsides like totem poles. It is November: smoke rises from lonely tobacco barns; a hound bays from the fields where corn stands yellow in the shock.

Perhaps our boyhood is a stream in northern Michigan, Big Two-Hearted River, flowing through burned-over lands dotted with islands of pine into a tamarack swamp. The water is swift and chill in July; a trout lurks in a hollow log, ready to take the grasshopper floating toward him at the end of your line. Perhaps we remember a fat farm in Wisconsin, or a Nebraska prairie, or a plantation house among the canebrakes. Wherever it lies, the country is our own; its people speak our language, recognize our values, yes, and our grandmother's eyes, our uncle's trick of pausing in a discussion to make a point impressive. "The Hopkinses was alluz an arguin' family," they say, and suddenly you laugh with a feeling of tension relaxed and pretenses vanished. This is your home . . . but does it exist outside your memory? On reaching the hilltop or the bend in the road, will you find the people gone, the landscape altered, the hemlock trees cut down and only stumps, dried tree-tops, branches and fireweed where the woods had been? Or, if the country remains the same, will you find yourself so changed and uprooted that it refuses to take you back, to reincorporate you into its common life? No matter: the country of our childhood survives, if only in our minds, and retains our loyalty even when casting us into exile; we carry its image from city to city as our most essential baggage:

> *Wanderers outside the gates, in hollow*
> *landscapes without memory, we carry*
> *each of us an urn of native soil,*
> *of not impalpable dust a double handful*
>
> *anciently gathered—was it garden mold*
> *or wood soil fresh with hemlock needles, pine*
> *and princess pine, this little earth we bore*
> *in silence, blindly, over the frontier?*

—a parcel of the soil not wide enough
or firm enough to build a dwelling on,
or deep enough to dig a grave, but cool
and sweet enough to sink the nostrils in
and find the smell of home, or in the ears,
rumors of home, like oceans in a shell.

2: Big-Town High School

I was born in a farmhouse near Belsano, in Cambria County, Pennsylvania, on the western slope of the Alleghenies. All my summers were spent there, and sometimes the long autumns too—fishing, shooting cottontails and pine squirrels, or simply wandering through the woods by myself; I thought of Belsano as my home. But my father was a doctor in Pittsburgh and I attended a big-town high school.

It must have been like two hundred other high schools west of the mountains. It was new, it was well equipped, it was average in size, having in those days about a thousand pupils. In retrospect it seems that all sorts of people went there—I can remember the daughter of a millionaire coal operator, a future All-American halfback, a handsome Italian who later became a big-time mobster, a tall, serious and stupid Negro boy, two girls who wore cotton-print dresses all year round and whom we suspected of being sewed into their winter underwear—but the atmosphere of the school was prosperous and middle class. Everyone was friendly. There were, on the other hand, all sorts of separate crowds, the football crowd, the social crowd, the second-best social crowd, and the literary crowd composed of boys who made good marks in English Composition, read books that weren't assigned for reading, were shy, noisy, ill dressed and helped to edit the school magazine.

That of course was the crowd to which I belonged—with Kenneth Burke and Jimmy Light (who later became a theatrical director), Russell Farrell (the valedictorian of the class, who changed his mind and didn't become a priest), Jake Davis and three or four others. In the high schools west of the mountains there must have been, at that time, scores of these groups of adolescent writers. Let us see what we were like at seventeen.

I suppose we had all the normal aberrations of our age and type. We were wholly self-centered, absorbed in our own personalities, and appalled by the thought that these would some day be obliterated. We brooded often on death, often on slights to our timid vanity. We yearned: pimpled and awkward we yearned for someone to accept our caresses, be conquered by our cleverness, our real distinction, our reserves of feeling hidden from the world. We dreamed of escape, into European cities with crooked streets, into Eastern islands where the breasts of the women were small and firm as inverted teacups. We felt a bashful veneration for everything illicit, whether it was the prostitute living in the next block or the crimes of Nero or the bottle of blackberry cordial we passed from hand to hand on Sunday afternoons. We felt that we were different from other boys: we admired and hated these happy ones, these people competent for every situation, who drove their fathers' cars and led the cheers at football games and never wrote poems or questioned themselves.

Symptoms much like these have recurred in the adolescence of writers for at least two centuries; they could probably be traced much farther into the past. But we had other symptoms too, more characteristic of our time and nation.

Thus, we felt a certain humility in the face of life, a disinclination to make demands on the world about us. Art and life were two realms; art was looked down upon by the ordinary public, the "lifelings," and justly so, since it could never have any effect on them. Art was uncommercial, almost secret, and we hoped to become artists. That was our own concern. An artist, a poet, should not advertise his profession by his clothes, should not wear a black cloak or flowing tie or let his hair grow over his collar. The artist had a world of his own: his ambitions in the real world should be humble. One of my friends confided to me that he wanted to earn seven thousand dollars a year and go to a symphony concert every week: I thought he showed presumption. Another friend, like Somerset Maugham's hero in *Of Human Bondage,* wanted to be a ship's doctor and visit strange ports; another would be satisfied to enter his father's business. For my part I was determined to be the dramatic critic of a newspaper, metropolitan or provincial: I should earn about three thousand dollars a year and have a mistress. Meanwhile I should be writing; all my friends would be writing—but about what?

Every new generation has its own sentimentality, its symbols that move it to compassion or self-compassion. For early Romantic writers beginning with Byron, the favorite symbol was the Haunted Castle—inaccessible, lonely, dwelled in by a young aristocrat of fabulous lineage, a Manfred seeking absolution for an inner sense of guilt, but wholly contemptuous of humankind. For the socially minded writers who followed Ibsen, the stock situation was that of the misunderstood reformer, the Enemy of the People, who tries to help his neighbors and is crucified for his good intentions. The situation of the artist frustrated by society has been popular with the late Romantics. All these symbols seemed foreign to ourselves, even slightly ridiculous. Our sensibilities were touched by older situations—girls mourning their lost lovers, men crippled in battle, death, the longing for home, prostitutes weeping at songs about marriage

and babies. . . . Those were the themes we should normally
have employed, but our sensibility, at that point, was checked by
our ideas.

In describing the ideas I run the danger of making them seem
too reasoned and definite. Essentially they were not ideas at all:
they were attitudes or emotions, persistently but vaguely felt
and often existing only in germ. They are important because
they help to explain what followed—because, after a period of
imitation and before a period of change, they reappeared in
what we wrote, and because what we felt at seventeen is an
explanation and criticism of what we should later believe.

At seventeen we were disillusioned and weary. In the midst
of basketball, puppy love and discussions of life—washed down
with chocolate sodas on warm afternoons—we had come to
question almost everything we were taught at home and in
school. Religion—we had argued about it so much, Catholics
against agnostics against Lutherans against Christian Scientists,
that we were all converted to indifferentism. Morality, which
we identified with chasteness, was a lie told to our bodies. Our
studies were useless or misdirected, especially our studies in English Literature: the authors we were forced to read, and Shakespeare most of all, were unpleasant to our palate; they had the
taste of chlorinated water.

We were still too immature to understand the doctrine of
complete despair about the modern world that would later be
advanced by the followers of T. S. Eliot (before their recon-
ciliation with the Church), but we shared in the mood that lay
behind them. During the brief moments we devoted to the fate
of mankind in general, we suffered from a sense of oppression. We felt that the world was rigorously controlled by
scientific laws of which we had no grasp, that our lives were
directed by Puritan standards that were not our own, that so-

ciety in general was terribly secure, unexciting, middle class, a vast reflection of the families from which we came. Society obeyed the impersonal law of progress. Cities expanded relentlessly year by year; fortunes grew larger; more and more automobiles appeared in the streets; people were wiser and better than their ancestors—eventually, by automatic stages, we should reach an intolerable utopia of dull citizens, without crime or suffering or drama. The progression, of course, might be reversed. The period in which we were living might prove to resemble Rome under the Five Good Emperors; it might be followed by upheavals, catastrophes, a general decline. But the decay of society was psychologically equivalent to its progress: both were automatic processes that we ourselves could neither hasten nor retard. Society was something alien, which our own lives and writings could never affect: it was a sort of parlor car in which we rode, over smooth tracks, toward a destination we should never have chosen for ourselves.

Literature, our profession, was living in the shadow of its own great past. The symbols that moved us, the great themes of love and death and parting, had been used and exhausted. Where could we find new themes when everything, so it seemed, had been said already? Having devoured the world, literature was dying for lack of nourishment. Nothing was left to ourselves —nothing except to deal with marginal experiences and abnormal cases, or else to say the old things over again with a clever and apologetic twist of our own. Nothing remained except the minor note. . . . And so, having adopted it humbly, we contributed artificial little pieces to the high-school paper, in which vice triumphed over virtue, but discreetly, so as not to be censored by the faculty adviser.

We were launching or drifting into the sea of letters with no fixed destination and without a pilot. To whom could we turn

for advice? The few authors we admired were separated from
us either by time or else just as effectively by space and language.
Among the American writers of the day there were several who
had produced a good book or two good books. Except for
Howells, whom we regarded as one of our enemies (if we regarded him at all), and Henry James, whom we did not read
(and who lived in exile), not one of them had achieved a career.
There seemed to be no writer with our own background. There
was no one who spoke directly to our youth, no one for us to
follow with a single heart, no one, even, against whom we could
intelligently and fruitfully rebel.

Yet we read tirelessly, hour after hour; we were engaged in
a desperate search for guidance. We read English authors at
first, Kipling and Stevenson, then Meredith, Hardy and Gissing.
In *The Private Papers of Henry Ryecroft* we found an opinion
with which we agreed completely. "I have never learned to regard myself," Gissing said, "as a 'member of society.' For me
there have always been two entities—myself and the world—
and the normal relation between the two has been hostile."

Forgetting the hostile world, we continued our searching. We
read Conrad; we read Wilde and Shaw, who were always mentioned together. From one or the other of these dramatists—
or perhaps from Mencken and Nathan, then editors of *Smart
Set*—we derived the sense of paradox, which became a standard
for judging the writers we afterward encountered. If they were
paradoxical—if they turned platitudes upside down, showed the
damage wrought by virtue, made heroes of their villains—then
they were "moderns"; they deserved our respect. Congreve, we
learned, was a modern. Ibsen was modern also, but we were a
little repelled by his symbolism and not aroused by his social
message; we read him dutifully, self-consciously. Strindberg
was more exciting, and we plunged into Schnitzler's early plays
as if we were exploring forbidden countries in which we hoped

to dwell. Reading, we imagined boys in other cities, beneath the green lamps of public libraries, scheming like ourselves to get hold of the books "not to be issued to minors," and being introduced into a special world of epigrams and *süsse Mädl*, where love affairs were taken for granted and everyone had the sense of paradox.

For us, paradox reduced itself to the simplest terms: it was the ability to say what was not expected, to fool one's audience. If, during a thunder shower, another boy looked out the classroom window and said, "It isn't raining, is it?" expecting us to answer "no," we would say "yes." By so doing, we were giving what we called a First Convolution answer.

The theory of convolutions was evolved in Pittsburgh, at Peabody High School, but it might have appeared in any city during those years before the war. It was generally explained by reference to the game of Odd or Even. You have held an even number of beans or grains of corn in your hand; you have won; therefore you take an even number again. That is the simplest argument by analogy; it is no convolution at all. But if you say to yourself, "I had an even number before and won; my opponent will expect me to have an even number again; therefore I'll take an odd number," you have entered the First Convolution. If you say, "Since I won with an even number before, my opponent will expect me to try to fool him by having an odd number this time; therefore I'll be even," you are Second Convolution. The process seems capable of indefinite extension; it can be applied, moreover, to any form of art, so long as one is less interested in what one says than in one's ability to outwit an audience. We were not conscious of having anything special to say; we wanted merely to live in ourselves and be writers.

There is, however, a practical limit to the series of convolutions. If it leads at one moment to reading Oscar Wilde because other high-school pupils have never heard of him, it leads at

the next to disparaging Wilde because you admired him once
and because First Convolution people still admire him. You
have entered the Second Convolution: you read Schnitzler and
"go beyond him" without ever understanding what he has to
say. In this manner we passed through a whole series of enthusiasms—Mencken, Huneker, Somerset Maugham, Laforgue
(after we learned French)—till we encountered Dostoevski,
who didn't fit into our scheme, and Flaubert, whose patience
overawed us.

The sense of paradox ends by having nothing left to feed
upon; eventually it is self-devouring. The desire to surprise or
deceive leads often to a final deception—which consists in being exactly like everybody else. This was the stage that several
of us had reached by our eighteenth year. We dressed like everybody else; we talked about girls, automobiles and the World's
Series. Petting was not yet fashionable: it was called "loving up"
and was permitted only by unattractive girls who had to offer
special inducements; but there were dances and we attended
them; we rooted for the basketball team; we engaged in all the
common activities (and were sorry when the time came to leave
them behind). We were like others, we were normal—yet we
clung to the feeling that as apprentice writers we were abnormal and secretly distinguished: we lived in the special world
of art; we belonged to the freemasonry of those who had read
modern authors and admired a paradox.

It was during the first years of the European war. In New
York the House of Morgan was busy making loans; in Washington the President was revising his ideas of neutrality: already
it was written that several million young Americans would be
called from their homes, fed by the government and taught to
be irresponsible heroes. In Detroit Henry Ford had begun to
manufacture I don't know how many thousand or million identical motors per day or year. Greenwich Village, crowded with

foreign artists, was beginning to develop new standards of living. Young women all over the country were reading Freud and attempting to lose their inhibitions. Einstein was studying in Berlin, Proust was writing in Paris, and Joyce, having lost his job as a tutor in Trieste, was in Switzerland, working sixteen hours a day on *Ulysses*. The Socialist parties of the world were supporting the war and entering cabinets of national defense, but the Russian front buckled and crumbled; Lenin from his exile was calculating the moment for a Communist revolution. All the divergent forces that would direct the history of our generation were already in action. Meanwhile, in Boston, Pittsburgh, Nashville, Chicago, we boys of seventeen and eighteen were enormously ignorant of what was going on in the world. We were reading, dancing, preparing for college-entrance examinations and, in our spare time, arguing about ourselves, ourselves and life, ourselves as artists, as lovers, the sublimation of sex and what we could possibly write about that was new.

3: Apprentice of the Arts

Digging through some old papers, I found a letter from Kenneth Burke that I hadn't filed away with the others. It was written some fourteen months after we had graduated from Peabody, but still, better than any other document possibly could, it evokes the atmosphere of our high-school years.

"Of course," it begins, "you are going to stop here for a few days on your way to Harvard. There is nothing to do—I have no money to entertain with, and no character to love you with—except walk, play tennis and read. Nothing hindering, I should love to take a couple of real venturesome walks with you; you know, start out for God knows where and get home in time for dinner. You could bring your sneaks along and perhaps we could play some tennis. Your playing would be distressingly bad, *ça se voit,* but what of that? As to reading, I can lend you books written after your heart, for I have become somewhat of an authority on unpresentable French novels."

Kenneth was already a critic and a pundit, although he hated to think of teaching or even of being taught. After a year of college he was back with his parents, having decided that he would learn more and have more time for writing if he stayed at home. The Burkes had moved to Weehawken, New Jersey, where they lived in an apartment on the Palisades overlooking the river and Manhattan. There Kenneth wrote in the mornings—stories, poems, essays, fables, plays, all of them lopsided, brilliant, immature and full of characters who explained themselves in paradoxes. In the afternoons, after his mother cooked lunch for him, he studied or wrote letters like this. Letters, except for an occasional game of tennis, were almost his only social life.

But he now had a project to boast about. "Did you know, by the way, that my going to France is no longer a mere *Eintagsfliege?* It has become not only a certainty but even an actual propelling force, an aim which is already affecting my conduct. I have begun hunting a job now. Some of my wages I shall save, some I shall spend for books and beer, and some I shall invest in Berlitz French. *J'ai une idée fixe. Dame! Mais oui."*

France was then fighting a war, but that didn't enter his calculations. The France he knew was the unmilitary France of novelists and poets. "I am not going there to stay, as I first intended. That is much too drastic. If I went to France to stay, and my money ran out, and I had no job, I should have to starve, or come home in disgrace. And besides, I shouldn't like to leave my father and mother so definitely. I like them both a lot, you know. And Pa, since I have lost my temperament, seems really clever to me. No," it was to be the sort of walk on which you start out for God knows where and get back in time for dinner. "I shall not live in France. I shall go to France on a *visit*. I shall have so much money saved up with which to pay for this visit. Then if I have a chance in France to get a job and thus prolong my visit, I shall take it. If when that job fails, I get a chance for another job, I shall take it and prolong my visit a little more. As long as I can get money, I shall prolong my visit, and when money ceases, my visit is over. By this arrangement I run no chance of defeat. I gamble with loaded dice. I bet against doped horses. I take a decisive step without suffering the usual vacillation. *Nom d'un chien, comme je suis habile!*

"I shall stop now, *mon cher M;* it is a glorious afternoon for tennis. But tonight, perhaps I shall write you again; for I shall probably be all alone, and there is an awfully tempting moon, *une âme toute nue,* that haunts the boulevard these nights. A lavish donor of delicious sadness she is, M, and I should love to watch her with you over the chilly somnolent farms. I love the moon, and the memory of *ma petite jolie,* and the lesser Chopin, and the cross-eyed girl next door. All that doesn't fit me for literature, Malcolm, but oh Christ, it makes it hard to renounce."

Those moonlit walks along Boulevard East were the crown of his days and the moment when his adolescence flowered. Years later he described them in another letter. "When I meant business (and every evening I meant business) I went along the Palisades, past the stone where Alexander Hamilton laid his historic and misleading head—and I stopped at the very end of the street, where it went off into nothing. Directly opposite Forty-second Street, looking down upon the exposed ribs of half-sunken barges (an era of postwar prosperity has since replaced them with concrete docks, and I trust that the bankers have got out from under the bond issue successfully), I stood silent and bareheaded, while the armies of melancholy attacked me. This was the Latrine of Endymion—necessarily, since the poet stood here for quite a while, in the cold fall air."

He was like Balzac's young man, climbing the heights of Montmartre to survey the city he would conquer, mapping out Paris street by lighted street; but the quality of his ambition was different, bitterly defensive; there was no thought of conquest in his mind, nor was New York his chosen city. Yet he would soon be plunged into its life. Next week—it had been decided that evening at the dinner table—he would go to work as a bank runner, but he would not rise by diligent ruthlessness to the control of corporations and a seat on the Exchange; he would perhaps rise to a clerkship. Later he might go to Paris (but only for a visit), he might live in a garret (but not starve there spectacularly), he might write plays (but not have the world fall at his feet nor yet be garlanded with the arms of pretty actresses). The glory and the drama were for others, those who lived in the world without question. Living in himself, he could hope only to preserve his self-integrity—to yield, if it was necessary to yield, but make his enemies pay for their triumph; to lie or cheat as a last resort, but never write sloppy prose. Meanwhile he was privileged to feel a sentimental regret for what he was losing.—"Surveying the city (night—sharp lights against the water) the poet meditated upon New York's sinfulness, its prodigality and its cruel ability to get along so well without him. He thought of autumn carnivals in vaguely located woods, of soft, breathless, cold-nosed girls, of a dewy, wide-eyed moon with sportive figures shivering and cuddling in its flannel light. Retaining the vocabulary of Grecian deities as preserved in Keats (or should I say in *The Golden Treasury*?), he considered indeterminately Artemis and gaslit chopsuey houses, stage doors and marbles in a grove, bacchantic dances and his job as a bank runner."

The chill of the sidewalks was striking through the damp soles of his shoes. About midnight he went home to brush his teeth in front of the bathroom-cabinet mirror, question his face for new pimples, repeat a phrase from Laforgue and go to bed. He was alone, four hundred miles from his boyhood.

4: American College, 1916

It often seems to me that our years in school and after school, in college and later in the army, might be regarded as a long process of deracination. Looking backward, I feel that our whole training was involuntarily directed toward destroying whatever roots we had in the soil, toward eradicating our local and regional peculiarities, toward making us homeless citizens of the world.

In school, unless we happened to be Southerners, we were divested of any local pride. We studied Ancient History and American History, but not, in my own case, the history of western Pennsylvania. We learned by name the rivers of Siberia— Obi, Yenisei, Lena, Amur—but not the Ohio with its navigable tributaries, or why most of them had ceased to be navigated, or why Pittsburgh was built at its forks. We had high-school courses in Latin, German, Chemistry, good courses all of them, and a class in Civics where we learned to list the amendments to the Constitution and name the members of the Supreme Court; but we never learned how Presidents were really chosen or how a law was put through Congress. If one of us had later come into contact with the practical side of government—that

is, if he wished to get a street paved, an assessment reduced, a
friend out of trouble with the police or a relative appointed to
office—well, fortunately the ward boss wouldn't take much time
to set him straight.

Of the English texts we studied, I can remember only one,
"The Legend of Sleepy Hollow," that gave us any idea that an
American valley could be as effectively clothed in romance as
Ivanhoe's castle or the London of Henry Esmond. It seemed to
us that America was beneath the level of great fiction; it seemed
that literature in general, and art and learning, were things existing at an infinite distance from our daily lives. For those of us
who read independently, this impression became even stronger:
the only authors to admire were foreign authors. We came to
feel that wisdom was an attribute of Greece and art of the
Renaissance, that glamour belonged only to Paris or Vienna
and that glory was confined to the dim past. If we tried, not-
withstanding, to write about more immediate subjects, we were
forced to use a language not properly our own. A definite effort
was being made to destroy all trace of local idiom or pronuncia-
tion and have us speak "correctly"—that is, in a standardized
Amerenglish as colorless as Esperanto. Some of our instructors
had themselves acquired this public-school dialect only by dint
of practice, and now set forth its rules with an iron pedantry, as
if they were teaching a dead language.

In college the process of deracination went on remorselessly.
We were not being prepared for citizenship in a town, a state
or a nation; we were not being trained for an industry or profession essential to the common life; instead we were being ex-
horted to enter that international republic of learning whose
traditions are those of Athens, Florence, Paris, Berlin and Oxford. The immigrant into that high disembodied realm is supposed to come with empty hands and naked mind, like a recruit
into the army. He is clothed and fed by his preceptors, who

furnish him only with the best of intellectual supplies. Nothing must enter that world in its raw state; everything must be refined by time and distance, by theory and research, until it loses its own special qualities, its life, and is transformed into the dead material of culture. The ideal university is regarded as having no regional or economic ties. With its faculty, students, classrooms and stadium, it exists in a town as if by accident, its real existence being in the immaterial world of scholarship—or such, at any rate, was the idea to be gained in those years by any impressionable student.

Take my own experience at Harvard. Here was a university that had grown immediately out of a local situation, out of the colonists' need for trained ministers of the Gospel. It had transformed itself from generation to generation with the transformations of New England culture. Farming money, fishing money, trading money, privateering money, wool, cotton, shoe and banking money, had all contributed to its vast endowment. It had grown with Boston, a city whose records were written on the face of its buildings. Sometimes on Sundays I used to wander through the old sections of Beacon Hill and the North End and admire the magnificent doorways, built in the chastest Puritan style with profits from the trade in China tea. Behind some of them Armenians now lived, or Jews; the Old North Church was in an Italian quarter, near the house of Paul Revere, a silversmith. Back Bay had been reclaimed from marshland and covered with mansions during the prosperous years after the Civil War (shoes, uniforms, railroads, speculation in government bonds). On Brattle Street, in Cambridge, Longfellow's house was open to the public, and I might have visited Brook Farm. All these things, Emerson, doorways, factory hands and fortunes, the Elective System, the Porcellian Club, were bound together into one civilization, but of this I received no hint. I was studying Goethe's *Dichtung und Wahrheit* and the Eliza-

bethan drama, and perhaps, on my way to classes in the morning, passing a Catholic church outside of which two Irish boys
stood and looked at me with unfriendly eyes. Why was Cambridge an Irish provincial city, almost like Cork or Limerick?
What was the reason, in all the territory round Boston, for the
hostility between "nice people" and "muckers"? When a development of houses for nice Cambridge people came out on
the main street of Somerville (as one of them did), why did it
turn its back on the street, build a brick wall against the sidewalk, and face on an interior lawn where nurses could watch
nice children playing? I didn't know; I was hurrying off to a
section meeting in European History and wondering whether
I could give the dates of the German peasant wars.

I am not suggesting that we should have been encouraged
to take more "practical" courses—Bookkeeping or Restaurant
Management or Sewage Disposal or any of the hundreds that
clutter the curriculum of a big university. These specialized
techniques could wait till later, after we had chosen our life
work. What we were seeking, as sophomores and juniors, was
something vastly more general, a key to unlock the world, a
picture to guide us in fitting its jigsaw parts together. It happened that our professors were eager to furnish us with such a
key or guide; they were highly trained, earnest, devoted to their
calling. Essentially the trouble was that the world they pictured
for our benefit was the special world of scholarship—timeless,
placeless, elaborate, incomplete and bearing only the vaguest
relationship to that other world in which fortunes were made,
universities endowed and city governments run by muckers.

It lay at a distance, even, from the college world in which we
were doing our best to get ahead. The rigorous methods and
high doctrines taught by our professors applied only to parts
of our lives. We had to fill in the gaps as best we could, usually
by accepting the unspoken doctrines of those about us. In prac-

tice the college standards were set, not by the faculty, but by the leaders among the students, and particularly by the rich boys from half-English preparatory schools, for whose benefit the system seemed to be run. The rest of us, boys from public high schools, ran the risk of losing our own culture, such as it was, in our bedazzlement with this new puzzling world, and of receiving nothing real in exchange.

Young writers were especially tempted to regard their own experience as something negligible, not worth the trouble of recording in the sort of verse or prose they were taught to imitate from the English masters. A Jewish boy from Brooklyn might win a scholarship by virtue of his literary talent. Behind him there would lie whole generations of rabbis versed in the Torah and the Talmud, representatives of the oldest Western culture now surviving. Behind him, too, lay the memories of an exciting childhood: street gangs in Brownsville, chants in a Chassidic synagogue, the struggle of his parents against poverty, his cousin's struggle, perhaps, to build a labor union and his uncle's fight against it—all the emotions, smells and noises of the ghetto. Before him lay contact with another great culture, and four years of leisure in which to study, write and form a picture of himself. But what he would write in those four years were Keatsian sonnets about English abbeys, which he had never seen, and nightingales he had never heard.

I remember a boy from my own city, in this case a gentile and a graduate of Central High School, which then occupied a group of antiquated buildings on the edge of the business section. Southeast of it was a Jewish quarter; to the north, across the railroad, was the Strip, home of steelworkers, saloons and small-time politicians; to the east lay the Hill, already inhabited by Negroes, with a small red-light district along the lower slopes of it, through which the boys occasionally wandered at lunchtime. The students themselves were drawn partly from these various slums, but chiefly from residential districts in East Liberty and on Squirrel Hill. They followed an out-of-date curriculum under the direction of teachers renowned for thoroughness and severity; they had every chance to combine four years of sound classical discipline with a personal observation of city morals and sociology and politics in action.

This particular student was brilliant in his classes, editor of the school paper, captain of the debating team; he had the sort of reputation that spreads to other high schools; everybody said he was sure to be famous some day. He entered Harvard two or three years before my time and became a fairly important figure. When I went out for the *Harvard Crimson* (incidentally, without making it) I was sent to get some news about an activity for which he was the spokesman. Maybe he would take an interest in a boy from the same city, who had debated and written for the school paper and won a scholarship like himself. I hurried to his room on Mt. Auburn Street. He was wearing—this was my first impression—a suit of clothes cut by a very good tailor, so well cut, indeed, that it made the features above it seem undistinguished. He eyed me carelessly—my own suit was bought in a department store—and began talking from a distance in a rich Oxford accent put on like his clothes. I went away without my news, feeling ashamed. The story wasn't printed.

Years later I saw him again when I was writing book reviews for a New York newspaper. He came into the office looking very English, like the boss's son. A friendly reporter told me that he was a second-string dramatic critic who would never become first-string. "He ought to get wise to himself," the reporter said. "He's got too much culture for this game."

In college we never grasped the idea that culture was the outgrowth of a situation—that an artisan knowing his tools and having the feel of his materials might be a cultured man; that a farmer among his animals and his fields, stopping his plow at the fence corner to meditate over death and life and next year's crop, might have culture without even reading a newspaper. Essentially we were taught to regard culture as a veneer, a badge of class distinction—as something assumed like an Oxford accent or a suit of English clothes.

Those salesrooms and fitting rooms of culture where we would spend four years were not ground-floor shops, open to the life of the street. They existed, as it were, at the top of very high buildings, looking down at a far panorama of boulevards and Georgian houses and Greek temples of banking—with people outside them the size of gnats—and, vague in the distance, the fields, mines, factories that labored unobtrusively to support us. We never glanced out at them. On the heights, while tailors transformed us into the semblance of cultured men, we exercised happily, studied in moderation, slept soundly and grumbled at our food. There was nothing else to do except pay the bills rendered semi-annually, and our parents attended to that.

College students, especially in the big Eastern universities, inhabit an easy world of their own. Except for very rich people and certain types of childless wives, they have been the only American class that could take leisure for granted. There have always been many among them who earned their board and tuition by tending furnaces, waiting on table or running back kickoffs for a touchdown; what I am about to say does not apply to them. The others—at most times the ruling clique of a big university, the students who set the tone for the rest—are supported practically without efforts of their own. They write a few begging letters; perhaps they study a little harder in order to win a scholarship; but usually they don't stop to think where the money comes from. Above them, the president knows the source of the hard cash that runs this great educational factory; he knows that the stream of donations can be stopped by a crash

in the stock market or reduced in volume by newspaper reports
of a professor gone bolshevik; he knows what he has to tell his
trustees or the state legislators when he goes to them begging
for funds. The scrubwomen in the library, the chambermaids
and janitors, know how they earn their food; but the students
themselves, and many of their professors, are blind to economic
forces and they never think of society in concrete terms, as the
source of food and football fields and professors' salaries.

The university itself forms a temporary society with standards
of its own. In my time at Harvard the virtues instilled into
students were good taste, good manners, cleanliness, chastity,
gentlemanliness (or niceness), reticence and the spirit of competition in sports; they are virtues often prized by a leisure class.
When a student failed to meet the leisure-class standards someone would say, "He talks too much," or more conclusively, "He
needs a bath." Even boys from very good Back Bay families
would fail to make a club if they paid too much attention to
chorus girls. Years later, during the controversy over the New
Humanism, I read several books by Professor Irving Babbitt, the
founder of the school, and found myself carried back into the
atmosphere of the classroom. Babbitt and his disciples liked
to talk about poise, proportionateness, the imitation of great
models, decorum and the Inner Check. Those too were leisure-
class ideals and I decided that they were simply the student
virtues rephrased in loftier language. The truth was that the
New Humanism grew out of Eastern university life, where it
flourished as in a penthouse garden.

Nor was it the only growth that adorned these high mansions
of culture. There was also, for example, the college liberalism
that always drew back from action. There was the missionary
attitude of Phillips Brooks House and the college Y.M.C.A.'s,
that of reaching down and helping others to climb not quite
up to our level. There was later the life-is-a-circus type of cyni-

cism rendered popular by the *American Mercury:* everything
is rotten, people are fools; let's all get quietly drunk and laugh
at them. Then, too, there was a type of aestheticism very popular during my own college years. The Harvard Aesthetes of
1916 were trying to create in Cambridge, Massachusetts, an
after-image of Oxford in the 1890s. They read the *Yellow Book,*
they read Casanova's memoirs and *Les Liaisons Dangereuses,*
both in French, and Petronius in Latin; they gathered at tea-
time in one another's rooms, or at punches in the office of the
Harvard Monthly; they drank, instead of weak punch, seidels
of straight gin topped with a maraschino cherry; they discussed
the harmonies of Pater, the rhythms of Aubrey Beardsley and,
growing louder, the voluptuousness of the Church, the essential
virtue of prostitution. They had crucifixes in their bedrooms,
and ticket stubs from last Saturday's burlesque show at the Old
Howard. They wrote, too; dozens of them were prematurely
decayed poets, each with his invocation to Antinoüs, his mourn-
ful descriptions of Venetian lagoons, his sonnets to a chorus girl
in which he addressed her as "little painted poem of God." In
spite of these beginnings, a few of them became good writers.

They were apparently very different from the Humanists,
who never wrote poems at all, and yet, in respect to their opinions, they were simply Humanists turned upside down. For each
of the Humanist virtues they had an antithesis. Thus, for poise
they substituted *ecstasy;* for proportionateness, the Golden
Mean, a worship of *immoderation;* for imitating great models,
the opposite virtue of following each impulse, of *living in the
moment.* Instead of decorum, they mildly preached a *revolt*
from middle-class standards, which led them toward a sentimental reverence for sordid things; instead of the Inner Check,
they believed in the duty of *self-expression.* Yet the Humanist
and the Aesthete were both products of the same milieu, one in
which the productive forces of society were regarded as some-

thing alien to poetry and learning. And both of them, though they found different solutions, were obsessed by the same problem, that of their individual salvation or damnation, success or failure, in a world in which neither was at home.

Whatever the doctrines we adopted during our college years, whatever the illusions we had of growing toward culture and self-sufficiency, the same process of deracination was continuing for all of us. We were like so many tumbleweeds sprouting in the rich summer soil, our leaves spreading while our roots slowly dried and became brittle. Normally the deracination would have ended when we left college; outside in the practical world we should have been forced to acquire new roots in order to survive. But we weren't destined to have the fate of the usual college generation and, instead of ceasing, the process would be intensified. Soon the war would be upon us; soon the winds would tear us up and send us rolling and drifting over the wide land.

5: Ambulance Service

During the winter of 1916–17 our professors stopped talking about the international republic of letters and began preaching patriotism. We ourselves prepared to change our uniforms of culture for military uniforms; but neither of these changes was so radical as it seemed. The patriotism urged upon us was not, like that of French peasants, a matter of saving one's own fields from an invader. It was an abstract patriotism that concerned world democracy and the right to self-determination of small nations, but apparently had nothing to do with our daily lives at home, nothing to do with better schools, lower taxes, higher pay for factory hands (and professors) or restocking Elk Run with trout. And the uniforms we assumed were not, in many cases, those of our own country.

When the war came the young writers then in college were attracted by the idea of enlisting in one of the ambulance corps attached to a foreign army—the American Ambulance Service or the Norton-Harjes, both serving under the French and receiving French army pay, or the Red Cross ambulance sections on the Italian front. Those were the organizations that promised to carry us abroad with the least delay. We were eager to get into action, as a character in one of Dos Passos's novels expressed it, "before the whole thing goes belly up."

In Paris we found that the demand for ambulance drivers had temporarily slackened. We were urged, and many of us consented, to join the French military transport, in which our work would be not vastly different: while driving munition trucks we would retain our status of gentleman volunteers. We drank to our new service in the *bistro* round the corner. Two weeks later, on our way to a training camp behind the lines, we passed in a green wheatfield the grave of an aviator *mort pour la patrie,* his wooden cross wreathed with the first lilies of the valley. A few miles north of us the guns were booming. Here was death among the flowers, danger in spring, the sweet wine of sentiment neither spiced with paradox nor yet insipid, the death being real, the danger near at hand.

We found on reaching the front that we were serving in what was perhaps the most literary branch of any army. My own section of thirty-six men will serve as an example. I have never attended a reunion of T. M. U. 526, if one was ever held, but at various times I have encountered several of my former comrades. One is an advertising man specializing in book publishers' copy. One is an architect, one a successful lecturer who has written a first novel, one an editor, one an unsuccessful dramatist.

The war itself put an end to other careers. A Rhodes scholar with a distinguished record was killed in action. The member of the section who was generally believed to have the greatest promise was a boy of seventeen, a poet who had himself transferred into the Foreign Legion and died in an airplane accident. Yet T. M. U. 526 was in no way exceptional. My friends in other sections where there was a higher percentage of young writers often pitied me for having to serve with such a bunch of philistines.

It would be interesting to list the authors who were ambulance or camion drivers in 1917. Dos Passos, Hemingway, Julian Green, William Seabrook, E. E. Cummings, Slater Brown, Harry Crosby, John Howard Lawson, Sidney Howard, Louis Bromfield, Robert Hillyer, Dashiell Hammett . . . one might almost say that the ambulance corps and the French military transport were college-extension courses for a generation of writers. But what did these courses teach?

They carried us to a foreign country, the first that most of us had seen; they taught us to make love, stammer love, in a foreign language. They fed and lodged us at the expense of a government in which we had no share. They made us more irresponsible than before: livelihood was not a problem; we had a minimum of choices to make; we could let the future take care of itself, feeling certain that it would bear us into new adventures. They taught us courage, extravagance, fatalism, these being the virtues of men at war; they taught us to regard as vices the civilian virtues of thrift, caution and sobriety; they made us fear boredom more than death. All these lessons might have been learned in any branch of the army, but ambulance service had a lesson of its own: it instilled into us what might be called a *spectatorial* attitude.

. . . Sometimes for three days at a time, a column of men and guns wound through the village where we were quartered.

Chasseurs slouching along in their dark-blue uniforms, canteens and helmets banging against their hips; a regiment of Senegalese, huge men with blue-black faces, pink eyeballs and white teeth; then a convoy of camions in first and second gear, keeping pace with the moving files. Behind them, dust rose from an interminable line of seventy-fives drawn by great bay horses, with very blond Flemish artillerymen riding the caissons; then came a supply train; then, in horizon blue, an infantry regiment from Provence, three thousand men with sullen features; then rolling kitchens and wagons heaped with bread the color of faded straw. The Annamites, little mud-colored men with the faces of perverted babies, watched from the ditches where they were breaking stone; the airplanes of three nations kept watch overhead, and we ourselves were watchers. It did not seem that we could ever be part of all this. The long parade of races was a spectacle which it was our privilege to survey, a special circus like the exhibition of Moroccan horsemen given for our benefit on the Fourth of July, before we all sat down at a long table to toast *la France héroïque* and *nos amis américains* in warm champagne. In the morning we should continue our work of carrying trench-mortar bombs from the railhead to the munition dumps just back of the Chemin des Dames—that too would be a spectacle.

Behind the scenes, that early summer, a great drama was being played. The Russians had had their February revolution, the French and British their April offensive; the second had been turned into ridicule when the Germans safely withdrew to stronger positions. There were grumblings in the armies round Verdun and in the Ile de France. Too many men were being killed. The battalion of chasseurs once stationed in our village—those dark stocky men who asked how much longer it would go on, and begged a little gasoline for their cigarette lighters, and got drunk with us while telling of their losses in

the last attack—had mutinied the following week. A division
from the Midi had refused to go into the trenches. Everywhere
there was discontent; it was a question whether the troops would
imitate the Russians or fight on patiently till the arrival from
America of the help that everybody said would end the war.
We ourselves, as representatives of America at the front, were
being used to soften this discontent, were being displayed as
first-tokens of victory, but we did not realize that we were serving a political purpose. We were treated well, that was all we
knew. We were seeing a great show.

I remember a drizzling afternoon when our convoy grumbled into an artillery park with a consignment of 155-millimeter
shells. Soldiers came to unload our camions, old dirty Territorials with gunny sacks over their heads. We watched them wea-
rily, having driven and stopped and driven since four in the
morning. A shell suddenly burst on the north side of the park.
The Territorials disappeared into holes in the ground like so
many woodchucks; we ourselves found shelter under an over-
hanging bank. The bombardment continued: shrapnel mixed
with high explosive was bursting in the road every two minutes,
regularly. Somebody found that by rushing into the center of
the road after each explosion, he could gather warm fragments
of steel and return to the shelter of the bank before the next
shell burst in the same spot. The rest of us followed his example,
fighting over our trophies. A tiny change in the elevation of the
German guns and the whole park would be destroyed, ourselves
along with it, but we knew that the guns wouldn't change: our
lives were charmed. Spectators, we were collecting souvenirs of
death, like guests bringing back a piece of wedding cake or a
crushed flower from the bride's bouquet.

On a July evening, at dusk, I remember halting in the courtyard of a half-ruined château, through which zigzagged the
trenches held by the Germans before their retreat two miles

northward to stronger positions. Shells were harmlessly rumbling overhead: the German and the French heavy batteries, three miles behind their respective lines, were shelling each other like the Brushton gang throwing rocks at the Car Barn gang; here, in the empty courtyard between them, it was as if we were underneath a freight yard where heavy trains were being shunted back and forth. We looked indifferently at the lake, now empty of swans, and the formal statues chipped by machine-gun fire, and talked in quiet voices—about Mallarmé, the Russian ballet, the respective virtues of two college magazines. On the steps of the château, in the last dim sunlight, a red-faced boy from Harvard was studying Russian out of a French textbook. Four other gentlemen volunteers were rolling dice on an outspread blanket. A French artillery brigade on a hillside nearby—rapid-firing seventy-fives—was laying down a barrage; the guns flashed like fireflies among the trees. We talked about the Lafayette Escadrille with admiration, and about our own service bitterly.

Yet our service was, in its own fashion, almost ideal. It provided us with fairly good food, a congenial occupation, furloughs to Paris and uniforms that admitted us to the best hotels. It permitted us to enjoy the once-in-a-lifetime spectacle of the Western Front. Being attached to the French army, it freed us from the severe and stupid forms of discipline then imposed on American shavetails and buck privates. It confronted us with hardships, but not more of them than it was exhilarating for young men to endure, and with danger, but not too much of it: seldom were there more than two or three serious casualties in a section during the year—and that was really the burden of our complaint. We didn't want to be slackers, *embusqués*. The war created in young men a thirst for abstract danger, not suffered for a cause but courted for itself; if later they believed in the cause, it was partly in recognition of the danger it con-

ferred on them. Danger was a relief from boredom, a stimulus
to the emotions, a color mixed with all others to make them
brighter. There were moments in France when the senses were
immeasurably sharpened by the thought of dying next day, or
possibly next week. The trees were green, not like ordinary
trees, but like trees in the still moment before a hurricane; the
sky was a special and ineffable blue; the grass smelled of life
itself; the image of death at twenty, the image of love, mingled
together into a keen, precarious delight. And this perhaps was
the greatest of the lessons that the war taught to young writers.
It revivified the subjects that had seemed forbidden because they
were soiled by many hands and robbed of meaning: danger
made it possible to write once more about love, adventure, death.
Most of my friends were preparing to follow danger into other
branches of the army—of any army—that were richer in fatali-
ties.

They scattered a few months later: when the ambulance and
camion services were taken over by the American Expeditionary
Force, not many of them re-enlisted. Instead they entered the
Lafayette Escadrille, the French or Canadian field artillery, the
tanks, the British balloon service, the Foreign Legion, the Royal
Air Force; a very few volunteered for the American infantry,
doing a simple thing for paradoxical reasons. I had friends in
distant sectors: one of them flew for the Belgians, another in
Serbia, and several moved on to the Italian front, where John
Dos Passos drove an ambulance. Ernest Hemingway was also
an ambulance driver on that front, until the July night when an
Austrian mortar bomb exploded in the observation post beyond
the front lines where he was visiting at the time, like a spectator
invited to gossip with the actors behind the scenes. E. E. Cummings was given no choice of service. Having mildly revolted
against the discipline of the Norton-Harjes Ambulance Corps,
and having become the friend of a boy from Columbia Univer-

sity who wrote letters to Emma Goldman, he was shipped off to a French military prison, where he had the adventures later described in *The Enormous Room.* . . . But even in prison threatened with scurvy, or lying wounded in hospitals, or flying combat planes above the trenches, these young Americans retained their curious attitude of non-participation, of being friendly visitors who, though they might be killed at any moment, still had no share in what was taking place.

Somewhere behind them was another country, a real country of barns, cornfields, hemlock woods and brooks tumbling across birch logs into pools where the big trout lay. Somewhere, at an incredible distance, was the country of their childhood, where they had once been part of the landscape and the life, part of a spectacle at which nobody looked on.

This spectatorial attitude, this monumental indifference toward the cause for which young Americans were risking their lives, is reflected in more than one of the books written by former ambulance drivers. Five of the principal characters in Dos Passos's *1919*—the Grenadine Guards, as he calls them—Dick Savage (a Harvard aesthete), Fred Summers, Ed Schuyler, Steve Warner (another Harvard man, but not of the same college set), and Ripley (a Columbia freshman) first enlist in the Norton-Harjes Ambulance Corps, and then, when the American army takes it over, go south to the Italian front. In February of the last wartime year, Steve Warner reads that the Empress Taitu of Abyssinia is dead, and the Grenadine Guards hold a wake for her:

They drank all the rum they had and keened until the rest of the section thought they'd gone crazy. They sat in the dark round the open moonlit window wrapped in blankets and drinking warm zabaglione. Some Austrian planes that had been droning overhead suddenly cut off their motors and dumped a load of bombs right in front of them. The anti-aircraft guns had been barking for some time and shrapnel sparkling in the moonhazy sky overhead but they'd been too drunk to notice. One bomb fell geflump into the Brenta and the others filled the space in front of the window with red leaping glare and shook the villa with three roaring snorts. Plaster fell from the ceiling. They could hear the tiles scuttering down off the roof overhead.

"Jesus, that was almost good night," said Summers. Steve started singing, *Come away from that window my light and my life,* but the rest of them drowned it out with an out of tune *Deutschland, Deutschland über Alles*. They suddenly all felt crazy drunk. . . .

"Fellers," Fred Summers kept saying, "this ain't a war, it's a goddam madhouse . . . it's a goddam Cook's tour." It remained, for many of us, a goddam crazy Cook's tour of Western Europe, but for those who served longer it became something else as well.

Ernest Hemingway's hero, in *A Farewell to Arms*, is an American acting as lieutenant of an Italian ambulance section. He likes the Italians, at least until Caporetto; he is contemptuous of the Austrians, fears and admires the Germans; of political conviction he has hardly a trace. When a friend tells him, "What has been done this summer cannot have been done in vain," he makes no answer:

I was always embarrassed by the words sacred, glorious, and sacrifice, and the expression in vain. We had heard them, sometimes standing in the rain almost out of earshot, so that only the shouted words came through, and had read them, on proclamations that were slapped up by billposters over other proclamations, now for a long time, and I had seen nothing sacred, and the things that were glorious had no glory and the sacrifices were like the stockyards at Chicago if nothing was done with the meat except to bury it. . . . Abstract

words such as glory, honor, courage, or hallow were obscene beside
the concrete names of villages, the numbers of roads, the names of
rivers, the numbers of regiments and the dates. Gino was a patriot,
so he said things that separated us sometimes, but he was also a fine
boy and I understood his being a patriot. He was born one. He left
with Peduzzi in the car. . . .

Two days later the Germans broke through at Caporetto.

The passage dealing with the Italian retreat from river to river,
from the mountains beyond the Isonzo along rain-washed narrow roads to the plains of the Tagliamento, is one of the few
great war stories in American literature: only *The Red Badge
of Courage* and a few short pieces by Ambrose Bierce can be
compared with it. Hemingway describes not an army but a
whole people in motion: guns nuzzling the heads of patient
farm horses, munition trucks with their radiator caps an inch
from the tailboard of wagons loaded with chairs, tables, sew-
ing machines, farm implements; then behind them ambulances,
mountain artillery, cattle and army trucks, all pointed south;
and groups of scared peasants and interminable files of gray
infantrymen moving in the rain past the miles of stalled vehicles.
Lieutenant Frederick Henry is part of the retreat, commanding three motor ambulances and half a dozen men, losing his
vehicles in muddy lanes, losing his men, too, by death and deser-
tion, shooting an Italian sergeant who tries to run away—but
in spirit he remains a non-participant. He had been studying
architecture in Rome, had become a gentleman volunteer in
order to see the war, had served two years, been wounded and
decorated: now he is sick of the whole thing, eager only to get
away.

As he moves southward, the southbound Germans go past
him, marching on parallel roads, their helmets visible above the
walls. Frightened Italians open fire on him. The rain falls end-

lessly, and the whole experience, Europe, Italy, the war, becomes a nightmare, with himself as helpless as a man among
nightmare shapes. It is only in snatches of dream that he finds
anything real—love being real, and the memories of his boyhood. "The hay smelled good and lying in a barn in the hay took
away all the years in between. We had lain in hay and talked
and shot sparrows with an air rifle when they perched in the
triangle cut high up in the wall of the barn. The barn was gone
now and one year they had cut the hemlock woods and there
were only stumps, dried tree-tops, branches and fireweed where
the woods had been. You could not go back"; the country of
his boyhood was gone and he was attached to no other.

And that, I believe, was the final effect on us of the war; that
was the honest emotion behind a pretentious phrase like "the
lost generation." School and college had uprooted us in spirit;
now we were physically uprooted, hundreds of us, millions,
plucked from our own soil as if by a clamshell bucket and
dumped, scattered among strange people. All our roots were
dead now, even the Anglo-Saxon tradition of our literary ancestors, even the habits of slow thrift that characterized our social
class. We were fed, lodged, clothed by strangers, commanded
by strangers, infected with the poison of irresponsibility—the
poison of travel, too, for we had learned that problems could be
left behind us merely by moving elsewhere—and the poison of
danger, excitement, that made our old life seem intolerable.
Then, as suddenly as it began for us, the war ended.

When we first heard of the Armistice we felt a sense of relief
too deep to express, and we all got drunk. We had come through,
we were still alive, and nobody at all would be killed tomorrow. The composite fatherland for which we had fought and
in which some of us still believed—France, Italy, the Allies, our
English homeland, democracy, the self-determination of small
nations—had triumphed. We danced in the streets, embraced

old women and pretty girls, swore blood brotherhood with soldiers in little bars, drank with our elbows locked in theirs, reeled through the streets with bottles of champagne, fell asleep somewhere. On the next day, after we got over our hangovers, we didn't know what to do, so we got drunk. But slowly, as the days went by, the intoxication passed, and the tears of joy: it appeared that our composite fatherland was dissolving into quarreling statesmen and oil and steel magnates. Our own nation had passed the Prohibition Amendment as if to publish a bill of separation between itself and ourselves; it wasn't our country any longer. Nevertheless we returned to it: there was nowhere else to go. We returned to New York, appropriately —to the homeland of the uprooted, where everyone you met came from another town and tried to forget it; where nobody seemed to have parents, or a past more distant than last night's swell party, or a future beyond the swell party this evening and the disillusioned book he would write tomorrow.

II: War in Bohemia

1: The Long Furlough

After college and the war, most of us drifted to Manhattan, to the crooked streets south of Fourteenth, where you could rent a furnished hall-bedroom for two or three dollars weekly or the top floor of a rickety house for thirty dollars a month. We came to the Village without any intention of becoming Villagers. We came because living was cheap, because friends of ours had come already (and written us letters full of enchantment), because it seemed that New York was the only city where a young writer could be published. There were some who stayed in Europe after the war and others who carried their college diplomas straight to Paris: they had money. But the rest of us belonged to the proletariat of the arts and we lived in Greenwich Village where everyone else was poor.

"There were," I wrote some years ago, "two schools among us: those who painted the floors black (they were the last of the aesthetes) and those who did not paint the floors. Our college textbooks and the complete works of Jules Laforgue gathered dust on the mantelpiece among a litter of unemptied ashtrays. The streets outside were those of Glenn Coleman's early paintings: low red-brick early nineteenth-century houses, crazy doorways, sidewalks covered with black snow and, in the foreground, an old woman bending under a sack of rags."

The black snow melted: February blustered into March. It was as if the war had never been fought, or had been fought by others. We were about to continue the work begun in high school, of training ourselves as writers, choosing masters to imitate, deciding what we wanted to say and persuading magazines to let us say it. We should have to earn money, think about getting jobs: the war was over. But besides the memories we scarcely mentioned, it had left us with a vast unconcern for the future and an enormous appetite for pleasure. We were like soldiers with a few more days to spend in Blighty: every moment was borrowed from death. It didn't matter that we were penniless: we danced to old squeaky victrola records—*You called me Baby Doll a year ago; Hello, Central, give me No Man's Land*—we had our first love affairs, we stopped in the midst of arguments to laugh at jokes as broad and pointless as the ocean, we were continually drunk with high spirits, transported by the miracle of no longer wearing a uniform. As we walked down Greenwich Avenue we stopped to enjoy the smell of hot bread outside of Cushman's bakery. In the spring morning it seemed that every ash barrel was green-wreathed with spinach.

It was April now, and the long furlough continued. . . . You woke at ten o'clock between soiled sheets in a borrowed apartment; the sun dripped over the edges of the green windowshade. On the dresser was a half-dollar borrowed the night before from the last guest to go downstairs singing: even at wartime prices it was enough to buy breakfast for two—eggs, butter, a loaf of bread, a grapefruit. When the second pot of coffee was emptied a visitor would come, then another; you would borrow fifty-five cents for the cheapest bottle of sherry. Somebody would suggest a ride across the bay to Staten Island. Dinner provided itself, and there was always a program for the evening. On Fridays there were dances in Webster Hall attended by terrible uptown people who came to watch the Villagers at their revels and buy them drinks in return for being insulted; on Saturdays everybody gathered at Luke O'Connor's saloon, the Working Girls' Home; on Sunday nights there were poker games played for imaginary stakes and interrupted from moment to moment by gossip, jokes, plans; everything in those days was an excuse for talking. There were always parties, and if they lasted into the morning they might end in a "community sleep": the mattresses were pulled off the beds and laid side by side on the floor, then double blankets were unfolded and stretched lengthwise across them, so that a dozen people could sleep there in discomfort, provided nobody snored. One night, having fallen asleep, you gave a snore so tremendous that you wakened to its echo, and listened to your companions drowsily cursing the snorer, and for good measure cursed him yourself. But always, before going to bed, you borrowed fifty cents for breakfast. Eight hours' foresight was sufficient. Always, after the coffee pot was drained, a visitor would come with money enough for a bottle of sherry.

But it couldn't go on forever. Some drizzly morning late in April you woke up to find yourself married (and your wife, perhaps, suffering from a dry cough that threatened consumption). If there had been checks from home, there would be no more of them. Or else it happened after a siege of influenza, which that year had curious effects: it left you weak in body, clear in mind, revolted by humanity and yourself. Tottering from the hospital, you sat in the back room of a saloon and, from the whitewood table sour with spilled beer, surveyed your blank prospects. You had been living on borrowed money, on borrowed time, in a borrowed apartment: in three months you had exhausted both your credit and your capacity to beg. There was no army now to clothe and feed you like a kind-hateful parent. No matter where the next meal came from, you would pay for it yourself.

In the following weeks you didn't exactly starve; ways could be found of earning a few dollars. Once a week you went round to the editorial offices of the *Dial,* which was then appearing every two weeks in a format something like that of the *Nation.* One of the editors was a friend of your wife's and he would give you half a dozen bad novels to review in fifty or a hundred words apiece. When the reviews were published you would be paid a dollar for each of them, but that mightn't be for weeks or months, and meanwhile you had to eat. So you would carry the books to a bench in Union Square and page through them hastily, making notes—in two or three hours you would be finished with the whole armful and then you would take them to a secondhand bookstore on Fourth Avenue, where the proprietor paid a flat rate of thirty-five cents for each review copy; you thought it was more than the novels were worth. With exactly $2.10 in your pocket you would buy bread and butter and lamb chops and Bull Durham for cigarettes and order a bag of coal; then at home you would broil the lamb chops over the grate because the landlady had neglected to pay her gas bill, just as you had neglected to pay the rent. You were all good friends and she would be invited to share in the feast. Next morning you would write the reviews, then start on the search for a few dollars more.

You began to feel that one meal a day was all that anyone needed and you wondered why anyone bothered to eat more. Late on a June day you were sitting in Sheridan Square trying to write a poem. "Move along, young fella," said the cop, and the poem was forgotten. Walking southward with the Woolworth Building visible in the distance you imagined a revolution in New York. Revolution was in the air that summer; the general strike had failed in Seattle, but a steel strike was being prepared, and a coal strike, and the railroad men were demanding government ownership—that was all right, but you imagined another kind of revolt, one that would start with a dance through the streets and barrels of cider opened at every corner, and beside each barrel a back-country ham fresh from the oven; the juice squirted out of it when you carved the first slice. Then—but only after you had finished the last of the ham and drained a pitcher of cider and stuffed your mouth with apple pie—then you would set about hanging policemen from the lamp posts, or better still from the crossties of the Elevated, and beside each policeman would be hanged a Methodist preacher, and beside each preacher a pansy poet. Editors would be poisoned with printer's ink: they would die horribly, vomiting ink on white paper. You hated editors, pansipoetical poets, policemen, preachers, you hated city streets . . . and suddenly the street went black. You hadn't even time to feel faint. The pavement rose and hit you between the eyes.

Nobody came to help, nobody even noticed that you had fallen. You scrambled to your feet, limped into a lunch wagon and spent your last dime for a roll and a cup of coffee. The revolution was postponed (on account of I was hungry, sergeant, honest I was too hungry) and the war was ended (listen, sojer, you're out of that man's army now, you're going back behind the plow, you gotta get rich, you son of a bitch). The war was over now and your long furlough was over. It was time to get a job.

2: The Greenwich Village Idea

In those days when division after division was landing in Hoboken and marching up Fifth Avenue in full battle equipment, when Americans were fighting the Bolshies in Siberia and guarding the Rhine—in those still belligerent days that followed the Armistice there was a private war between Greenwich Village and the *Saturday Evening Post*.

Other magazines fought in the same cause, but the *Post* was persistent and powerful enough to be regarded as chief of the aggressor nations. It published stories about the Villagers, editorials and articles against them, grave or flippant serials dealing with their customs in a mood of disparagement or alarm, humorous pieces done to order by its staff writers, cartoons in which the Villagers were depicted as long-haired men and short-haired women with ridiculous bone-rimmed spectacles—in all, a long campaign of invective beginning before the steel strike or the Palmer Raids and continuing through the jazz era, the boom and the depression. The burden of it was always the same: that the Village was the haunt of affectation; that it was inhabited by fools and fakers; that the fakers hid Moscow heresies under the disguise of cubism and free verse; that the fools would eventually be cured of their folly: they would forget this funny business about art and return to domesticity in South Bend, Indiana, and sell motorcars, and in the evenings sit with slippered feet while their children romped about them in paper caps made from the advertising pages of the *Saturday Evening Post*. The Village was dying, had died already, smelled to high heaven and Philadelphia. . . .

The Villagers did not answer this attack directly: instead they carried on a campaign of their own against the culture of which the *Post* seemed to be the final expression. They performed autopsies, they wrote obituaries of civilization in the United States, they shook the standardized dust of the country from their feet. Here, apparently, was a symbolic struggle: on the one side, the great megaphone of middle-class America; on the other, the American disciples of art and artistic living. Here, in its latest incarnation, was the eternal warfare of bohemian against bourgeois, poet against propriety—Villon and the

Bishop of Orléans, Keats and the quarterly reviewers, Rodolphe,
Mimi and the landlord. But perhaps, if we review the history
of the struggle, we shall find that the issue was other than it
seemed, and the enmity less ancient.

Alexander Pope, two centuries before, had taken the side of
property and propriety in a similar campaign against the slums
of art. When writing *The Dunciad* and the *Epistle to Dr. Ar-
buthnot,* he lumped together all his enemies—stingy patrons,
homosexual peers, hair-splitting pedants; but he reserved his
best-considered insults for the garret dwellers of Grub Street,
the dramatists whose lives were spent dodging the bailiff, the
epic poets "lulled by a zephyr through the broken pane." These
he accused of slander, dullness, theft, bootlicking, ingratitude,
every outrage to man and the Muses; almost the only charge
he did not press home against them was that of affectation.
They were not play-acting their poverty. The threadbare Miltons
of his day were rarely the children of prosperous parents; they
could not go home to Nottingham or Bristol and earn a comfortable living by selling hackney coaches; if they "turned a
Persian tale for half a crown," it was usually because they had
no other means of earning half a crown and so keeping themselves out of debtors' prison. And the substance of Pope's attack
against them is simply that they were poor, that they belonged
to a class beneath his own, without inherited wealth, that they
did not keep a gentleman's establishment, or possess a gentleman's easy manners, or the magnanimity of a gentleman sure
of tomorrow's dinner:

> Yet then did Gildon draw his venal quill;
> I wish'd the man a dinner, and sate still.
> Yet then did Dennis rave in furious fret;
> I never answer'd, I was not in debt.

Pope was a far wittier poet than any of his adversaries, but the forces he brought against them were not those of wit or poetry alone: behind him, massed in reserve, was all the prejudice of eighteenth-century gentlefolk against intruders into the polite world of letters. He was fighting a literary class war, and one that left deep wounds. To many a poor scribbler it meant the difference between starvation and the roast of mutton he lovingly appraised in a bake-shop window and promised himself to devour if his patron sent him a guinea: after *The Dunciad,* patrons closed their purses. Pope had inflicted a defeat on Grub Street but—the distinction is important—he had left bohemia untouched, for the simple reason that Queen Anne's and King George's London had no bohemia to defeat.

Grub Street is as old as the trade of letters—in Alexandria, in Rome, it was already a crowded quarter; bohemia is younger than the Romantic movement. Grub Street develops in the metropolis of any country or culture as soon as men are able to earn a precarious living with pen or pencil; bohemia is a revolt against certain features of industrial capitalism and can exist only in a capitalist society. Grub Street is a way of life unwillingly followed by the intellectual proletariat; bohemia attracts its citizens from all economic classes: there are not a few bohemian millionaires, but they are expected to imitate the customs of penniless artists. Bohemia is Grub Street romanticized, doctrinalized and rendered self-conscious; it is Grub Street on parade.

It originated in France, not England, and the approximate date of its birth was 1830: thus, it followed the rise of French industry after the Napoleonic Wars. The French Romantic poets complained of feeling oppressed—perhaps it was, as Musset believed, the fault of that great Emperor whose shadow fell across their childhood; perhaps it was Science, or the Industrial Revolution, or merely the money-grubbing, the stuffy morals

and stupid politics of the people about them; in any case they
had to escape from middle-class society. Some of them became
revolutionists; others took refuge in pure art; but most of them
demanded a real world of present satisfactions, in which they
could cherish aristocratic ideals while living among carpenters
and grisettes. The first bohemians, the first inhabitants of that
world, were the friends of Théophile Gautier and Gérard de
Nerval, young men of good family, bucks and dandies with
money enough to indulge their moods; but the legend of it was
spread abroad, some twenty years later, by a poor hack named
Henry Murger, the son of a German immigrant to Paris.

Having abandoned all hopes of a formal education when he
left primary school, and feeling no desire to follow his father's
trade of tailor, Murger began to write mediocre verse and paint
incredible pictures, meanwhile supporting himself by his wits.
Soon he joined a group that called itself the Water Drinkers because it could rarely afford another beverage. A dozen young
men with little talent and extravagant ambitions, they lived in
hovels or in lofts over a cow stable, worked under the lash of
hunger, and wasted their few francs in modest debauchery. One
winter they had a stove for the first time: it was a hole cut in the
floor, through which the animal heat of the stable rose into their
chamber. They suffered from the occupational diseases of poor
artists—consumption, syphilis, pneumonia—all of them aggravated by undernourishment. Joseph Desbrosses died in the
winter of 1844; he was an able sculptor, possibly the one genius
of the group. His funeral was the third in six weeks among the
Water Drinkers, and they emptied their pockets to buy a wooden
cross for the grave. When the last sod clumped down, the gravediggers stood waiting for their tip. There was not a sou in the
party.

"That's all right," said the gravediggers generously, recognizing the mourners. "It will be for the next time."

Spring came and their feelings rose with the mercury. One evening when his friends were making war maps in water color, Murger began unexpectedly to tell them stories. They listened, chuckled and roared for two good hours, till somebody advised him, seriously between gales of laughter, to abandon poetry for fiction. A little later he followed this advice, writing about the life of his friends, the only life he knew. Personally he hated this existence on the cold fringes of starvation and planned to escape from it as soon as he could, but for the public he tried to render it attractive.

In *Scènes de la Vie de Bohême,* he succeeded beyond his ambition. He succeeded not only in writing a popular book, one that was translated into twenty languages, successfully dramatized, candied into an opera, one that enabled its author to live in bourgeois comfort, but also in changing an image in the public mind. Grub Street, where dinnerless Gildon drew his venal quill, contemptible Grub Street, the haunt of apprentices and failures and Henry Murger, was transformed into glamorous bohemia. The unwilling expedient became a permanent way of life, became a cult with rituals and costumes, a doctrine adhered to not only by artists, young and old, rich and poor, but also in later years by designers, stylists, trade-paper sub-editors, interior decorators, wolves, fairies, millionaire patrons of art, sadists, nymphomaniacs, bridge sharks, anarchists, women living on alimony, tired reformers, educational cranks, economists, hopheads, dipsomaniac playwrights, nudists, restaurant keepers, stockbrokers and dentists craving self-expression.

Even during Murger's lifetime, the bohemian cult was spreading from France into other European countries. Having occupied a whole section of Paris—three sections, in fact, for it moved from the Boul' Mich' to Montmartre and thence to Montparnasse—it founded new colonies in Munich, Berlin, London, St.

Petersburg. In the late 1850s it reached New York, where it established headquarters in Charlie Pfaff's lager-beer saloon under
the sidewalk of lower Broadway. Again in 1894 the "Trilby"
craze spawned forth dozens of bohemian groups and magazines;
in New York a writer explained that the true bohemia may exist
at millionaires' tables; in Philadelphia young married couples
south of Market Street would encourage their guests: "Don't
stand on ceremony; you know we are thorough bohemians." All
over the Western world, bohemia was carrying on a long warfare with conventional society, but year by year it was making
more converts from the ranks of the enemy.

When the American magazines launched their counteroffen-
sive, in 1919, a curious phenomenon was to be observed. The
New York bohemians, the Greenwich Villagers, came from exactly the same social class as the readers of the *Saturday Evening
Post*. Their political opinions were vague and by no means dangerous to Ford Motors or General Electric: the war had destroyed their belief in political action. They were trying to get
ahead, and the proletariat be damned. Their economic standards
were those of the small American businessman.

The art-shop era was just beginning. Having fled from Du-
buque and Denver to escape the stultifying effects of a civilization ruled by business, many of the Villagers had already entered business for themselves, and many more were about to
enter it. They would open tea shops, antique shops, book shops,
yes, and bridge parlors, dance halls, night clubs and real-estate
offices. By hiring shop assistants, they would become the ex-
ploiters of labor. If successful, they tried to expand their one
restaurant into a chain of restaurants, all with a delightfully free
and intimate atmosphere, but run on the best principles of business accounting. Some of them leased houses, remodeled them
into studio apartments, and raised the rents three or four hundred per cent to their new tenants. Others clung faithfully to

their profession of painting or writing, rose in it slowly, and at last had their stories or illustrations accepted by *Collier's* or the *Saturday Evening Post*. There were occasions, I believe, when Greenwich Village writers were editorially encouraged to write stories making fun of the Village, and some of them were glad to follow the suggestion. Of course they complained, when slightly tipsy, that they were killing themselves—but how else could they maintain their standard of living? What they meant was that they could not live like *Vanity Fair* readers without writing for the *Saturday Evening Post*.

And so it was that many of them lived during the prosperous decade that followed. If the book succeeded or if they got a fat advertising contract, they bought houses in Connecticut, preferably not too far from the Sound. They hired butlers; they sent their children to St. Somebody's; they collected highboys, lowboys, tester beds; they joined the local Hunt and rode in red coats across New England stone fences and through wine-red sumacs in pursuit of a bag of imported aniseed. In the midst of these new pleasures they continued to bewail the standardization of American life, while the magazines continued their polemic against Greenwich Village. You came to suspect that some of the Villagers themselves, even those who remained below Fourteenth Street, were not indignant at a publicity that brought tourists to the Pirates' Den and customers to Ye Olde Curiowe Shoppe and increased the value of the land in which a few of them had begun to speculate. The whole thing seemed like a sham battle. Yet beneath it was a real conflict of ideas and one that would soon be mirrored in the customs of a whole country.

Greenwich Village was not only a place, a mood, a way of life: like all bohemias, it was also a doctrine. Since the days of Gautier and Murger, this doctrine had remained the same in spirit, but it had changed in several details. By 1920, it had become a system of ideas that could roughly be summarized as follows:

1. The idea of salvation by the child.—Each of us at birth has special potentialities which are slowly crushed and destroyed by a standardized society and mechanical methods of teaching. If a new educational system can be introduced, one by which children are encouraged to develop their own personalities, to blossom freely like flowers, then the world will be saved by this new, free generation.

2. The idea of self-expression.—Each man's, each woman's, purpose in life is to express himself, to realize his full individuality through creative work and beautiful living in beautiful surroundings.

3. The idea of paganism.—The body is a temple in which there is nothing unclean, a shrine to be adorned for the ritual of love.

4. The idea of living for the moment.—It is stupid to pile up treasures that we can enjoy only in old age, when we have lost the capacity for enjoyment. Better to seize the moment as it comes, to dwell in it intensely, even at the cost of future suffering. Better to live extravagantly, gather June rosebuds, "burn my candle at both ends. . . . It gives a lovely light."

5. The idea of liberty.—Every law, convention or rule of art that prevents self-expression or the full enjoyment of the moment should be shattered and abolished. Puritanism is the great enemy. The crusade against puritanism is the only crusade with which free individuals are justified in allying themselves.

6. The idea of female equality.—Women should be the economic and moral equals of men. They should have the same pay, the same working conditions, the same opportunity for drinking, smoking, taking or dismissing lovers.

7. The idea of psychological adjustment.—We are unhappy because we are maladjusted, and maladjusted because we are

repressed. If our individual repressions can be removed—by confessing them to a Freudian psychologist—then we can adjust ourselves to any situation, and be happy in it. (But Freudianism is only one method of adjustment. What is wrong with us may be our glands, and by a slight operation, or merely by taking a daily dose of thyroid, we may alter our whole personalities. Again, we may adjust ourselves by some such psycho-physical discipline as was taught by Gurdjieff. The implication of all these methods is the same—that the environment itself need not be altered. That explains why most radicals who became converted to psychoanalysis or glands or Gurdjieff [1] gradually abandoned their political radicalism.)

8. The idea of changing place.—"They do things better in Europe." England and Germany have the wisdom of old cultures; the Latin peoples have admirably preserved their pagan heritage. By expatriating himself, by living in Paris, Capri or the South of France, the artist can break the puritan shackles, drink, live freely and be wholly creative.

All these, from the standpoint of the business-Christian ethic then represented by the *Saturday Evening Post,* were corrupt ideas. This older ethic is familiar to most people, but one feature of it has not been sufficiently emphasized. Substantially, it was a *production* ethic. The great virtues it taught were industry, foresight, thrift and personal initiative. The workman should be industrious in order to produce more for his employer; he should look ahead to the future; he should save money in order to become a capitalist himself; then he should exercise personal initiative and found new factories where other workmen would toil industriously, and save, and become capitalists in their turn.

[1] George Ivanovich Gurdjieff, a Russian living in France, had worked out a system of practical mysticism based largely on Yoga. His chief disciple was A. E. Orage, the editor of the *New English Weekly.* In the spring of 1924, when Orage was in New York, he gained a great many converts, chiefly among older members of the Greenwich Village set.

During the process many people would suffer privations: most workers would live meagerly and wrack their bodies with labor; even the employers would deny themselves luxuries that they could easily purchase, choosing instead to put back the money into their business; but after all, our bodies were not to be pampered; they were temporary dwelling places, and we should be rewarded in Heaven for our self-denial. On earth, our duty was to accumulate more wealth and produce more goods, the ultimate use of which was no subject for worry. They would somehow be absorbed, by new markets opened in the West, or overseas in new countries, or by the increased purchasing power of workmen who had saved and bettered their position.

That was the ethic of a young capitalism, and it worked admirably, so long as the territory and population of the country were expanding faster than its industrial plant. But after the war the situation changed. Our industries had grown enormously to satisfy a demand that suddenly ceased. To keep the factory wheels turning, a new domestic market had to be created. Industry and thrift were no longer adequate. There must be a new ethic that encouraged people to buy, a *consumption* ethic.

It happened that many of the Greenwich Village ideas proved useful in the altered situation. Thus, *self-expression* and *paganism* encouraged a demand for all sorts of products—modern furniture, beach pajamas, cosmetics, colored bathrooms with toilet paper to match. *Living for the moment* meant buying an automobile, radio or house, using it now and paying for it tomorrow. *Female equality* was capable of doubling the consumption of products—cigarettes, for example—that had formerly been used by men alone. Even *changing place* would help to stimulate business in the country from which the artist was being expatriated. The exiles of art were also trade missionaries: involuntarily they increased the foreign demand for fountain pens, silk stockings, grapefruit and portable typewriters. They drew after them an invading army of tourists, thus swelling the profits of steamship lines and travel agencies. Everything fitted into the business picture.

I don't mean to say that Greenwich Village was the source of the revolution in morals that affected all our lives in the decade after the war, and neither do I mean that big business deliberately plotted to render the nation extravagant, pleasure worshiping and reckless of tomorrow.

The new moral standards arose from conditions that had nothing to do with the Village. They were, as a matter of fact, not really new. Always, even in the great age of the Puritans, there had been currents of licentiousness that were favored by the immoderate American climate and held in check only by hellfire preaching and the hardships of settling a new country. Old Boston, Providence, rural Connecticut, all had their underworlds. The reason puritanism became so strong in America was perhaps that it had to be strong in order to checkmate its enemies. But it was already weakening as the country grew richer in the twenty years before the war; and the war itself was the puritan crisis and defeat.

All standards were relaxed in the stormy-sultry wartime atmosphere. It wasn't only the boys of my age, those serving in the army, who were transformed by events: their sisters and younger brothers were affected in a different fashion. With their fathers away, perhaps, and their mothers making bandages or tea-dancing with lonely officers, it was possible for boys and girls to do what they pleased. For the first time they could go to dances unchaperoned, drive the family car and park it by the roadside while they made love, and come home after midnight, a little tipsy, with nobody to reproach them in the hallway.

They took advantage of these stolen liberties—indeed, one might say that the revolution in morals began as a middle-class children's revolt.

But everything conspired to further it. Prohibition came and surrounded the new customs with illicit glamour; prosperity made it possible to practice them; Freudian psychology provided a philosophical justification and made it unfashionable to be repressed; still later the sex magazines and the movies, even the pulpit, would advertise a revolution that had taken place silently and triumphed without a struggle. In all this Greenwich Village had no part. The revolution would have occurred if the Village had never existed, but—the point is important—it would not have followed the same course. The Village, older in revolt, gave form to the movement, created its fashions, and supplied the writers and illustrators who would render them popular. As for American business, though it laid no plots in advance, it was quick enough to use the situation, to exploit the new markets for cigarettes and cosmetics, and to realize that, in advertising pages and movie palaces, sex appeal was now the surest appeal.

The Greenwich Village standards, with the help of business, had spread through the country. Young women east and west had bobbed their hair, let it grow and bobbed it again; they had passed through the period when corsets were checked in the cloakroom at dances and the period when corsets were not worn. They were not very self-conscious when they talked about taking a lover; and the conversations ran from mother fixations to birth control while they smoked cigarettes between the courses of luncheons eaten in black-and-orange tea shops just like those in the Village. People of forty had been affected by the younger generation: they spent too much money, drank too much gin, made love to one another's wives and talked about their neuroses. Houses were furnished to look like studios. Stenographers went on parties, following the example of the boss and his girl friend and her husband. The "party," conceived as a gathering together of men and women to drink gin cocktails, flirt, dance to the phonograph or radio and gossip about their absent friends, had in fact become one of the most popular American institutions; nobody stopped to think how short its history had been in this country. It developed out of the "orgies" celebrated by the French 1830 Romantics, but it was introduced into this country by Greenwich Villagers—before being adopted by salesmen from Kokomo and the younger country-club set in Kansas City.

Wherever one turned the Greenwich Village ideas were making their way: even the *Saturday Evening Post* was feeling their influence. Long before Repeal, it began to wobble on Prohibition. It allowed drinking, petting and unfaithfulness to be mentioned in the stories it published; its illustrations showed women smoking. Its advertising columns admitted one after another of the strictly pagan products—cosmetics, toilet tissues, cigarettes —yet still it continued to thunder against Greenwich Village and bohemian immorality. It even nourished the illusion that its long campaign had been successful. On more than one occasion it announced that the Village was dead and buried: "The sad truth is," it said in the autumn of 1931, "that the Village was a flop." Perhaps it was true that the Village was moribund—of that we can't be sure, for creeds and ways of life among artists are hard to kill. If, however, the Village was really dying, it was dying of success. It was dying because it became so popular that too many people insisted on living there. It was dying because women smoked cigarettes on the streets of the Bronx, drank gin cocktails in Omaha and had perfectly swell parties in Seattle and Middletown—in other words, because American business and the whole of middle-class America had been going Greenwich Village.

3: The League of Youth

But the Village, when we first came there to live, was undergoing a crisis. People were talking about the good old days of
1916. It seemed unlikely that they would ever return.

The Village, before America entered the war, contained two
mingled currents: one of those had now disappeared. It contained two types of revolt, the individual and the social—or the
aesthetic and the political, or the revolt against puritanism and
the revolt against capitalism—we might tag the two of them
briefly as *bohemianism* and *radicalism*. In those prewar days,
however, the two currents were hard to distinguish. Bohemians
read Marx and all the radicals had a touch of the bohemian: it
seemed that both types were fighting in the same cause. Social-
ism, free love, anarchism, syndicalism, free verse—all these creeds
were lumped together by the public, and all were physically
dangerous to practice. Bill Haywood, the one-eyed man-moun-
tain, the Cyclops of the IWW, appeared regularly at Mabel
Dodge's Wednesday nights, in a crowd of assorted poets and
Cubist painters who, listening to his slow speech, might fancy
themselves in the midst of the fight at Cœur d'Alene. During
the bread riots of 1915 the Wobblies made their headquarters
in Mary Vorse's studio on Tenth Street; and Villagers might get
their heads broken in Union Square by the police before appearing at the Liberal Club to recite Swinburne in bloody bandages. The Liberal Club was the social center of the Village, just
as the *Masses,* which also represented both tendencies, was its
intellectual center.

But the war, and especially the Draft Law, separated the two currents. People were suddenly forced to decide what kind of rebels they were: if they were merely rebels against puritanism they could continue to exist safely in Mr. Wilson's world. The political rebels had no place in it. Some of them yielded, joined the crusade for democracy, fought the Bolsheviks at Archangel, or volunteered to help the Intelligence Service by spying on their former associates and submitting typewritten reports about them to the Adjutant General's office. Others evaded the draft by fleeing to Mexico, where they were joined by a number of the former aesthetes, who had suddenly discovered that they were political rebels too. Still others stood by their opinions and went to Leavenworth Prison. Whatever course they followed, almost all the radicals of 1917 were defeated by events. The bohemian tendency triumphed in the Village, and talk about revolution gave way to talk about psychoanalysis. The *Masses,* after being suppressed, and after temporarily reappearing as the *Liberator,* gave way to magazines like the *Playboy,* the *Pagan* (their names expressed them adequately) and the *Little Review.*

After the war the Village was full of former people. There were former anarchists who had made fortunes manufacturing munitions, former Wobblies about to open speakeasies, former noblewomen divorced or widowed, former suffragists who had been arrested after picketing the White House, former conscientious objectors paroled from Leavenworth, former aviators and soldiers of fortune, former settlement workers, German spies, strike leaders, poets, city editors of Socialist dailies. But the distinguished foreign artists who had worked in the Village from 1914 till 1917, and given it a new character, had disappeared along with the active labor leaders. Nobody seemed to be doing anything now, except lamenting the time's decay. For the moment the Village was empty of young men.

But the young men were arriving from week to week, as colleges held commencement exercises or troops were demobilized.

One of the first results of their appearance was the final dissolution of the Liberal Club.

Its members had been resigning or leaving their dues unpaid. As a means of paying off its debts, the club voted to hold a dance —not an ordinary Webster Hall affair, but a big dance, uptown at the Hotel Commodore, with a pageant, and thousands of tickets sold, and none given away. But of course they were given away in the end. Everybody in the Village expected to be invited to every Village function, simply by right of residence, and the Liberal Club was forced to yield to a mass demand that was accompanied by threats of gate-crashings and riots.

On one of our free tickets we took with us a young lady who had just graduated from Radcliffe.

The dance at the Commodore was something new in Village history: there were so many youngsters, such high spirits, so many people not drinking quietly as in the old days, but with a frantic desire to get drunk and enjoy themselves. After midnight there were little commotions everywhere in the ballroom. Laurence Vail was deciding that people were disagreeable and was telling them so in a most polite way, but some of them didn't like being called smug—it took four detectives to throw him out, and he left behind him a great handful of bloodstained yellow hair. I noticed people gathering about the Radcliffe young lady admiringly, and later I saw them avoiding her; she had developed the habit of biting them in the arm and shrieking. Once, having bitten a strange Pierrot, she jumped backward with a shriek into a great Chinese vase. It crashed to the floor.

We never saw her after that night. She had met a copy-desk man and later I heard that he was asking the address of an abortionist; still later she wrote that she was married and had a baby. There were many people like that; they appeared in the Village, made themselves the center of a dance or a crowd, everybody liked or hated them and told stories about them; then suddenly they were gone, living in Flatbush, Queens or Keokuk, holding down jobs or wheeling baby carriages. But the vase was the end of the Liberal Club, the broken vase that cost so much to replace and the free tickets. The dance at the Commodore had been a great success and had emptied the treasury. After that the social centers of the Village were two saloons: the Hell Hole, on Sixth Avenue at the corner of West Fourth Street, and the Working Girls' Home, at Greenwich Avenue and Christopher Street. The Hell Hole was tough and dirty; the proprietor kept a pig in the cellar and fed it scraps from the free-lunch counter. The boys in the back room were small-time gamblers and petty thieves, but the saloon was also patronized by actors and writers from the Provincetown Playhouse, which was just around the corner. Sometimes the two groups mingled. The gangsters admired Dorothy Day because she could drink them under the table; but they felt more at home with Eugene O'Neill, who listened to their troubles and never criticized. They pitied him, too, because he was thin and shabbily dressed. One of them said to him, "You go to any department store, Gene, and pick yourself an overcoat and tell me what size it is and I steal it for you." The Hell Hole stayed in business during the first two or three years of prohibition, but then it was closed and I don't know where the gangsters met after that. The actors and playwrights moved on to the Working Girls' Home, where the front door was locked, but where a side door on Christopher Street still led into a room where Luke O'Connor served Old Fashioneds and the best beer and stout he could buy from the wildcat breweries.

It was in the Working Girls' Home that I first became conscious of the difference between two generations. There were two sorts of people here: those who had lived in the Village before 1917 and those who had just arrived from France or college. For the first time I came to think of them as "they" and "we."

"They" wore funny clothes: it was the first thing that struck you about them. The women had evolved a regional costume, then widely cartooned in the magazines: hair cut in a Dutch bob, hat carried in the hand, a smock of some bright fabric (often embroidered Russian linen), a skirt rather shorter than the fashion of the day, gray cotton stockings and sandals. With heels set firmly on the ground and abdomens protruding a little —since they wore no corsets and dieting hadn't become popular —they had a look of unexampled solidity; it was terrifying to be advanced upon by six of them in close formation. But this costume wasn't universal. Some women preferred tight-fitting tailored suits with Buster Brown collars; one had a five-gallon hat which she wore on all occasions, and there was a girl who always appeared in riding boots, swinging a crop, as if she had galloped down Sixth Avenue, watered her horse and tied him to a pillar of the Elevated; I called her Yoicks. The men, as a rule, were more conventional, but tweedy and unpressed. They did not let their hair grow over their collars, but they had a good deal more of it than was permitted by fashion. There were a few Russian blouses among them, a few of the authentic Windsor ties that marked the bohemians of the 1890s.

"They" tried to be individual, but there is a moment when individualism becomes a uniform in spite of itself. "We" were accustomed to uniforms and content to wear that of the American middle classes. We dressed inconspicuously, as well as we were able.

"They" were older, and this simple fact continued to impress me long after I ceased to notice their clothes. Their ages ran from sixty down to twenty-three; at one end of the scale there was hardly any difference. But the Village had a pervading atmosphere of middle-agedness. To stay in New York during the war was a greater moral strain than to enter the army: there were more decisions to be made and uneasily justified; also there were defeats to be concealed. The Village in 1919 was like a conquered country. Its inhabitants were discouraged and drank joylessly. "We" came among them with an unexpended store of energy: we had left our youth at home, and for two years it had been accumulating at compound interest; now we were eager to lavish it even on trivial objects.

And what did the older Villagers think of us? We had fresh faces and a fresh store of jokes and filthy songs collected in the army; we were nice to take on parties, to be amused by and to lecture. Sometimes they were cruel to us in a deliberately thoughtless way. Sometimes they gave us advice which was never taken because it was obviously a form of boasting. I don't believe they thought much about us at all.

But these differences in costume, age and mood were only the symbols of another difference. Though our paths had momentarily converged, they were not the same. "We" had followed the highroad; "they" had revolted and tried to break new trails.

"They" had once been rebels, political, moral, artistic or religious—in any case they had paid the price of their rebellion. They had separated themselves from parents, husbands, wives; they had slammed doors like Nora in *A Doll's House;* they never got letters from home. "We," on the other hand, had never broken with our parents, never walked stormily out of church, never been expelled from school for writing essays on anarchism. We had avoided issues and got what we wanted in a quiet way, simply by taking it. During the ten years that preceded the war something had happened to the relations between parents and children. The older Villagers had been so close to their fathers and mothers that, in a way, they had been forced to quarrel with and reject them. "We" had been placed at a greater distance from our elders; we liked and even loved them without in the least

respecting their opinions; we said, "Yes, sir," if we were Southerners, "All right," if we lived in a Northern city, and did what
we pleased.

"They" had been rebels: they wanted to change the world,
be leaders in the fight for justice and art, help to create a society
in which individuals could express themselves. "We" were convinced at the time that society could never be changed by an effort of the will.

"They" had been rebels, full of proud illusions. They made
demands on life itself, that it furnish them with beautiful adventures, honest friendships, love freely given and returned in
an appropriate setting. Now, with illusions shattered, they were
cynics. "We," on the contrary, were greatly humble and did not
ask of Nature that she gild our happy moments or wildly re-
echo our passions. We did not feel that our arguments on aesthetics should take place in aesthetic surroundings: we were content to sit in the kitchen, two or three young men with our feet
on the bare table, discussing the problem of abstract beauty while
we rolled Bull Durham into cigarettes and let the flakes sift
down into our laps. We had lost our ideals at a very early age,
and painlessly. If any of them survived the war, they had disappeared in the midst of the bickerings at Versailles, or later with
the steel strike, the Palmer Raids, the Centralia massacre. But
they did not leave us bitter. We believed that we had fought for
an empty cause, that the Germans were no worse than the Allies,
no better, that the world consisted of fools and scoundrels ruled
by scoundrels and fools, that everybody was selfish and could
be bought for a price, that we were as bad as the others—all this
we took for granted. But it was fun all the same. We were content to build our modest happiness in the wreck of "their" lost
illusions, a cottage in the ruins of a palace.

Among the furnishings of this cottage—it was more likely to
be three upright coffin-shaped rooms at the top of an Italian tene-

ment, with the walls painted green or tenement brown and sweating in winter when the gas stove was burning, while in summer the odors of thirty Italian suppers mingled in the hall-way and seeped through the open transom—among the college textbooks, the crossed German bayonets, the complete works of Jules Laforgue, there was not much room for what I have called the Greenwich Village ideas. It was not so much that we re-jected them: they simply did not touch us. The idea of salvation by the child was embodied in "progressive education," a topic that put us to sleep. The idea of self-expression caused people to be "arty"—it was our generation that invented the word. We might act like pagans, we might live for the moment, but we tried not to be self-conscious about it. We couldn't see much use in crusading against puritanism: it had ceased to interfere with our personal lives and, though it seemed to be triumphant, it had suffered a moral defeat and would slowly disappear. Female equality was a good idea, perhaps, but the feminists we knew wore spectacles and flat-heeled shoes. As for psychological ad-justment, we were too young to have felt the need of it.

Later we should be affected by the Greenwich Village ideas, but only at second hand and only after they had begun to affect the rest of the country. The truth is that "we," the newcomers to the Village, were not bohemians. We lived in top-floor tene-ments along the Sixth Avenue Elevated because we couldn't af-ford to live elsewhere. Either we thought of our real home as existing in the insubstantial world of art, or else we were simply young men on the make, the humble citizens not of bohemia but of Grub Street.

4: The French Line Pier, 1921

But there was one idea that was held in common by the older
and the younger inhabitants of the Village—the idea of salvation by exile. "They do things better in Europe: let's go there."
This was not only the undertone of discussions at Luke O'Connor's saloon; it was also the recurrent melody of an ambitious
work, a real symposium, then being prepared for the printer.

Civilization in the United States was written by thirty intellectuals, of whom only a few, say ten at the most, had been living in the Village. There were no Communists or even right-
wing Socialists among the thirty. "Desirous of avoiding merely
irrelevant criticism," said Harold Stearns in his Preface, "we
provided that all contributors to the volume must be American
citizens. For the same reason, we likewise provided that in the
list there should be no professional propagandists . . . no martyrs, and no one who was merely disgruntled." All Village cranks
were strictly excluded. But Harold Stearns, the editor, lived in
a remodeled house at 31 Jones Street. The editorial meetings
were conducted in his basement while often a Village party
squeaked and thundered on the floor above. And the book that
resulted from the labors of these thirty intellectuals embodied
what might be called the more sober side of Village opinion.

Rereading it today, one is chiefly impressed by the limited
vision of these men who were trying to survey and evaluate the
whole of American civilization. They knew nothing about vast
sections of the country, particularly the South and the Southwest. They knew little about the life of the upper classes and
nothing (except statistically) about the life of the industrial proletariat. They were city men: if any one of the thirty had been

familiar with farming, he would have prevented the glaring pomicultural error made by Lewis Mumford on the second page of the book.[2] They were ridiculously ignorant of the younger generation. The civilization which they really surveyed was the civilization shared in by people over thirty, with incomes between two thousand and twenty thousand dollars, living in cities north of the Ohio and east of the Rockies.

As a matter of fact, their book was more modest than its pretentious title. They were not trying to present or solve the problem of American civilization as a whole. They were trying to answer one question that touched them more closely: why was there, in America, no satisfying career open to talent? Every year hundreds, thousands of gifted young men and women graduated from our colleges; they entered life as these thirty intellectuals had entered it; they brought with them a rich endowment, but they accomplished little. Why did all this promise result in so few notable careers?

It was Van Wyck Brooks, in his essay on "The Literary Life," who stated the problem most eloquently and with the deepest conviction:

What immediately strikes one as one surveys the history of our literature during the last half century, is the singular impotence of

---

[2] Mumford said, ". . . the story of the Western movement is somehow summed up in the legend of Johnny Appleseed, who planted dry apple seeds, instead of slips from the living tree, and hedged the roads he traveled with wild apples, harsh and puny and inedible." The statement is large and empty, historically and horticulturally. The real John Chapman planted orchards, not hedges, and he returned to take care of them. He couldn't have traveled through the wilderness carrying thousands of "slips from the living tree." Slips have no roots and wouldn't have grown unless grafted on other living trees. The fruit from seedling apple trees isn't always "harsh and puny and inedible." Some of it is delicious; all of it can be used for making cider, apple butter and vinegar, the products that were useful to the pioneers.

its creative spirit. . . . One can count on one's two hands the American writers who are able to carry on the development and unfolding of their individualities, year in, year out, as every competent man of affairs carries on his business. What fate overtakes the rest? Shall I begin to run over some of those names, familiar to us all, names that have signified so much promise and are lost in what Gautier calls "the limbo where moan (in the company of babes) stillborn vocations, abortive attempts, larvae of ideas that have won neither wings nor shapes"? Shall I mention the writers—but they are countless!— who have lapsed into silence, or have involved themselves in barren eccentricities, or have been turned into machines? The poets who, at the very outset of their careers, find themselves extinguished like so many candles? The novelists who have been unable to grow up, and remain withered boys of seventeen? The critics who find themselves overtaken in mid-career by a hardening of the spiritual arteries? . . . Weeds and wild flowers! Weeds without beauty or fragrance, and wild flowers that cannot survive the heat of the day.

Nowhere else is the problem stated with such deep feeling. But the other contributors are conscious of it: each in his own field they make the same report. "Journalism in America is no longer a profession through which a man can win to a place of real dignity among his neighbors." As for politics, the average congressman "is incompetent and imbecile, and not only incompetent and imbecile, but also incurably dishonest. . . . It is almost impossible to imagine a man of genuine self-respect and dignity offering himself as a candidate for the lower house." In music, art, medicine, scholarship, advertising, the theater, everywhere the story is the same: there is no scope for individualism; ignorance, unculture or, at the best, mediocrity has triumphed; the doors are closed to talent. And what is the explanation?

Here again the thirty intellectuals have the same story to tell. 'In view both of the fact that every contributor has full liberty of opinion and that the personalities and points of view finding expression in these essays are all highly individualistic, the underlying unity which binds the volume together is really surprising." The individualistic army has its own uniform. There were three or four who didn't wear it—thus, Conrad Aiken's essay on American Poetry is an appraisal, not an indictment, and has about it an air of final justice; Leo Wolman writing on Labor and George Soule on Radicalism are objective and critical, and analyze the weaknesses of these movements with an eye to the possibility of correcting them in the future. But most of the contributors may be treated conjointly and anonymously. One after another they come forward to tell us that American civilization itself is responsible for the tragedy of American talent.

Life in this country is joyless and colorless, universally standardized, tawdry, uncreative, given over to the worship of wealth and machinery. "The highest achievements of our material civilization . . . count as so many symbols of its spiritual failure." It is possible that this failure can be explained by a fundamental sexual inadequacy. The wife of the American businessman "finds him so sexually inapt that she refuses to bear him children and so driveling in every way except as a money-getter that she compels him to expend his energies solely in that direction while she leads a discontented, sterile, stunted life." She seeks compensation by making herself the empress of culture. "Hardly any intelligent foreigner has failed to observe and comment upon the extraordinary feminization of American social life, and oftenest he has coupled this observation with a few biting remarks concerning the intellectual anemia or torpor that seems to accompany it."—"In almost every branch of American life there is a sharp dichotomy between preaching and practice . . . the moral code resolves itself into the one cardinal heresy of being found out."—"The most moving and pathetic fact in the social life of America today is emotional and aesthetic starvation." And what is the remedy?

On this topic the chorus, so united in attack, becomes weak and discordant. Since the thirty contributors are city men, and for the most part New Yorkers, they feel that some good might be done by increasing the influence of the city at the expense of the small town, of the metropolis at the expense of the provinces. Since they are intellectuals and extremely class-conscious, they feel that the various professions should organize to better their own position and support intellectual standards. Being critics, they assume that criticism will help "in making a real civilization possible . . . a field cannot be plowed until it has first been cleared of rocks." They have a vague belief in aristocracy and in the possibility of producing real aristocrats through education. Beyond this point, their remedies differ. Van Wyck Brooks gives a moral lecture to writers, adjuring them to be creative. H. L. Mencken believes that our political life might be made over merely by abolishing the residential qualification for elective offices. Harold Stearns is inclined to cynicism. "One shudders slightly," he says, "and turns to the impeccable style, the slightly tired and sensuous irony of Anatole France for relief." On the whole, they question the efficacy of their own prescriptions. "One can feel the whole industrial and economic system as so maladjusted to the primary and simple needs of men and women"—that we ought to change the system? No, these are sensible men, not propagandists, and they see no possibility of changing the system. Instead they bring forth a milder remedy—"that the futility of a rationalistic attack on these infantilisms of compensation becomes obvious. There must be an entirely new deal of the cards in one sense; we must change our hearts." But is this remedy really simpler? Is a change in heart any easier to accomplish than a change in the system?

The intellectuals had explored many paths; they had found no way of escape; one after another they had opened doors that led only into the cupboards and linen closets of the mind. "What should a young man do?" asked Harold Stearns in an article written for the *Freeman*. This time his answer was simple and uncompromising. A young man had no future in this country of hypocrisy and repression. He should take ship for Europe, where people know how to live.

Early in July 1921, just after finishing his Preface and delivering the completed manuscript to the publisher, Mr. Stearns left this country, perhaps forever. His was no ordinary departure: he was Alexander marching into Persia and Byron shaking the dust of England from his feet. Reporters came to the gangplank to jot down his last words. Everywhere young men were preparing to follow his example. Among the contributors to *Civilization in the United States,* not many could go: most of them were moderately successful men who had achieved security without achieving freedom. But the younger and footloose intellectuals went streaming up the longest gangplank in the world; they were preparing a great migration eastward into new prairies of the mind.

"I'm going to Paris," they said at first, and then, "I'm going to the South of France. . . . I'm sailing Wednesday—next month —as soon as I can scrape together money enough to buy a ticket." Money wasn't impossible to scrape together; some of it could be saved from one's salary or borrowed from one's parents or one's friends. Newspapers and magazines were interested in reports from Europe, two or three foundations had fellowships for study abroad, and publishers sometimes made advances against the future royalties of an unwritten book. In those days publishers were looking for future authors, and the authors insisted that their books would have to be finished in France, where one could live for next to nothing. "Good-by, so long," they said, "I'll meet you on the Left Bank. I'll drink your health in good red Burgundy, I'll kiss all the girls for you. I'm sick of this country. I'm going abroad to write one good novel."

And we ourselves, the newcomers to the Village, were leaving it if we could. The long process of deracination had reached its climax. School and college had uprooted us in spirit; the war had physically uprooted us, carried us into strange countries and left us finally in the metropolis of the uprooted. Now even New York seemed too American, too close to home. On its river side, Greenwich Village was bounded by the French Line pier.

In the late spring of 1921 I was awarded an American Field Service fellowship for study at a French university. It was only twelve thousand francs, or about a thousand dollars at that year's rate of exchange, but it also entitled my wife and me to a reduction of fifty per cent in our cabin-class steamship fares. We planned to live as economically as a French couple, and we did. With the help of a few small checks from American magazines, the fellowship kept us in modest comfort, even permitting us to travel, and it was renewed for the following year. When we left New York hardly anyone came to the ship to say good-by. Most of our friends had sailed already; the others were wistful people who promised to follow us in a few months. The Village was almost deserted, except for the pounding feet of young men from Davenport and Pocatello who came to make a name for themselves and live in glamour—who came because there was nowhere else to go.

III: Traveller's Cheque

1: Valuta

The exiles of 1921 came to Europe seeking one thing and found another. They came to recover the good life and the traditions of art, to free themselves from organized stupidity, to win their deserved place in the hierarchy of the intellect. Having come in search of values, they found valuta.

Exchange! It happened that old Europe, the continent of immemorial standards, had lost them all: it had only prices, which changed from country to country, from village to village, it seemed from hour to hour. Tuesday in Hamburg you might order a banquet for eight cents (or was it five?); Thursday in Paris you might buy twenty cigarettes for the price of a week's lodging in Vienna. You might gamble in Munich for high stakes, win half the fortune of a Czechoslovakian profiteer, then, if you could not spend your winnings for champagne and Picasso, you might give them day after tomorrow to a beggar and not be thanked. Once in Berlin a man was about to pay ten marks for a box of matches when he stopped to look at the banknote in his hand. On it was written, "For these ten marks I sold my virtue." He wrote a long virtuous story about it, was paid ten million marks, and bought his mistress a pair of artificial silk stockings.

Nobody was honest in those days: the seller could not cheat

enough to profit, nor the buyer give anything but paper. Those who had gold, or currency redeemable in gold, hastened toward the cheapest markets. There sprang into being a new race of tourists, the *Valutaschweine,* the parasites of the exchange, who wandered from France to Rumania, from Italy to Poland, in quest of the vilest prices and the most admirable gangrenes of society. Suddenly indifferent to the past of Europe, they were seen in fashionable hotels, in money-changers' booths, in night clubs oftener than in museums; but especially you saw them in the railway station at Innsbruck: Danes, Hindus, Yankees, South Americans, wine-cheeked Englishmen, more Yankees, waiting by the hundreds for the international express that would bear them toward the falling paper-mark or the unstabilized lira. We too were waiting: a few dollars in our pockets, the equivalent of how many thousand crowns or pengos, we went drifting onward with the army of exploitation:

Following the dollar, ah, following the dollar, I learned three fashions of eating with the knife and ordered beer in four languages from a Hungarian waiter while following the dollar eastward along the 48th degree of north latitude— where it buys most, there is the Fatherland—

Following the dollar, we saw a chaotic Europe that was feverishly seeking the future of art, finance and the state. We saw machine guns in the streets of Berlin, Black Shirts in Italy, were stopped by male prostitutes along the Kurfürstendam, sat in a café at Montpellier with an Egyptian revolutionist who said, "Let's imagine this vermouth is the blood of an English baby," drained the glass deep—"Bravo!" we said, and drifted down to Pamplona for the bullfights. Sometimes in a Vienna coffeehouse full of dark little paunchy men and golden whores, in the smoke above these shaven or marceled heads we saw another country, not just painted, revolving, but solid with little hills and the earth brown beneath the plow. "I shall never return, never, to my strange land"—but sometimes beside an unreal Alpine lake they asked us, "Everybody is rich in your country, say?" and steam shovels suddenly bit into the hills, gold washed itself from the rivers, skyscrapers rose, heiresses were kidnaped—we saw the America they wished us to see and admired it through their distant eyes:

Following the dollar by gray Channel seas, by blue seas in Italy,
by Alpine lakes as blue as aniline blue, by lakes as green as
a bottle of green ink, with ink-stained mountains rising on
either hand,

I dipped my finger in the lake and wrote, I shall never return,
never, to my strange land.

We had come three thousand miles in search of Europe and had found America, in a vision half-remembered, half-falsified and romanced. Should we ever return to our own far country?

Four angels glory-haunted guard my land:

at the north gate Theodore Roosevelt, at the south gate Jack
Johnson, at the west gate Charlie Chaplin and

at the middle gate a back-country fiddler from Clarion County
fiddling, with a turkey in the straw and a haw, haw, haw
and a turkey in the hay and I shall never hear it fiddled, ah,
farther than Atlantis is my land,

where I could return tomorrow if I chose,

but I shall return to it never,

never shall wed my pale Alaska virgin,

in thine arms never lie, O Texas Rose.

2: Historical Parallel

After the middle of the nineteenth century the younger Russians began to speak of "going to Europe" in the same spirit and even the same words as American writers of the 1920s. They inhabited what seemed to be a new continent raised from the ocean of prehistory; they too stood face to face, not with Germany alone, or France or Great Britain, but with "Europe"—that is, with the whole of West European culture. And they made their long pilgrimage, they settled themselves in Dresden or Geneva, just as American expatriates would cluster in Montparnasse.

In April 1867, long after the beginning of this migration, a couple newly married took the westbound express from St. Petersburg. Each was distinguished, among ten thousand exiles, by a characteristic of interest to posterity. The husband was beginning to be recognized as a man of genius: he was Fëdor Mikhailovich Dostoevski. His second wife, Anna Grigorevna, kept a diary in shorthand and recorded their life together, their first impressions of Europe, with the fullness and directness of a vulgar woman writing for herself. At the end of the 1920s the diary was transcribed and published by the Central Archives of the Soviets; it was translated into English from the German edition.

It begins, as travel diaries do, with an accumulation of details chiefly concerning the price of things. The bride and groom entered Germany at Eydtkuhnen, where the station had "enormous restaurants with two rows of windows one above the other, and a marvelous painted ceiling and everything wonderfully done." On reaching Berlin they went to the Grand Union Hotel; their room cost one thaler and ten silver groschen. "Fëdor again began grumbling about the Germans, the hotel and the weather." They went on to Dresden, where the droshky that took them from the station cost "the awful price of twenty-two silver groschen." The hotel room was expensive, and the hotel tea really too weak to drink, but they soon found two furnished rooms at the moderate price of seventeen thalers per month, washing included. . . . Every fact recorded is an implied comparison—as if Anna Grigorevna were saying, *our* tea is stronger, *our* people are less grasping, these Europeans have no business looking down on *us*.

Once established in Dresden, they rushed off to the museum. The Sistine Madonna, they thought, was perhaps the greatest picture ever painted. Holbein's Madonna they admired at first, but later they decided that it had a German look, and they didn't like Germany. They spent some time in front of a letter "painted so lifelike that in the distance one would have taken it for a real letter, stuck to the wall." Then finally they "went and looked at the pictures of Watteau, the French court painter of the early part of last century. For the most part he paints scenes of court life, some marquis or other making love to some dazzling beauty." So far the story has been that of any impecunious and disagreeably self-assertive young couple confronted for the first time with the marvels of European civilization—the sort of couple that servants avoid and cabbies like to overcharge. But soon the diary assumes the accents of a Dostoevski novel. They reach Baden-Baden and Fëdor Mikhailovich goes to the Rooms.

Having lost his money at roulette, he raises a few more thalers and, with Christian humility in the face of temptation, returns to the gaming tables.

The process was really longer and more cyclical. One morning, for example, the total fortune of the Dostoevskis consists of sixty gold pieces, locally known as ducats. Fëdor Mikhailovich takes ten of these and sets out for the Rooms. He returns with a despondent face, having lost them all. After a somber luncheon he takes ten more gold pieces and disappears. This time he does not return till after sunset. He begs Anna Grigorevna to forgive him, but he must have twenty ducats more; it is time for his luck to change. He is back in ten minutes, having staked and lost the money on one throw. They have only twenty ducats in the world. Fëdor Mikhailovich falls on his knees; he begs God and Anna Grigorevna to forgive him for having robbed her; he kisses her shoes; he swears that after tonight he will never gamble again. Then, taking five ducats more, he goes back to the Rooms.

The following morning they have only five silver thalers, and their rent due, and no food in the house. Fëdor Mikhailovich takes her wedding ring—having pawned his own already—and goes out to find a Jew. He is gone all day, while Anna Grigorevna walks up and down their sitting room. Late in the evening he returns, holding a great bunch of roses in one hand; little boys follow him with baskets of plums, peaches, grapes, a great cheese, a pound of Russian tea. After these purchases he has forty ducats left from his winnings; it is time to stop gambling forever. Fëdor Mikhailovich decides that he wants to win just enough for a bottle of wine. He disappears. . . .

Two days later they are once more reduced to five silver thalers. Anna Grigorevna's earrings and Fëdor Mikhailovich's overcoat have followed the two wedding rings. Returning after another bout of play, physically and mentally overwhelmed by

his losses, the husband falls into one of his epileptic fits. "He began to fling himself about so violently that it became impossible
for me to hold him. . . . I undid his waistcoat and trousers,
that he might breathe more freely. For the first time I now
noticed that his lips were quite blue and his face much redder
than usual. . . . He called me Anya, and then begged my pardon, and couldn't in the least understand what I said. Finally
he begged for some more money to go and play with. A fine
piece of work that would have been!" It seems that everyone
who met Dostoevski ended by talking like a character in a
Dostoevski novel. "And yet," says Anna Grigorevna, "none the
less I had a feeling that he would have won."

He often won; he was not an especially unfortunate gambler;
but he rarely had strength of mind to leave the Rooms before
his winnings were frittered away. It was only the fortunate arrival of money from Russia that enabled them to continue their
journey, after redeeming most of their belongings from the
pawnbrokers and settling with the landlady before whom they
had trembled for a month. The diary ends with the Dostoevskis
in Switzerland, in Basel, staring at the Town Hall. "There is
no doubt from the style of it," wrote Anna Grigorevna, "that it
dates from very far back."

Among these details concerning Dostoevski's life (and the
emotional background of his novels) there is a quantity of
material that bears upon the general problem of provincialism
and expatriation—not only as it affected his Russian contemporaries, but also as it was met by the American exiles to Montparnasse.

That problem, in literary Russia during the 1860s, was omnipresent. Among people of breeding—the land-owning class,
that is, and the new bourgeoisie—the language itself was becoming a despised, almost a foreign tongue. Stavrogin, the hero

of *The Possessed,* was an aristocrat of wide education and yet he could not write Russian correctly: the fact is mentioned more than once in the novel. Anna Grigorevna observes of the compatriots she met in Dresden: "They would say the Russian 'God be with you,' then immediately start talking in French; it really doesn't seem the custom to speak Russian." In order to appeal to such an audience—there was no other—writers published their works under French titles, adopted a gallicized style and interlarded their sentences with German, French and English phrases. One might say that they were workmen forced to struggle with half-foreign tools—but the same remark could of course be applied to the American writers of a later day who hesitated whether to use the English expressions they learned in school or the words they heard in the streets.

The Russians had other difficulties, however, arising from the fact that their country was in the full sense a colony of Europe. It exported furs, fish, wheat and rough-sawed lumber; it imported not only machinery, shoes, furniture, Sèvres china, but also governesses, portrait painters, wives for the nobility, fine wines, fashions in clothes and books—everything, in a word, that composed its new culture. And the Russian traders and officials, the chief proprietors of this culture, had enriched themselves by acting as mere agents for European capitalism. They were a class limited in function, in number, and they were almost the only class to which writers could look for support.

In spite of all the difficulties there were novelists and poets in Russia whose greatness was generally recognized. But the middle class of letters, the men who had neither failed nor succeeded, led a troubled existence. If they stayed at home, they had the feeling of being provincials doomed to follow last year's Paris styles. If they emigrated, many of their problems were solved: they lived nearer the source of literary fashions, lived in an atmosphere that seemed more favorable to art, lived more cheaply; and finally they acquired a certain distinction at home from the very fact that they had shaken from their feet the mud of Moscow. On the other hand, they lost contact with their own people, were uprooted from the Russian land. . . .

These alternatives were discussed by every Russian writer, just as they were discussed in America during the 1920s. The majority chose at least a temporary expatriation. Time went on and there were several generations of expatriates; Dostoevski belonged to what might be called the second. It was distinguished by the practical nature of its motives. Fëdor Mikhailovich left Russia neither on account of his political convictions nor in the hope of broadening his culture: he went to Europe to play roulette and escape his creditors. In Baden-Baden, between two bouts of gambling, he paid a visit to Ivan Turgenev. Their encounter, described in Anna Grigorevna's diary, was symbolic; it was the younger generation of expatriates confronting the elder; with allowance for the literary stature and opinions of the men involved, it was like a meeting, let us say, between Henry James and Ernest Hemingway.

Turgenev, like James, had definitely cast his fortunes with Europe; he spoke rather coldly of the homeland. Dostoevski suggested that he get himself a telescope so that he could see what was going on in Russia. Turgenev smiled politely. Dostoevski mentioned the new Turgenev novel; he didn't think much of it. Turgenev smiled politely. Dostoevski burst into a sudden torrent of imprecations against the Germans, "that detestable race . . . who exalt themselves at our expense." This time, instead of smiling, Turgenev went white with rage. "Insofar as you talk like that," he shouted, "you mean to insult me personally! Here and now let me tell you that I have settled in Baden-Baden for good and all, and that I no longer regard myself as a Russian, but as a German, and am proud of it."

Dostoevski was still calm enough to apologize. He shook

hands, pronounced a definite farewell, then hurried off to risk
five ducats in the Rooms.

Not all of his long exile in Europe was wasted in gambling
and repenting. It was shortly after leaving Basel for Geneva—in
other words, after the end of Anna Grigorevna's published
record—that he set to work on *The Idiot,* a novel more Russian
than anything he had written in Petersburg—so Russian, in fact,
that many years would pass before it was translated into the
Western languages, and still more years before it began to be admired. The effect of living in Europe had been to emphasize the
most national—it would be wiser to say the most personal—
elements in his character.

A similar effect was produced on many American expatriates
of the second generation; and the parallel lines of growth go
even farther. After his return to Dresden, in 1870, Dostoevski
began a novel which, in its conception, was not unlike *Main
Street.* It is true that *The Possessed* belongs to a higher category
of fiction, but its distinguishing qualities did not appear in the
original plan, nor do they appear in the first two hundred pages
of the book as published. It opens as a satire on Russian provincial life rather less skillful than Sinclair Lewis's satire. It opens
in a town that is evidently smaller than George F. Babbitt's
Zenith, and somewhat larger than Gopher Prairie. It opens with
a character, Stepan Trofimovich Verkhovensky, who is in many
ways the Russian elder brother of Carol Kennicott. "Always,"
Dostoevski says, "he had filled a particular role among us, that
of the progressive patriot, so to say, and he was passionately
fond of playing the part."

Stepan Trofimovich was surrounded by half a dozen serious
Russian thinkers. There was Shatov, "one of those idealistic be-
ings common in Russia who are suddenly struck by some over-
mastering idea." There was Virginsky, the henpecked liberal.

"His wife and all the ladies of his family professed the very latest convictions, but in a rather crude form. They got it all out of books, and at the first hint coming from any of our little progressive corners in Petersburg they were prepared to throw anything overboard." There was a Jew called Lyamshin who played the piano, and a Captain Kartusov sometimes joined in the discussion. "An old gentleman of inquiring mind used to come at one time, but he died. . . . It was reported about the town that our little circle was a hotbed of nihilism, profligacy and godlessness, and the rumor gained more and more strength. And yet we did nothing but indulge in the most harmless, agreeable, typically Russian lighthearted liberal chatter. The 'higher liberalism' and the 'higher liberal'—that is, a liberal without any definite aim—are possible only in Russia."

The tone of all this is unmistakable. Change the names to Perkins or Schmaltz, change "Russia" to "America" or "the Middle West," and it might have been written by Sinclair Lewis. Change the style to something more colloquial, objective, and it might almost have been written by a young American in Montparnasse as he leaned his elbows on a café table of imitation marble ringed with coffee stains. But there is a difference, even at the beginning of *The Possessed*. Instead of ridiculing a Russian Gopher Prairie, Dostoevski is ridiculing the Russian Carol Kennicotts, the denationalized intellectuals who dreamed of escaping to Europe. And there is another difference which, as the story proceeds, becomes enormous.

Sinclair Lewis planned to write a good satirical novel, and, by keeping a firm grip on plot and characters, successfully executed his plan. Dostoevski, after the first few chapters, let his characters take hold of the story, let them transform it page by page, let them carry it toward realms into which lesser novelists cannot venture. But it was only on rewriting the novel (he mentions the fact elsewhere) that he introduced the figure of Nikolai

Stavrogin, the most terrible of all his creations. This proud, humble, godless and mystical hero destroyed by his own undirected power seems to have been the pattern after which thousands upon thousands of Russian intellectuals came to model themselves. One might say in a certain sense, and after a hundred reservations, that in creating Stavrogin over his writing desk in Dresden Dostoevski revealed or invented what used to be known as the Russian soul. He himself used another word, though his meaning was almost the same: he spoke of finding the Russian god. . . . "God is the synthetic personality of the whole people, taken from its beginning to its end. . . . The object of every national movement, in every people and at every period of its existence, is to seek for its God, who must be its own God, and for the faith in Him as its only true faith."

Today it is easy to see that the soul or god invented by Dostoevski was only one aspect of the Russian people. Any great people has many personalities of this order; often they are in conflict, and the nation may reveal different personalities one after the other as new classes become socially dominant. The Stavrogin personality was the myth of the old intelligentsia. After the 1917 revolution it was the idol they would carry with them into a harsher sort of exile—sitting in the Russian Isba or the Caveau Ukrainien, Vera and Olga and the Caucasian Princess would pour out many libations of vodka to this tragic buffoon-god that had ceased to be worshiped by their cousins in Moscow. There in the homeland another myth would be installed: that of the bustling, practical commissar who was equally ruthless to himself and others. What the intellectuals had once accepted as "the synthetic personality of the whole people, taken from its beginning to its end," was merely the personality adopted for a time by their own caste. That was a lesson learned by some of the intellectuals in their new exile, and it was also a lesson that the commissars might some day learn about themselves as national gods and heroes.

But I am going beyond my story, having merely wished to suggest that Dostoevski's achievement was not exactly what it seemed. He did not reveal the total personality of the Russian people or even put an end to the feeling of inferiority to "Europeans" that weighed upon the intellectuals of his own generation and the one that followed. Nevertheless, with his myth and his great novels, he had changed something. A burden was lifted from the shoulders of Russian literature, a feeling of backwardness and provincialism. Russia after his day was still a colonial nation in the economic sense, but writers in Petersburg and Moscow were no longer condemned to follow European fashions: they could create their own fashions, could write for the world.

3: Transatlantic Review

There is a point beyond which historical parallels cannot be carried. The United States in 1921, unlike Russia in 1867, had ceased to be a colony of European capitalism. It exported not only raw materials but finished products, and the machinery with which to finish them, and the methods by which to distribute them, and the entire capital required in the process. In addition to wheat and automobiles, it had begun to export cultural goods, hot and sweet jazz bands, financial experts, movies and political ideals. There were even American myths, among others that of the hardheaded, softhearted businessman enslaved by his wife. Yet our literature had not registered the changed status of the nation. American intellectuals as a group continued to labor under a burden of provincialism as heavy and jagged as that which oppressed the compatriots of Dostoevski.

Almost everywhere, after the war, one heard the intellectual life of America unfavorably compared with that of Europe. The critics often called for a great American novel or opera; they were doggedly enthusiastic, like cheer leaders urging Princeton to carry the ball over the line; but at heart they felt that Princeton was beaten, the game was in the bag for Oxford and the Sorbonne; at heart they were not convinced that even the subject matter of a great novel could be supplied by this country. American themes—so the older critics felt—were lacking in dignity. Art and ideas were products manufactured under a European patent; all we could furnish toward them was raw talent destined usually to be wasted. Everywhere, in every department of cultural life, Europe offered the models to imitate—in painting, composing, philosophy, folk music, folk drinking, the drama, sex, politics, national consciousness—indeed, some doubted that this country was even a nation; it had no traditions except the fatal tradition of the pioneer. As for our contemporary literature, thousands were willing to echo Van Wyck Brooks when he said that in comparison with the literature of any European country, "it is indeed one long list of spiritual casualties. For it is not that the talent is wanting, but that somehow this talent fails to fulfill itself."

Ten years later this feeling had gone and even its memory was fading. American intellectuals still complained, but their enemy was no longer "civilization in the United States"; it was "our business civilization," it was efficiency, standardization, mass production, the machine—it was something that dominated our nation more than others, but affected the others also. Germany had yielded to it, Britain was yielding, even France was being poisoned—it was no use fleeing to London or Paris, though perhaps there was a secure village in the South of France, perhaps there was safety in Majorca. . . . People still said in 1930 that it was impossible to live in the United States, but not that it was impossible to write or paint there. Comparisons with European literature continued to be drawn, but not so often or so unfavorably. Ten years after the first migration to Montparnasse, I met a talented, rather naïve young woman just returned from London, where she had published her first novel. Yes, it had been fairly successful—it was good enough for the English, she said, but she didn't want to publish it over here until she had time to rewrite it completely; it wasn't good enough for New York. I knew that she did not intend to be smart; she was a simple person trying to state her impressions and those of the circle in which she moved.

Something had changed, and the exiles of the 1920s had played their part in changing it. They had produced no Dostoevski, but for this simpler task no genius was required; they had merely to travel, compare, evaluate and honestly record what they saw. In the midst of this process the burden of inferiority somehow disappeared—it was not so much dropped as it leaked away like sand from a bag carried on the shoulder—suddenly it was gone and nobody noticed the difference. Nobody even felt the need for inventing an American god, a myth to replace that of the businessman; instead the exiles invented the international myth of the Lost Generation.

These young Americans had begun by discovering a crazy Europe in which the intellectuals of their own middle class were more defeated and demoralized than those at home. Later, after discounting the effects of the war, they decided that all nations were fairly equal, some excelling in one quality, some in another—the Germans in mechanical efficiency, the French in self-assurance, the English in political acumen; the Americans excelled in wealth, but in most qualities they ranked midway in the scale: they were simply a nation among the other capitalist West European nations. Having registered this impression, the exiles were ready to find that their own nation had every attribute they had been taught to admire in those of Europe. It had developed its national types—who could fail to recognize an American in a crowd?—it possessed a folklore, and traditions, and the songs that embodied them; it had even produced new forms of art which the Europeans were glad to borrow. Some of the exiles had reached a turning point in their adventure and were preparing to embark on a voyage of rediscovery. Standing as it were on the Tour Eiffel, they looked southwestward across the wheatfields of Beauce and the rain-drenched little hills of Brittany, until somewhere in the mist they saw the country of their childhood, which should henceforth be the country of their art. American themes, like other themes, had exactly the dignity that talent could lend them.

. . . That was the general conclusion, but it was reached after a process that extended over a period of years and had many variations. Indeed, there were several waves or successive groups of exiles, and their different points of view were reflected in a whole series of little exiled magazines. The myth of the Lost Generation was adopted by the second wave, by the friends of Ernest Hemingway who contributed in 1924 to the *Transatlantic Review;* this was also the magazine that showed the greatest interest in colloquial writing about American themes. *Transition,* which came later, was more international. It included among its contributors many of the dyed-in-the-wool expatriates, those who had deliberately cut every tie binding them to the homeland except one tie: their incomes still came from the United States. They were like colts who had jumped the fence without breaking their tethers: one day the tethers would be tightened and they would have to jump back again. Our own earlier wave of exiles wrote for magazines like *Broom, Gargoyle* and *Secession.* The years we spent in Europe were adventurous and busy, and our return to America proceeded by stages as clearly marked as those of a well-prepared debate.

For me the process began under a grape arbor in Dijon, when I tried to define the ideas with which I had come to Europe.

4: Form and Matter

Early on a hot August morning in 1921 I started to write an essay on "This Youngest Generation." Six weeks had passed since leaving New York: it was still too early to be affected by a new intellectual climate. But the essay expressed clearly enough the ideas which the exiles of that year had packed in their baggage and carried duty-free across the Atlantic.

"As an organized body of opinion," I said, "the youngest generation in American letters does not exist. There is no group, but there are individuals. There is no solidarity, but there are prevailing habits of thought. Certain characteristics held in common unify the work of the youngest writers, the generation that has just turned twenty."

Most of these traits, I found, were negative. "One can safely assert that these new writers are not gathered in a solid phalanx behind H. L. Mencken to assault our American puritanism. Certainly they are not puritans themselves, but they are willing to leave the battle to their elder cousins and occupy themselves elsewhere. In the same way the controversy about Queen Victoria does not excite them. She died when they were still in bloomers, and the majority of the Browning Clubs died with her. Time has allowed enough perspective for them to praise Tennyson a little and Browning a great deal."

I am setting all this down as I wrote it that morning under the grape arbor, when everything was simpler and it was possible to annihilate in a phrase the life work of an internationally famous man of letters, without fear of being in turn annihilated. "It follows as a corollary," I said, "that they have little sympathy with the belated revolt of the Georgians. Little with the huge, uninspired documents of the Georgian novelists, as informative and formless as a cookbook. Little with the divine journalism of Mr. Wells. None with the *fausse-naïveté* of Georgian poets. It does not follow that they dislike the 'movements' popular among Georgians on both sides the water, and yet one meets few that are either feminist, Freudian or Communist.

"Let us picture the American writer at the age of twenty-five." In reality I was just about to celebrate my twenty-third birthday, and was in no way precocious. "He has already adopted," I said, "the enthusiasms of the generation that preceded him, and has abandoned them one by one—at least they no longer exist in his mind as enthusiasms. He cannot be described as Wildean, Wellsian, Shavian, Georgian or Menckenian, as aesthetic, ecstatic or naturalistic. The great literary controversies of the last generation he has solved by the simplest of all logical processes; he ignores them. Thus, he is neither puritan nor anti-puritan, romantic nor realistic. He has a great many literary prejudices and could easily write little essays beginning with 'I hate people who . . .' or smart poems whose refrain is 'I am tired of. . . .' Unfortunately, he equally hates and is tired of this form of literary inanity. He has no movement of his own to support and he has no audience. . . . It is the picture of a very negative young man; but it is only one side of the picture."

I began to sketch in some positive traits. "The writers of this newest generation show more respect, if not reverence, for the work of the past. Before the war the belief was rapidly gaining ground that literature and the drama began together on that night when Nora first slammed the door of the doll's house. To be a rebel from convention, one had only to say that one liked Shakespeare better than Ibsen or Shaw. . . . The youngest writers not only prefer to read Shakespeare: they may even prefer Jonson, Webster and Marlowe, Racine and Molière. They are more interested in Swift and Defoe than in Samuel Butler. Their enthusiasm for the New Russians is temperate, even lukewarm. In other words, the past that they respect ended about forty years ago—not long after Nora slammed the door.

"If strange modern gods must be imported and worshiped, they are more likely to be French than Slavic, Scandinavian or English. In this respect, however, the youngest writers are developing the tendency of their elders rather than revolting from it. The last half-century of American literature might be diagramed as a progression away from London. This new interest in French prose and poetry almost completes the progression, for no city is intellectually so far from London as is Paris.

"They read Flaubert. They read Remy de Gourmont. These writers usually serve as their introduction to modern French literature; these are the two fixed points from which their reading diverges. Gourmont's *Book of Masks* may set them to following French poetry from Baudelaire and Laforgue down through the most recent and most involved Parisian schools. Or they may read the New Catholics, beginning with Huysmans. . . . Certainly the French influence is acting on us today; there remains to be seen just what effect it will bring forth."

It was very still under the arbor; flies were buzzing outside among the late Glory of Dijon roses; New York was centuries away. I tried to remember Manhattan conversations and translate them into terms of prophecy. "One of these effects," I said, "is almost sure to be a new interest in form. Flaubert and Gour-

mont spent too much time thinking of the balance and movement of their work for this subject to be neglected by their pupils.
Already the tendency is manifesting itself strongly among the
younger writers: they seem to have little desire to record inchoate
episodes out of their own lives. I have heard one of them speak
learnedly of line and mass, of planes, circles and tangents. Without going to the geometrical extremes of Kenneth Burke, one
can forecast safely that our younger literature will be at least as
well composed as a good landscape; it may even attain to the
logical organization of music.

"Another characteristic of the younger writers is their desire
for simplification; this also is partly a result of the French influence. 'What is needed of art,' said T. S. Eliot in the *Dial*, 'is a
simplification of current life into something rich and strange.'
One hears the same idea expressed elsewhere; it is coupled usually with a desire for greater abstractness.

"Form, simplification, strangeness, respect for literature as an
art with traditions, abstractness . . . these are the catchwords
repeated most often among the younger writers. They represent
ideas that have characterized French literature hitherto, rather
than English or American. They are the nearest approach to
articulate doctrine of a generation without a school and without
a manifesto."

There was more of the essay, but that was the heart of it. Rereading it now, after many years, I am struck by two questions,
both of which concern a larger question absent from our calculations: I mean the position of the artist in society. Why did our
theories, slogans and catchwords all center about the unfruitful
distinction between form and matter? Why did we abandon
them, not without a struggle, but swiftly none the less, in the
course of a few months?

The questions are not impossible to answer. . . . I have said that ours was a humble generation, but the truth is that all writers are ambitious: if they were really humble they would choose a craft that involved less risk of failure and milder penalties for the crime of being average. All writers thirst to excel. In many, even the greatest, this passion takes a vulgar form: they want to get rich quick, be invited to meet the Duchess—thus, Voltaire was a war profiteer; Shakespeare disgracefully wangled himself a coat of arms. But always, mingled with cheaper ambitions, is the desire to exert an influence on the world outside, to alter the course of history. And always, when this path seems definitely closed, ambition turns elsewhere, eating its way like a torrent into other channels—till it finally bursts forth, if not in life, at least in the imagination. "Art for art's sake," "pure art," "form triumphant over matter"—all these slogans bear some relation to an old process of thought. "Matter" is equivalent to the outside world in which the writer is powerless; but in his rich interior world he can satisfy his ambition by subjugating "matter," by making it the slave of "form," of himself.

The writers of our generation were humble in the sense that they did not hope to alter the course of events or even to build themselves an honored place in society. Their class, the urban middle class, was lacking in political power; it was indeed so empty of political ideas as not to realize that such power was being exercised by others. Society was either regarded as a sort of self-operating, self-repairing, self-perpetuating machine, or else it was not regarded. Perhaps in their apprentice years, during Mr. Wilson's crusade or the Russian Revolution, the younger writers had the brief vision of a world adventurously controlled by men, guided by men in conflict, but the vision died. Once more society became an engine whose course they could not direct, whether to glory or destruction—nor did they much care, since the splendors and defeats of history were equally the material for art, the stone for the chisel. And, though their lives might be dingy and cluttered, they had one privilege: to write a poem in which all was but order and beauty, a poem rising like a clean tower above the tin cans and broken dishes of their days. In the world of "form," their failures, our failures, would be avenged.

This, I think, was the emotional attitude lying behind the ideas I was trying to express that morning in the grape arbor at Dijon, while flies buzzed among the August roses. The arbor itself, and the garden with its graveled walks, its fruit trees geometrically trained against the north wall, were triumphs of art over nature, were matter subjugated to form. Indeed, to young writers like ourselves, a long sojourn in France was almost a pilgrimage to Holy Land.

France was the birthplace of our creed. It was in France that poets had labored for days over a single stanza, while bailiffs hammered at the door; in France that novelists like Gourmont had lived as anchorites, while imagining seductions more golden and mistresses more harmoniously yielding than life could ever reproduce; in France that Flaubert had described "the quaint mania of passing one's life wearing oneself out over words," and had transformed the mania into a religion. Everything admirable in literature began in France, was developed in France; and though we knew that the great French writers quarreled among themselves, Parnassians giving way to Decadents, who gave way to Symbolists, who in turn were giving way to the new school, whatever it was, that would soon reign in Paris—though none achieved perfection, we were eager to admire them all. And this, precisely, was the privilege we should not be granted.

In the year 1921 Flaubert had ceased to be admired by the younger writers and Gourmont was almost despised. The religion of art is an unstable religion which yearly makes over its calendar of saints. Changes come rapidly, convolutions are piled on convolutions; schools, leaders, manifestoes, follow and cancel one another—and into this mad steeplechase we arrived with our innocent belief that Flaubert was great and that form ought to be cultivated at the expense of matter. In a few months we were exposed to the feverish intellectual development of half a century.

That suggests, I think, the answer to my second question, why we abandoned our theories after so brief a struggle. As school superseded school, the religion of art had extended its domain. Aesthetic standards of judgment, after being applied to works of art, had been applied to the careers of their authors and finally to the world at large. Cities, nations, were admired for the qualities that were then being accepted as making books admirable —for being picturesque, surprising, dramatic, swift, exuberant, vigorous, "original." What nation more than America possessed these qualities? It happened that the American writers who admired French literature were confronted by young French writers who admired American civilization. "Gourmont," we said, "is a great stylist."—"Nonsense, my dear friend. New York has houses of fifty-six stories."

It was a contest of politeness, an Alphonse-Gaston argument in which, at the end, we were glad to yield. America was after all our country, and we were beginning to feel a little homesick for it. But our friends in New York were unaware of the change.

5: Rumors of Home

"I must apologize for my failure to write you sooner"—all letters from your friends begin that way; strangers apologize for writing you at all—"but I have been frantically busy. Boobery is soaring to its seventh heaven and I am making frantic efforts to maintain my hold on its tail feathers so that I may be in at the killing of the gentle bird."

It was Ray Johnson, J. Raymond Johnson, one of the professionals who wrote and directed the writing of daily propaganda stories for the newspapers without ever signing his name. The barons and dowager baronesses of industry had turned, after the war, to the new task of molding the public mind. Needing advice, they had hired the services of anonymous freebooters. These for the most part were intelligent, poetic, were men of soul. They despised the barons, hated the work of wheedling money from the public for patriotic causes—but they performed it efficiently and solaced themselves by making fun of it in their cups.

"My latest venture," Ray Johnson continued, "is a projected Good Will Mission under the auspices of the American Committee for Devastated France. Our own beloved Ambassador is president of this kindly enterprise, which looks forward to raising $500,000—good God! how many francs is that?—to be spent by Anne Morgan and others in the Department of the Aisne. Drives are no longer popular and so we are staging 300 newpapers contests in 300 cities to select a delegate (at ten cents a vote) to represent each city in the Good Will Mission. Not so bad, what? The delegate will get a free trip to the battlefields and all we ask are the shekels she wrings from her friends.

"We've been having merry times since you left the Village. The Fatty Arbuckle rape case has crowded the deliberations of the Disarmament Conference from the first page, so the delegates are sneaking back to Europe with a fine collection of photographs and a taste for grapefruit, bathtubs and Jersey lightning. Harold Stearns's book, 'America and the YOUNG INTELLECTUAL' (the caps are the publisher's), has appeared,[1] but

---

[1] It was a collection of essays explaining why intellectuals should live in more civilized countries. When it was published Stearns was in Paris

there is still space in literary columns for little pieces about Van Loon's 'Story of Mankind,' Howard Pyle's 'Book of Pirates' and Al Jennings's (the train robber's) book about O. Henry."

Months had passed since we left New York and nothing there had really changed. The dance continued, perhaps to a faster beat, but the dancers were the same, and when the orchestra momentarily stopped they talked about the same topics: Prohibition, Village gossip, American stupidity and they do things better in Europe. "The w.k. poet Harry Kemp is occupying a chimney recess at 31 Jones Street. Frances is getting fat, has a new tea set, paint on the floor, a new cupboard in the bedroom, trouble with the gas in cold weather and all that sort of thing. There were only twenty deaths from wood alcohol during the Christmas holidays, but there's a hundred in the hospitals and you never can tell. New Year's Eve was a bright and festive event. The prohibition agents promised a dry evening, but there were so many old-fashioned drunks that the cops had no place to put 'em after midnight. Nobody seems to know where the stuff comes from, but most of our leading citizens have been indicted for bootlegging in the last few days. Everybody is shouting prosperity, but the bank presidents are all Swiss hotelkeepers and the best you can do on a loan is 50 per cent. The Elevated still runs down Sixth Avenue and turns into Third Street at a point not far from the château of one J. Smith, who, by the way, has learned to make synthetic gin and has regained much of his old-time gaiety. Broadway ticket speculators at last have been put out of business and now you only have to pay $6.60 for a $2 seat. The newspapers announced that the government had abolished the amusement tax to take effect January 1, but

---

and, in Hemingway's phrase, "had gone into the period of his unreliability." He appears as Harvey Stone in Hemingway's novel *The Sun Also Rises*. People used to look down at him sleeping on a café terrace and say, "There lies civilization in the United States."

when you try to buy a ticket the box-office overlord tells you that the ruling applies only to seats costing less than ten cents. After a lapse of eighteen years our benevolent government is once more coining silver dollars. About a million of them arrived in the New York banks. There's a rumor that the new coin will take the place of the once popular nickel."

Nothing in New York had changed very much. In Europe we were learning to regard the dragon of American industry as a picturesque and even noble monster; but our friends at home had not the advantage of perspective; for them the dragon blotted out the sky; they looked up and all they could see was the scales of its belly, freshly alemited and enameled with Duco. They dreamed of escaping into older lands which the dragon hadn't yet invaded—while we, in older lands, were already dreaming of a voyage home. Soon we began to argue back and forth across the water.

The debate burst forth in the early months of 1923. My share in it was provoked by two sentences in an article that Kenneth Burke contributed to *Vanity Fair*. "There is in America," he wrote, "not a trace of that really dignified richness which makes for peasants, household gods, traditions. America has become the wonder of the world simply because America is the purest concentration point for the vices and vulgarities of the world." He was expressing, from New York, ideas in which both of us had concurred two years before. And I answered, from Europe, with a letter of almost incoherent dissent.

"Since when, Kenneth, have you become a furniture salesman? *That really dignified richness!* You seem to have the disease of the American lady I met in Giverny.—'You know, in America the wall papuh hardly seems to last a minute, it fades or peels off so quickly, but heah the good European papuh dyed with European dyes and put on with *that good European glue,* why, it just seems to last forevuh.' Let me assure you that the chiefest benefit of my two years in Europe was that it freed me from the prejudices of the lady whose European flour paste was so much better than the made-in-the-U.S.A. product, and of the thirty American intellectuals under the general editorship of Harold Stearns.

"America is just as god-damned good as Europe—worse in some ways, better in others, just as appreciative, fresher material, inclined to stay at peace instead of marching into the Ruhr. As for its being the concentration point for all the vices and vulgarities—nuts. New York is refinement itself beside Berlin. French taste in most details is unbearable. London is a huge Gopher Prairie. I'm not ashamed to take off my coat anywhere and tell these degenerate Europeans that I'm an American citizen. Wave Old Glory! Peace! Normalcy!

"America shares an inferiority complex with Germany. Not about machinery or living standards, but about Art. *Secession,* being edited by Americans, is less important than any little magazine edited by Frenchmen. John Marin, being American, is a minor figure beside even such a minor French water colorist as Dunoyer de Segonzac. The only excuse for living two years in France is to remove this feeling of inferiority and to find, for example, that Tristan Tzara, who resembles you in features like two drops of water, talks a shade less intelligently. To discover that the Dada crowd has more fun than the Secession crowd because the former, strangely, has more American pep. . . . The only salvation for American literature is to BORROW A LITTLE PUNCH AND CONFIDENCE FROM AMERICAN BUSINESS. American literature—I mean Anderson, Dreiser, Frank, *et al.*—is morally weak, and before it learns the niceties of form its moral has to be doctored, or all the niceties in the world will do it no good at all."

The old argument about form and matter was already being pushed into the background. For two years, in the midst of a

Europe where values shifted from day to day, we had been looking for guidance, for examples to imitate, for a stable intellectual
currency. And the guidance, when it came, was not what we had
expected it to be.

IV: Paris Pilgrimages

1: Examination Paper

People who read books without writing them are likely to form a simple picture of any celebrated author. He is John X or Jonathan Y, the man who wrote such a fascinating novel about Paris, about divorce, about the Georgia Crackers—the man who drinks, who ran off with the doctor's wife—the bald-headed man who lectured to the Wednesday Club. But to writers, especially to young writers in search of guidance, the established author presents a much more complicated image.

Their impressions of the great author are assembled from many sources. It is true that his books are a principal source, but there must also be considered his career, the point from which it started, the direction in which it seems to be moving. There is his personality, as revealed in chance interviews or as caricatured in gossip; there are the values that he assigns to other writers; and there is the value placed on himself by his younger colleagues in those kitchen or barroom gatherings at which they pass judgment with the harsh finality of a Supreme Court— John X has got real stuff, they say, but Jonathan Y is terrible— and they bring forward evidence to support these verdicts. The evidence is mulled over, all the details are fitted together like the pieces of a jigsaw puzzle, until they begin to form a picture, vague and broken at first, then growing more distinct as the years pass by: the X or Y picture, the James Joyce, Ezra Pound or T. S. Eliot picture. But it is not so much a picture when completed: it is rather a map or diagram which the apprentice writer will use in planning his own career.

If he is called upon to review a book by Joyce or Eliot, he will say certain things he believes to be accurate: they are not the things lying closest to his heart. Secretly he is wondering whether he can, whether he should, ever be great in the Joyce or Eliot fashion. What path should he follow to reach this goal? The great living authors, in the eyes of any young man apprenticed to the Muse, are a series of questions, an examination paper compiled by and submitted to himself:

1. What problems do these authors suggest?

2. With what problems are they consciously dealing?

3. Are they my own problems? Or if not, shall I make them my own?

4. What is the Joyce solution to these problems (or the Eliot, the Pound, the Gertrude Stein, the Paul Valéry solution)?

5. Shall I adopt it? Reject it and seek another master? Or must I furnish a new solution myself?

And it is as if the examiner had written: *Take your time, young man. Consider all questions carefully; there is all the time in the world. Don't fake or cheat; you are making these answers for yourself. Nobody will grade them but posterity.*

2: Readings from the Lives of the Saints

To American writers of my own age, or at any rate to those who went abroad in 1921, the author who seemed nearest to themselves was T. S. Eliot. Essentially the picture he presented was that of the local-boy-makes-good. He was born in St. Louis; he was in the class of 1910 at Harvard, where he took courses that any of us might have taken and belonged to three or four undistinguished clubs; he continued his studies at a French provincial university and got a job in London. Now, ten years after leaving Cambridge, he was winding himself in a slow cocoon of glory. But his glory, his making good, was not in the vulgar sense of making money, making a popular reputation: in 1921 the newspapers had never heard of this clerk in Barclay's Bank. His achievement was the writing of perfect poems, poems in which we could not find a line that betrayed immaturity, awkwardness, provincialism or platitude. Might a Midwestern boy become a flawless poet?—this was a question with which we could not fail to be preoccupied.

But it was not the only question that Eliot answered, or the only door by which he entered our secret minds. His early critical writings were concerned in large part with the dispute between form and matter, and he aligned himself with what we had learned to call our side of it. He effectively defended the intellect as against the emotions, and the conscious mind as against the libido, the dark Freudian wish. His poems, from the first, were admirably constructed. He seemed to regard them, moreover, as intellectual problems—having solved one problem, he devoted himself to another. From his early sketches in free verse, he moved on to "Portrait of a Lady" and "Prufrock"; thence he moved on to his Sweeney poems, thence to "Gerontion"; and it was certain that his new ambitious work soon to be published in the *Dial* would mark another departure. For he never repeated himself and never, in those days, persisted in any attitude or technique: once having suggested its possibilities, he moved on.

Eliot, of course, did not originate the idea of "moving on." It was part of the general literary atmosphere, part of a long tradition—for example, it closely resembled the "theory of convolutions" that developed among my high-school friends. But Eliot's influence had the effect of making the idea vastly popular among young writers. They began to picture the ideal poet as an explorer, a buffalo hunter pressing westward toward new frontiers—from the Shenandoah he marches into unknown Tennessee, thence into the Blue Grass, thence into Missouri, always leaving the land untilled behind him, but who cares?—there will be disciples to follow the plow. No other American poet had so many disciples as Eliot, in so many stages of his career. Until 1925 his influence seemed omnipresent, and it continued to be important in the years that followed. But in 1922, at the moment when he was least known to the general public and most fervently worshiped by young poets, there was a sudden crisis. More than half of his disciples began slowly to drop away.

When *The Waste Land* first appeared, we were confronted with a dilemma. Here was a poem that agreed with all our recipes and prescriptions of what a great modern poem should be. Its form was not only perfect but was far richer musically and architecturally than that of Eliot's earlier verse. Its diction was superb. It employed in a magisterial fashion the technical discoveries made by the French writers who followed Baudelaire. Strangeness, abstractness, simplification, respect for literature as an art with traditions—it had all the qualities demanded in our slogans. We were prepared fervently to defend it against the attacks of the people who didn't understand what Eliot was trying to do—but we made private reservations. The poem had forced us into a false position, had brought our consciously adopted principles into conflict with our instincts. At heart—not intellectually, but in a purely emotional fashion—we didn't like it. We didn't agree with what we regarded as the principal idea that the poem set forth.

The idea was a simple one. Beneath the rich symbolism of *The*

Waste Land, the wide learning expressed in seven languages, the actions conducted on three planes, the musical episodes, the geometrical structure—beneath and by means of all this, we felt the poet was saying that the present is inferior to the past. The past was dignified; the present is barren of emotion. The past was a landscape nourished by living fountains; now the fountains of spiritual grace are dry. . . . Often in his earlier poems Eliot had suggested this idea; he had used such symbols of dead glory as the Roman eagles and trumpets or the Lion of St. Mark's to emphasize the vulgarities of the present. In those early poems, however, the present was his real subject. Even though he seemed to abhor it, even though he thought "of all the hands that are raising dingy shades in a thousand furnished rooms" and was continually "aware of the damp souls of housemaids sprouting despondently at area gates," still he was writing about the life that all of us knew—and more than that, he was endowing our daily life with distinction by means of the same distinguished metaphors in which he decried and belittled it. *The Waste Land* marked a real change. This time he not only expressed the idea with all his mature resources but carried it to a new extreme. He not only abused the present but robbed it of vitality. It was as if he were saying, this time, that our age was prematurely senile and could not even find words of its own in which to bewail its impotence; that it was forever condemned to borrow and patch together the songs of dead poets.

The seven-page appendix to *The Waste Land,* in which Eliot paraded his scholarship and explained the Elizabethan or Italian sources of what had seemed to be his most personal phrases, was a painful dose for us to swallow. But the truth was that the poet had not changed so much as his younger readers. We were becoming less preoccupied with technique and were looking for poems that portrayed our own picture of the world. As for the question proposed to us by Eliot, whether the values of past ages

were superior or inferior to present values, we could bring no
objective evidence to bear on it. Values are created by living men.
If they believe—if their manner of life induces them to believe
—that greatness died with Virgil or Dante or Napoleon, who
can change their opinion or teach them new values? It happened
that we were excited by the adventure of living in the present.
The famous "postwar mood of aristocratic disillusionment" was
a mood we had never really shared. It happened that Eliot's subjective truth was not our own.

I say "it happened" although, as a matter of fact, our beliefs
grew out of the lives we had led. I say "we" although I can re-
fer only to a majority, perhaps two-thirds, of those already influenced by Eliot's poems. When *The Waste Land* was published
it revealed a social division among writers that was not a division
between rich and poor or—in the Marxian terms that would
later be popular—between capitalist and proletarian.[1] Not many
of the younger writers belonged to either the top or the bottom
layer of society. Some of them it is true, were the children of
factory workers or tenant farmers, but even those few had received the education of the middle class and had for the most
part adopted its standards. The middle class had come to domi-

---

[1] It seems to me now that the division was more a matter of temperament, and less a result of social background, than I believed in 1934.
The division was real, however, and it reflected attitudes toward life in
our own time. When *The Waste Land* appeared, complete with notes,
E. E. Cummings asked me why Eliot couldn't write his own lines instead
of borrowing from dead poets. In his remarks I sensed a feeling almost of
betrayal. Hemingway said in the *Transatlantic Review*, "If I knew that by
grinding Mr. Eliot into a fine dry powder and sprinkling that powder
over Mr. Conrad's grave Mr. Conrad would shortly appear, looking very
annoyed at the forced return, and commence writing, I would leave for
London early tomorrow with a sausage grinder." On the other hand John
Peale Bishop, of Princeton, who was also in Paris at the time, told me
that he was studying Italian so that he could get the full force of the
quotations from Dante identified in Eliot's notes.

nate the world of letters; the dominant educational background was that of the public high school and the big Midwestern university. And the writers of this class—roughly corresponding to Marx's petty bourgeoisie—were those who began to ask where Eliot was leading and whether they should follow.

But there were also many young writers who had been sent to good preparatory schools, usually Episcopalian, before they went on to Yale, Harvard, Princeton, Williams or Dartmouth. Whether rich or poor, they had received the training and acquired the standards of the small but powerful class in American society that might be described as the bourgeoisie proper. These, in general, were the "young poets old before their time" who not only admired *The Waste Land* but insisted on dwelling there in spirit; as Edmund Wilson said, they "took to inhabiting exclusively barren beaches, cactus-grown deserts and dusty attics overrun with rats." Their special education, their social environment and also, I think, their feeling of mingled privilege and insecurity had prepared them to follow Eliot in his desert pilgrimage toward the shrines of tradition and authority.

There were exceptions in both groups, and Eliot continued to be recited and praised behind the dingy shades of a thousand furnished rooms, but most of the struggling middle-class writers were beginning to look for other patterns of literary conduct. We were new men, without inherited traditions, and we were entering a new world of art that did not impress us as being a spiritual desert. Although we did not see our own path, we instinctively rejected Eliot's. In the future we should still honor his poems and the clearness and integrity of his prose, but the Eliot picture had ceased to be our guide.

James Joyce also presented us with a picture of the writer who never repeats himself. From *Chamber Music* through *Dubliners* and *A Portrait of the Artist as a Young Man,* each of his books had approached a new problem and had definitely ended a stage of his career. *Ulysses,* published in Paris in the winter of 1921–22, marked yet another stage. Although we had not time in the busy year that followed to read it carefully or digest more than a tenth of it, still we were certain of one thing: it was a book that without abusing the word could be called "great."

Thus we learned to couple Joyce and Eliot in a second fashion. Joyce, too, had become a success picture to fire the imagination of young writers, even though the success was on a different plane. He was another local-boy-makes-good, but not a St. Louis boy or a Harvard boy. His birthplace was the lower middle class; his home, above which he seemed to have soared, was the twentieth century. Can a writer of our own time produce a masterpiece fit to compare with those of other ages? Joyce was the first indication that there was another answer to this question than the one we were taught in school.

But—here were more difficult questions—what were the methods by and the motives for which he had written his indubitably great work? Had he set an example we should try to follow?

It seemed that from all his books three values disengaged themselves, three qualities of the man himself: his pride, his contempt for others, his ambition. Toward the end of *A Portrait of the Artist* they stood forth most clearly. The hero, Stephen Dedalus, was lonely and overweening in his pride; he despised the rabble of his richer schoolmates for being his inferiors in sensibility and intellect; and he set for himself the ambition, not of becoming a mere bishop, judge or general, but of pressing into his arms "the loveliness that has not yet come into the world." He would be the spiritual leader standing alone; he was leaving Ireland "to forge in the smithy of my soul the uncreated conscience of my race." Stephen Dedalus was obviously a more or less accurate picture of Joyce himself; but in life the author had chosen a still lonelier ambition. As he wandered through Italy, Austria, Switzerland and France, he continued to write about the Dublin of his youth and remembered the sound of Irish voices, but he half forgot that Irish race whose conscience was being forged in the smithy of revolution. He had chosen another destiny. Like Napoleon landing from Corsica, like Cortés or Pizarro marching into the highlands, he set himself a task of self-aggrandizement: he would be a genius!—he would carve out an empire, create a work of genius.

The intellectual resources at his command were not superhuman, and material resources were almost totally absent. He came of a family that had decayed with Ireland; all during his young manhood he was poor, desperately poor and unpopular. He was unusually sensitive, but no more so than half a dozen other Irish poets; he had a mind equaled in nimbleness by some of his Jesuit instructors; he had great learning of a type not impossible for any diligent student to acquire. But he was patient, obstinate —having chosen a goal he was willing to disregard all difficulties; he was a foreigner, penniless, in frail health; Europe was crumbling about his ears, thirteen million men died in the trenches, empires toppled over; he shut his window and worked on, sixteen hours a day, seven days a week, writing, polishing, elaborating. And it seemed to us that there was nothing mysterious in what he had accomplished. He had pride, contempt, ambition—and those were the qualities that continued to stand forth clearly from *Ulysses*. Here once more was the pride of Stephen Dedalus that raised itself above the Dublin public and especially above the Dublin intellectual public as represented by Buck Mulligan; here was the author's contempt for the world and for his readers—like a host being deliberately rude to his guests, he made no concession to their capacity for attention or their power of understanding; and here was an ambition willing to measure itself, not against any novelist of its age, not against any writer belonging to a modern national literature, but with the father of all the Western literatures, the archpoet of the European race.

And now this poor boy from the twentieth century had conquered his Peru and created his work of genius. We were not among the enthusiasts who placed him beside Homer, but this at least was certain: except possibly for Marcel Proust, there was no living author to be compared with him in depth, richness, complexity or scope. His achievement was there to urge us ahead; his ambition dignified our lesser ambitions. But obviously he had written *Ulysses* at a price—just how much had he paid in terms of bread and laughter? How did a man live who had written a masterpiece?

We fitted together passages from his books with sometimes erroneous information collected from magazine articles about him, bits of café gossip and the remarks of people allowed to meet him. The resulting picture, the Joyce picture of 1923, was not wholly pleasant. The great man lived in a cheap hotel, not picturesquely sordid, but cluttered and depressing. He was threatened with Homeric blindness, and much of his meager income was spent on doctors, for the disease from which he suffered was aggravated by hypochondria. He had no companions of his own intellectual stature and associated either with family friends or else with admiring disciples. Except in matters concerning literature and the opera, his opinions were those of a fourth or fifth-rate mind. It was as if he had starved everything else in his life to feed his ambition. It was as if he had made an inverted Faust's bargain, selling youth, riches and part of his common humanity to advance his pride of soul.

Having been granted an interview, I went to his hotel. He was waiting for me in a room that looked sour and moldy, as if the red-plush furniture had fermented in the twilight behind closed shutters. I saw a tall, emaciated man with a very high white forehead and smoked glasses; on his thin mouth and at the puckered corners of his eyes was a look of suffering so plainly marked that I forgot the questions with which I had come prepared. I was simply a younger person meeting an older person who needed help.

"Is there anything I can do for you, Mr. Joyce?" I said.

Yes, there was something I could do: he had no stamps, he didn't feel well enough to go out and there was nobody to run errands for him. I went out to buy stamps, with a sense of relief as I stepped into the street. He had achieved genius, I thought, but there was something about the genius as cold as the touch at parting of his long, smooth, cold, wet-marble fingers.

Ezra Pound presented a less intimidating picture, since he was known not so much for his own creations as for his advocacy of other writers and his sallies against the stupid public. His function seemed to be that of a schoolmaster, in a double sense of the word. He schooled the public in scolding it; he was always presenting it with new authors to admire, new readings of the classics, new and stricter rules for judging poetry. It was Gertrude Stein who said that he was "a village explainer, excellent if you were a village, but if you were not, not." Miss Stein herself seldom bothered to explain, although she liked to have young men sit at her feet and was not above being jealous of Pound's influence on the younger writers. The influence was extensive and well earned. He not only gave the best of advice to writers but often tried to organize them into groups or schools, each with its own manifesto and its own magazine; that is the second sense in which he might have been called schoolmaster.

In London he had started the Imagiste school and then, after relinquishing the name to Amy Lowell (who had dropped the "e" from it, together with most of the principles on which the group was founded), had assembled the Vorticists, who survived as a group until most of the members were called into military service. Besides these formal groups that Pound inspired he also had a circle of friends that included some of the greatest poets of our time. They deferred to Pound because they felt that he had shown an unselfish devotion to literature. He had fought to win recognition for the work of other writers at a time when much of his own work was going unpublished, and he had obtained financial support for others that he could as easily have had for himself. During most of his career he had earned hardly more than the wages of an English day laborer. "If I accept more than I need," he used to say, "I at once become a sponger."

He was in somewhat better financial circumstances in 1921, when he left London for Paris. During the next two years I went to see him several times, but the visit I remember is the last, in the summer of 1923. Pound was then living in the *pavillon,* or summer house, that stood in the courtyard of *70bis,* rue Notre-Dame-des-Champs, near the Luxembourg Gardens. A big young man with intent eyes and a toothbrush mustache was there when I arrived, and Pound introduced him as Ernest Hemingway; I said that I had heard about him. Hemingway gave a slow Mid-western grin. He was then working for the International News Service, but there were rumors that he had stories in manuscript and that Pound had spoken of them as being something new in American literature. He didn't talk about the stories that afternoon; he listened as if with his eyes while Pound discussed the literary world. Very soon he rose, made a date with Pound for tennis the following day and went out the door, walking on the balls of his feet like a boxer. Pound continued his monologue.

"I've found the lowdown on the Elizabethan drama," he said as he vanished beard-first into the rear of the pavilion; he was always finding the lowdown, the inside story and the simple reason why. A moment later he returned with a worm-eaten leather-bound folio. "It's all in here," he said, tapping the volume. "The whole business is cribbed from these Italian state papers."

The remark seemed so disproportionate that I let it go unchallenged, out of politeness. "What about your own work?" I asked.

Pound laid the book on a table piled with other books. "I try not to repeat myself," he said. He began walking back and forth in his red dressing gown, while his red beard jutted out like that of an archaic Greek soldier (or, as I afterward thought, like a fox's muzzle). There was no attempt to play the great man of letters. With an engaging lack of pretense to dignity he launched into the story of his writing life.

At the age of twenty-two he had written a poem, the "Ballad of the Goodly Fere," that had been widely discussed and had even been reprinted in the *International Sunday School*. It was the first of the masculine ballads in the genre that Masefield would afterward exploit, and Pound might have exploited it himself— "Having written this ballad about Christ," he said, "I had only to write similar ballads about James, Matthew, Mark, Luke and John and my fortune was made." If he had missed falling into the gulf of standardization it was partly because he didn't see it was there. Instead he had gone to England in 1908 and started a new career.

He was still convinced that he had been right to leave America. America was England thirty years before. America was England without the fifty most intelligent men. America didn't print his poems in magazines until they had been collected into books in England. Perhaps he had been misled by the early recognition he received there; perhaps it had made him willing for a time to write the sort of poems that friendly critics expected him to write. He had spent three years studying Oxford English before he learned that he was wasting his efforts; that English is not Latin and must be written as one speaks it.

He had lost many of his English readers when he published *Ripostes* in 1912. The public doesn't like to be surprised and the new poems had been surprising, even a little shocking; they had proved that Pound wasn't merely an author of masculine ballads or a new Browning who brought medieval characters to life in medieval phrases. Still more of his readers had dropped away when he published *Lustra* in 1916; they hadn't liked his use of colloquial language or the frankness with which he described the feelings of *l'homme moyen sensuel*. It was the same when he published the *Mauberley* poems and the first of the *Cantos:* with each successive book he lost old readers and, after a time, gained some new ones, who disappeared in their turn; he had always outdistanced his audience.

Pound talked about some of his associates. Gaudier-Brzeska, killed at the front in 1916, had been the most gifted of the new sculptors; Pound had helped to keep him alive when he was starving in London. Wyndham Lewis was the real Vorticist, a man of amazing intellectual force. Lewis had visited New York in the spring of 1917 and two weeks later—Pound paused for emphasis—the United States had declared war on the Central Powers. In earlier days Pound had worked to gain recognition for Lewis, just as he had worked for Joyce, Eliot and dozens of gifted writers. Now he was thirty-seven years old and it was time for him to stop doing so much for other men and for literature in general, stop trying to educate the public and simply write. It would take years for him to finish the *Cantos;* he wanted to write an opera and he had other plans. To carry them out it might be best for him to leave Paris and live on the Mediterranean, far from distractions, in a little town he had discovered when he was in *villeggiatura*. . . .

I went back to Giverny, the village about sixty miles from Paris where I was living that year (not in *villeggiatura*), and re-read all of Pound's poems that I had been able to collect in their

English editions. I liked them better than on first reading and was less irritated by their parade of eccentric scholarship. What impressed me now was their new phrases, new rhythms, new images, and their resolute omission of every word that he might have requisitioned from the stockroom of poetry. I could see how much Eliot had learned from them (although I didn't know at the time that he had sent the manuscript of *The Waste Land* to Pound for criticism and had accepted almost all the changes that Pound advised). I could also see that E. E. Cummings had used *Hugh Selwyn Mauberley* as a model in writing his own satirical poems and I could trace other derivations as well. Pound deserved the credit for discoveries which other poets were using, yet it seemed to me that some of the others—notably Eliot and Cummings—had a great deal more to say. For all his newness of phrase Pound kept making statements that were simply the commonplaces of the art-for-art's-sake tradition, when they did not belong to the older tradition of the tavern minstrel. He kept repeating that the public was stupid, that the poet was happier living in a garret, that he wrote to shock the public and that his songs would live when his readers were dead:

> Go, little naked and impudent songs,
> Go with a light foot!
> (Or with two light feet, if it please you!)
> Go and dance shamelessly!
> Go with an impertinent frolic!

> . . .

> Ruffle the skirts of prudes,
>   speak of their knees and ankles.
> But, above all, go to practical people—
>   go! jangle their door-bells!
> Say that you do no work
>   and that you will live forever.

In poems like this he was affronting the conventions in a fashion that was badly needed at the time and he was writing a declaration of independence for poets—but how could the songs live forever when they had so little fresh blood in their arteries? There was, moreover, another weakness in Pound's poetry that had been impressed on me by his remark about outdistancing his readers. He kept moving ahead into unexplored territory, like Eliot and Joyce, but it seemed to me that his motive was different. From his early ballads to *Ripostes,* to *Lustra,* to *Mauberley,* his poetic career might be explained, not as a search for something, but rather as a frantic effort to escape. I pictured him as a red fox pursued by the pack of his admirers; he led them through brambles and into marshes; some of them gave up the chase but others joined in. At present, in the *Cantos,* he had fled into high and rocky ground where the scent was lost and the hounds would cut their feet if they tried to follow, yet I felt that they would eventually find him even there and would crowd around muzzle to muzzle, not for the kill, but merely for the privilege of baying his praises. Then, with his weakness for defying the crowd, for finding crazily simple explanations and for holding eccentric opinions, to what new corner would the fox escape?

In November 1922 we heard that Marcel Proust had died, and it seemed that his death was the completion of a symbol. He represented an entirely different ambition from that of Pound or Joyce, for he strove neither to outdistance the public nor to create a work of genius by force of will. In Joyce the will had developed immoderately; in Proust it seemed almost to be atrophied. Not only his passions but his merest whims were stronger than his desire to control them, and he dispassionately watched himself doing silly things—it was almost as if the living Marcel Proust were an unpleasant but fascinating visitor in the house of his mind. Nevertheless, he had set himself a task and had carried it through. He had determined to take the living Marcel Proust that was weak and fickle and transform it, transform himself, into an enduring work of art.

Eager to execute this project while he still had strength for it, he shut himself off from friendships, public life, the world in general, spending most of his time in bed in a room hermetically sealed to prevent drafts—they say he would feel and suffer from a breath of fresh air three rooms away. Flowers, even, were prohibited, because they brought on his asthma. He rarely saw daylight. Sometimes very late in the evening, wrapped to the ears in a fur-lined overcoat, he attended a reception in the Faubourg St. Germain; but usually he spent his nights writing hurriedly in a study that was completely lined with cork in order to shut out the street noises. He was racing against time, his enemy. Here in seclusion he was trying to recapture and preserve his past in the moment before it vanished, like a mollusk making its shell before it dies. And his death, I wrote in an essay published at the time, "was only a process of externalization; he had turned himself inside out like an orange and sucked it dry, or inscribed himself on a monument; his observation, his sensibility, his affectations, everything about him that was weak or strong had passed into the created characters of his novel."

When I came to read the last section of his book, which was not published until the end of the decade, I found that Proust had expressed the same idea about himself in different words. "Let us allow our body to disintegrate, since each fresh particle that breaks off, now luminous and decipherable, comes and adds itself to our work to complete it at the cost of suffering superfluous to others more gifted, and to make it more and more substantial as emotions gradually chip away our life." The passage must have been written only a few weeks before his final illness. By then his life was almost wholly chipped away and all its luminous particles were added to his work, which, in the process, had become the longest novel that had been written. Dying at a moment when *Remembrance of Things Past* was practically completed (only two sections remained to be revised), Proust had become for us a symbol of fulfilled ambition. And yet the symbol was too cold and distant to touch us closely. We had neither the wish nor the financial nor yet the intellectual resources to shut ourselves in cork-lined chambers and examine our memories. And Proust, moreover, had closed a path to us merely by choosing it for himself. He had accomplished his task so thoroughly that it would never have to be done again.

In 1921 Paul Valéry was fifty years old and had recently entered his second literary career, which in a short time would carry him to the French Academy. His first career had begun some thirty years before; it had been brilliant and very brief. And it was his abandoning of that career, it was his deliberate, twenty-year-long refusal to write for publication, that impressed us even more than the high poems and the noble essays he had printed since consenting once more to become a writer like anybody else.

He had come to Paris in the autumn of 1892, a boy from the provinces with his road to make. Soon he attached himself to the circle of Symbolist poets surrounding Stéphane Mallarmé. Writing of that time he later said, "There was a certain austerity about the new generation of poets. . . . In the profound and scrupulous worship of all the arts, they thought to have found a discipline, and perhaps a truth, beyond the reach of doubt. A kind of religion was very nearly established." And again: "It was a time of theories, curiosity, glosses and passionate explanation. . . . More fervor, courage and learning, more researches into theory, more disputes and a more pious attention have rarely been devoted, in so short a time, to the problem of pure beauty. One might say that the problem was attacked from all sides."

Valéry himself chose the intellectual side. His ambition resembled that of T. S. Eliot's early days: he was obsessed by the idea of always moving through and "going beyond." Each poem could be translated into a problem capable of solution, capable of supplying a principle which could then be applied to the writing of other poems. But why bother to write them? "From the moment a principle has been recognized and grasped by someone," Valéry says that he said to himself, "it is quite useless to waste one's time applying it." Thus, he was always driven further, to attack new problems, discover new principles, until it became evident at a certain point in the process that literature itself was a problem capable of solution, and therefore was only an intermediate goal, a stage to be passed through and gone beyond. The poet was free to abandon poetry and devote himself to more essential aims.

For a young man of twenty-five, Valéry had won an enviable position; he had become a favorite disciple of Mallarmé and a leader among the younger Symbolists. His future seemed assured, and he abandoned it almost overnight. This deliberate choice, this apostasy, one might almost call it, exerted a powerful influence on the young French writers who followed him. Suddenly their highest value had been called into question, and not by the stupid public. Suddenly it seemed that the highest ambition might not be the writing of a great novel or poetic drama or the creation of any work of genius whatsoever. Apollo, after all, might be only a minor deity.

Valéry himself found his arguments so cogent that he had a hard time explaining, twenty years later, why he had once more begun writing essays and poems. He justified himself by saying on several occasions that literature was an *exercise,* a

game worth playing for the same reasons that one plays tennis
or chess or bridge. All these have difficult and arbitrary rules,
but we observe them for the sake of the game; and the arbitrary
and far more difficult conventions of classical poetry may be
observed for the same reasons. One might even assert that
these laws and constant requirements are the true object of the
poem. "It is indeed an exercise—intended as such, and worked
and reworked: a production entirely of deliberate effort; and
then of a second deliberate effort, whose hard task is to conceal
the first. He who knows how to read me will read an autobiography, in the form. The *matter* is of small importance."—His justification would have been more accurate, I think, if he had admitted from the first that the sport of writing was not altogether
non-professional: that he derived pleasure from the praise his
poems received, and wrote his essays for magazine editors who
ordered and paid well for them. But always, in reading Valéry,
one must learn to expect a certain high pretentiousness that
accompanies and dilutes and sometimes conceals his real acute-
ness.

Whether the new essays that he began to publish after 1917
were written for sport or hire, they contained a valuable record
of his thoughts during the years of silence.

It seems that the starting point of his researches, his first great
problem outside the field of poetry, was to re-create the mind
of "the universal man," to discover the *method* that unified the
extremely varied accomplishments in science, warfare, mechanics and the arts of a genius like Leonardo da Vinci. His essay on
Leonardo, written two or three years before the great renunci-
ation, is a magnificent defense of the conscious mind, and of
"the poet of the hypothesis" as against the specialized poet of
quatrains or the patient accumulator of facts. It also proposes
a new type of ambition. Might we not, by discovering his
method, produce a new Leonardo, able to work freely with the

infinitely rich materials of the present? But Valéry rejected the idea and seems to say that it would be useless to put the method into action. *To act,* for any individual of the first magnitude, is only an exercise, and one that may end by impoverishing the mind, since it is equivalent to choosing a single possibility and rejecting all the others with which the mind is teeming. Even "the universal man" becomes a problem capable of being reduced to a principle, to something that "it is quite useless to waste one's time applying."

Once more Valéry moved on, and this time to a problem he now regarded as the most far-reaching and difficult of all, "the study of the self for its own sake, the understanding of that attention itself, and the desire to trace clearly for oneself the nature of one's own existence." But it soon became evident that even this problem was capable of further refinement. Within the "self," what is the universal and changeless principle? It cannot be the body, which changes daily, or the senses, which tempt and deceive, or the mind, in which memories fade and ideas are dissipated; it cannot even be our *personality,* which we thoughtlessly mistake for our inmost characteristic— even the personality is only a *thing* that can be observed and reduced to tables and statistics. No, underneath all these is something else, the *I,* the naked ego, an essence that can finally be reduced to consciousness alone, to consciousness in its most abstract state. "This profound *tone* of our existence, as soon as it is heard, dominates all the complicated conditions and varieties of existence. To isolate this substantial attention from the strife of ordinary verities—is this not the ultimate and hidden task of the man with the greatest mind?"

Again he says:

Everything yields before the pure universality, the insurmountable generality, that consciousness feels itself to be. . . . It dares to con-

sider its "body" and its "world" as almost arbitrary restrictions imposed upon the extent of its functions . . . and this attention to its
external circumstances cannot react upon itself, so far has it drawn
aside from all things, so great are the pains it has taken *never to be
a part of anything it might conceive or do*. It is reduced to a black mass
that absorbs all light and gives nothing back.

And still again:

Carried away by his ambition to be unique, guided by his ardor for
omnipotence, the man of great mind has gone beyond all creations, all
works, even his own lofty designs; while at the same time he has
abandoned all tenderness for himself and all preference for his own
wishes. In an instant he immolates his individuality. . . . To this
point its pride has led the mind, and here pride is consumed. This
directing pride abandons it, astonished, bare, infinitely simple, on the
pole of its treasures.

This was the cheerless ambition, this was the path and the goal
that Paul Valéry was proposing to the young writers who followed him after an interval of thirty years. They should regard
poetry only as a beginning: from this they should move on to
the methods of poetry, thence to methods in general (and in
particular the methods of genius), thence to the universal self
that determines all methods, and thence to mere consciousness, which is the only unchanging element in the self. Having
reached this point, still undeterred by the bleakness of the way,
they will discover that consciousness itself is a perpetual process
of detachment from all things, from all emotions and sensations.
Then, lest they still persist, Valéry paints an image to drive
them back: "The man who is led by the demands of the indefatigable mind to this contact with living shadows and this
extreme of pure presence, perceives himself as destitute and
bare, reduced to the supreme poverty of being a force without

an object. . . . He exists without instincts, almost without images; and he no longer has an aim. He resembles nothing. I say *man,* and I say *he,* by analogy and through lack of words." The supreme genius has ceased even to be human.

But the perfected consciousness, which "differs from nothingness by the smallest possible of margins," is not merely a goal and an abstraction. Like all ideals, it is something to be embodied in a man who eats, lives and suffers. In *An Evening with M. Teste,* almost the only work he wrote for publication during his long retirement, Valéry performs this labor of incarnation. M. Teste, "Mr. Head," is the thinking man, the modern Leonardo, and he is an almost wholly dehumanized creature. He does nothing, desires nothing, occupies no position, is almost completely cut off from society (which nevertheless continues to nourish him). He looks at people as if they did not exist. At night, when he retires to his chamber, he is left alone with three realities: thought, sleeplessness and migraine. He suffers from incurable headaches.—And why, we asked ourselves when reading the story, does genius lead to this inhuman state in which suffering is the only reality? Why does it seem to exist in the atmosphere of a closed room, a sickroom, where the blinds are always drawn to exclude the movement and sunlight of the streets and where there is nothing living, not even a red geranium in a pot? Everything seemed to point in the same direction, James Joyce's blindness, Proust's asthma (no less real for being half imaginary), even Eliot's reiterated complaint of being devitalized, "an old man in a dry season"—all these seemed to possess the same symbolic value, as if life were taking revenge on these men for being eliminated from their calculations. These were the great literary men of our age and they resembled one another in proposing a future as cold as the touch of cold hands.

Without losing our admiration for them, we turned aside

to wonder what the writers of our own age were doing in France. They might have no genius, but they were younger certainly, and might be warmer and nearer to ourselves.

3: Paris-Express

I don't mean to give the impression that all my time or my friends' time in Europe was devoted to this search for literary guidance. I·wrote in the brief mornings, studied Molière and Racine, sat in cafés playing dominos, and traveled when we had money enough—there was always a new city where life was more agreeable or cheaper. After spending a month in Paris, and after the grape arbor at Dijon, I went south to Montpellier, where I registered at the university. The faculty adviser asked me whether I knew M. Mitchell, also a sympathetic young American. Of course I did: he was the poet Stewart Mitchell, whom I had known both at Harvard and later in New York, when he was managing editor of the *Dial*.

In March I took an examination and received a Diploma of French Studies. I intended to continue my university work, but the Mediterranean coast in May grew insufferably bright; people walked the streets in smoked glasses; Montpellier under the sun was like a city of the blind. My wife and I wandered northward, spending another month in Paris, three weeks in Brussels, two days in Munich, three days in Vienna. The trip to Vienna was a sort of mission; I carried with me the material assembled by Gorham B. Munson and Matthew Josephson for the third issue of their little magazine, *Secession*. Five hundred copies of the magazine could be printed in Vienna for twenty-five dollars. Next we spent six weeks at Imst, in the Austrian

Tyrol, where we heard that Josephson was going to be associate editor of another magazine, *Broom,* that was printed on rag paper and paid for contributions. It was on the shadowy veranda of the Gasthof Post, at Imst, that the proprietor's wife asked me whether I knew *Herr Braun von Amerika.* I answered, *"Jawohl, gnädige Frau,* I know Mr. Brown of America, I know him well." He was William Slater Brown, Bill Brown of Greenwich Village and Webster, Massachusetts, the Columbia boy who had been imprisoned with Cummings in the enormous room. In those days young American writers were drifting everywhere in West Europe and Middle Europe; they waved to each other from the windows of passing trains.

Again we traveled northward: it was October 1922, and Germany was entering its wildest period of inflation. When we crossed the border, German marks were selling eight hundred for the dollar; they had fallen to a thousand at Munich, twelve hundred at Ratisbon; in Berlin next morning a dollar would buy two thousand paper marks or an all-wool overcoat. In the station we were met by Josephson and by Harold Loeb, the publisher of *Broom;* together they were editing the magazine at a monthly cost of I don't and they didn't know how many marks or dollars. Art was a liquid product that flowed across international frontiers to find the lowest level of prices. For a salary of a hundred dollars a month in American currency, Josephson lived in a duplex apartment with two maids, riding lessons for his wife, dinners only in the most expensive restaurants, tips to the orchestra, pictures collected, charities to struggling German writers—it was an insane life for foreigners in Berlin and nobody could be happy there. We hurried back to France on an international express full of smugglers. An English officer had seven new suitcases full of German butter, which he purposed selling in Belgium at a profit of four shillings per kilogram. A Frenchman had a German baby carriage hidden under the seat. A French customs officer found it and forced him to pay duty under protest.—*La Patrie* was urging people to have children, and yet made them pay twice for a baby carriage! Why, it was outrageous, it was stupid, it was pro-German. —And it was good, I thought, to hear French voices raised once more in an argument involving patriotism, money and the Categorical Imperative.

We were spending the winter in Giverny, the village where Claude Monet was still painting at the age of eighty. His stepdaughter had married an American painter, Theodore Butler, and some of Butler's friends had settled nearby; before the war Giverny had been an art colony almost like Woodstock in the Catskills. Most of the American artists who remained were now sober and academic and they looked without favor on the new incursion of wild youngsters. The village lay on the Epte, a river not twelve yards wide that was the immemorial boundary between Normandy and France. On the west bank were straggling towns, the homes of farmer-freebooters who feared nobody, not God or the French; on the east bank the villages were close-huddled each about its church, for spiritual warmth and self-protection. Giverny was Norman and its people said of a horse or a woman from the village a scant mile across the river, "That horse is no good, it's a *French* horse, that woman is *French,* she sleeps with all the world." We lived in three rooms over the blacksmith shop. In the mornings I wrote or studied; in the short winter afternoons I bicycled into France or watched the alternate bands of storm and sunshine moving over the hillside. The almond trees blossomed early in February and soon afterward I began fishing in the river, where it was rumored that there were three trout: I caught one of them in June. Once a week, sometimes once a fortnight, I spent the day in Paris.

Those Paris ventures were periods of unexampled mental activity. . . . You rose before dawn, breakfasted on a quart of milk-and-coffee, just caught a branch-line train full of peasants dressed for market day, then changed at the junction for the Paris express—all this hurry and loss of sleep was a stimulant like cocaine. You could not sit still in your compartment, but picked your way up and down the crowded corridor, watching the Seine unwind as the train creaked faster, faster; thoughts, verses, situations were flashing into the mind, and there was never any time to write them down. Paris! You leaped into the first empty taxicab outside the station and ordered the driver to hurry. In Paris the subways were impossibly slow, and the taxis never drove fast enough as you raced from one appointment to another, from an art gallery to a bookshop where you had no time to linger, and thence to a concert you could never quite sit through—faster, faster, there was always something waiting that might be forever missed unless you hammered on the glass and told the driver to go faster. Paris was a great machine for stimulating the nerves and sharpening the senses. Paintings and music, street noises, shops, flower markets, modes, fabrics, poems, ideas, everything seemed to lead toward a half-sensual, half-intellectual swoon. Inside the cafés, color, perfume, taste and delirium could be poured together from one bottle or many bottles, from square, cylindrical, conical, tall, squat, brown, green or crimson bottles —but you drank black coffee by choice, believing that Paris itself was sufficient alcohol. And, as the evening wore on, it was more than sufficient. Late at night, you took the last train for Normandy, happy to be returning to your country routine.

It was during one of those Wednesdays in Paris that I was first introduced to the Dada group. "Matty Josephson is right about them," I said in a letter written that same week. "They are the most amusing people in Paris. André Breton, who is no longer thirty and has a mass of light-brown curly hair brushed back from a high forehead—Breton, their present *chef d'école,* had discovered a play of which he approved. At least he was not halfhearted in his approval, and he brought along his twenty friends with their wives and mistresses. He attended the dress rehearsal, the first night, the second night, the third; I joined the party on the fourth night, and Dada still possessed its thirty seats in the balcony. There was a stupid one-act curtain raiser which Dada hissed; then comes the great crazy drama. 'Attention, attention!' says the hero, and Dada bursts into a storm of applause. 'But they will never understand!' At this remark, which might apply to any book or poem or story by any member of the group, they clap and cheer so loudly that the police are forced to intervene. Breton orates for half an hour to the parquet. The audience separates into little groups of arguing men. Really it is huge fun."

That was early in December 1922. By the following February I was describing the Dadaists more seriously. I found that they were divided into two warring factions, of which the one headed by Breton was the larger and more uncompromising. "Paris," I wrote, "is a city one enters with elation and leaves without regret. My last visit there was spent chiefly with the Dadas. For the first time in eighteen months, Tzara, Ribemont-Dessaignes and Picabia met together with Breton, Aragon and their followers. They fought, of course, but finally decided to stage a joint manifestation. About twenty of us signed a paper. . . . Their love of literature is surprisingly disinterested. At this memorable meeting it was proposed that none of them should write for any except Dada publications during the next three months. No Dada publication is widely read or pays. The proposal would have been carried except for the objection of one man out of twenty. It was tiring and stimulating to meet them. I left Paris with fifty new ideas and hating the *groupe Dada*. They are a form of cocaine and personally take no stimulants except their own company. Last Wednesday all the Americans I know went to a tea and got divinely drunk. It was vastly more exciting to attend this three-hour French meeting at which not even water was served."

Tiring and stimulating, crazy, huge fun. . . . I began to feel that the Dada movement was the very essence of Paris. It existed on a level far below Joyce's ambition and Valéry's high researches into the metaphysics of the self, but at least it was young and adventurous, and human.

V: The Death of Dada

1: A Brief History of Dada

Tristan Tzara says that Dada was born in 1916, at the Cabaret Voltaire in Zurich. There is some dispute about this place and date, but Tzara's word ought to be final: after all, he founded Dada. He is a Rumanian, small and graceful, who belongs to a family of formerly rich merchants; educated in France and Switzerland, he adopted French as his native tongue. It is wholly fitting that this new school of art and letters should have been founded in a cabaret, by a young man so thoroughly expatriated that he could not speak more than three words of his native language. It is fitting, too, that Dada should have transferred itself to the two banks of the Seine.

But Tzara was still in Switzerland when he wrote the Dada Manifesto in March 1918. At that time André Breton and Louis Aragon, who would later become the French leaders of the movement, were serving at the front. When these very young soldiers came home after the Armistice, they joined forces with Philippe Soupault, Paul Eluard and others to found the magazine *Littérature,* which soon became known as a Dadaist review. At the beginning of 1920 they formally invited Tzara to Paris.

That was the period of the great Dada manifestations. At a matinee on January 23 Tzara was introduced to the public. He read aloud a newspaper article, while an electric bell kept ringing so that nobody could hear what he said. A meeting was held at the Grand Palace of the Champs Elysées; several thousand people attended it. Tzara afterward wrote in an article for *Vanity Fair* that they "manifested uproariously it is impossible to say exactly what, their joy or their disapproval, by unexpected cries and general laughter, which constituted a very pretty accompaniment to the manifestoes read by six people at once. The newspapers said that an old man in the audience gave himself up to behavior of a more or less intimate nature, that somebody set off some flashlight powder and that a pregnant woman had to be taken out." At the Théâtre de l'Œuvre two months later, twelve hundred people were turned away. "There were three spectators for every seat; it was suffocating. Enthusiastic members of the audience had brought musical instruments to interrupt us. The enemies of Dada threw down from the balconies copies of an anti-Dada paper called *Non* in which we were described as lunatics. The scandal reached proportions absolutely unimaginable." But the scandal was even greater at the Salle Gaveau. "For the first time in the history of the world, people threw at us not only eggs, vegetables and pennies, but beefsteaks as well. It was a very huge success."

Whether the public, the idiotic public, expressed its interest in terms of beefsteaks or applause, Dada was launched. It exactly suited the temper of a world disorganized by the war and ruled, so the Dadaists said, "by aggressive madmen"; now it was time for a literary movement that would outdo the politicians in lunacy. All over Europe Dadaist groups had sprung into being, and everywhere they repeated the same pattern of childishness and audacity: they played violently with art and politics and paper dollies. The Dadaists in Berlin had their own magazines, their publishing house and a Dada Club which soon brought to light great talents—Tzara believed that their many demonstrations helped to produce the German revolution. In Cologne an allied group was permitted by the city authorities to hold a Dada exhibition in a public urinal, with free admission. By 1922 there were Dadaists in all the European capitals, even Moscow; lectures on Dadaism were being delivered at the University of Tiflis, in Soviet Georgia, before a proletarian audience. A world congress of Dadaists was held in France. But at this conference, which demonstrated the strength of the movement, there was a split in the ranks, a division between those who wished to carry Dadaism into public life and those who were content to express their disgust in practical jokes, without being bothered by the police. Friendships were broken, adherents dropped away: at the very moment when Dada seemed most successful, it was dying at the heart. Soon it was replaced by a new movement, Surrealism, which in turn was causing its scandals and enlisting its adherents. One could write, "Here lies Dada, 1916–1924."

But the history of Dada was in reality much longer. Its existence was rendered possible by a succession of literary schools beginning before the middle of the nineteenth century. There had been the art-for-art's sake school of Théophile Gautier; there had been the Naturalist school (or at least the part of it which surrounded Flaubert and the Brothers Goncourt); there had been the Parnassians, the Decadents, the Symbolists; in England there had been the Pre-Raphaelite Brotherhood, the Oxford Aesthetes, the group surrounding the *Yellow Book*—then the tempo increased: there were the Post-Impressionists, the Cubists (schools of literature and schools of art were amalgamating), the Neo-Classicists, the Fantaisists; in Italy the Futurists, in England the Vorticists, in America the Imagists, in Germany the Expressionists, in Russia the Constructivists—still the dance moved faster, so that a single artist like Picasso might successively adhere to several schools, was even expected to *changer d'école* as one might change a coat—then, at the summit of

this long development, came Dada, like a last act that cast a
light of farce on the preceding acts, like a capstone self-crowned
with a dunce cap.

Edmund Wilson was the first American critic to show that a
single impulse persisted through eighty years of quarreling
doctrines and self-devouring schools. In *Axel's Castle* he suggested that the name Symbolism was broad enough to cover
this whole literary movement. His book was extraordinarily illuminating. Nobody before him had written a better exposition
of Yeats, Joyce, Proust; and he did not confine himself to
expository criticism: he placed these writers in historical perspective and considered the values that their work implied.
Yet *Axel's Castle* has an obvious weakness of structure. Midway
in the book, Wilson changes his conception of the subject; so
that although he continues to describe it by the same name,
he is really talking about two different things. In the first
chapter he is discussing Symbolism primarily as a *method,* as
"an attempt, by carefully studied means—a complicated association of ideas represented by a medley of metaphors—to communicate unique personal feelings." But at the end of the book
he is discussing Symbolism as an attitude, an ideology, in reality
a *way of life* that was adopted by a whole series of writers.

This changing conception of his subject led Wilson into
making two complementary mistakes. The Symbolistic *method*
is less important than he believes it to be: its history was shorter
and its influence less widespread in the world of international
letters. But the *attitude toward life* which he attributes to Yeats
and Valéry and Villiers de l'Isle-Adam was also that of many
writers who could not in any technical sense be regarded as
Symbolists. During the course of a long history, this attitude
affected not only poets and novelists of different schools, but
also painters, sculptors, composers, dramatists and ordinary

people who confessed with bitter humility that they weren't "creative," that they were unable to "express themselves artistically." Boys of my age in Pittsburgh and Chicago had acted in a certain fashion, read certain books—they had felt themselves to be cut off from and secretly superior to the dull mass of their schoolmates—because they were influenced by what might be called the religion of art.

One example is enough to show the difference between Wilson's two conceptions of the subject. In the first chapter he explains that Symbolism was a reaction from the Naturalism of novelists like Gustave Flaubert and the cold objectivity of poets like Théophile Gautier. But later, when he describes the anti-social philosophy connected with Symbolism, we can see that Gautier was one of its founders and Flaubert perhaps its principal sage. Among the many episodes preserved in the best informal record of those times, the *Journal* of the Brothers Goncourt, there is one that seems especially significant. It shows that the religion of art very quickly expressed itself as a way of life, and one that was essentially anti-human. . . . Flaubert with several of his friends once visited a brothel in Rouen. On a bet, before them all, he made love to a prostitute without removing his hat or taking the cigar from his mouth. The gesture was something more than an ugly boast. It announced a furious contempt for everything held sacred by society—as if he had said to the honest burghers of his time, "You think that life has meaning, that the act of love is holy, yet all of you together, the whole pack of lifelings, couldn't write one passable poem or even recognize the beauty of a sentence patiently carved in marble." It is as if he proclaimed that nothing had value in itself, that everything outside the world of art should be violently rejected. "Art is vast enough," he wrote in one of his letters, "to occupy the whole man."

Although such a doctrine might produce, and has in fact

produced, great works of art and ingenious technical discoveries, it does so at a sacrifice. The religion of art is too dehumanized to nourish rich careers or to bring forth characters that compel our admiration. The "pure poet," the "artist proper," goes stumbling through life, often under a burden of neurosis. Each new artist spies out the mistakes of his predecessors and tries to guard against them by making some theoretical change. He thinks that a little more foresight will render his position secure: he sets to work deepening the moat or razing some vulnerable outwork of his ivory tower, but nevertheless it crumbles—and still newer artists rebuild the ruins according to an improved design. Always there must be changes—and there is even a moment when change itself, change for its own sake, becomes an article of doctrine.

Nor was this the only tendency implied by the religion of art as it moved inevitably toward extremes. Once the artist had come to be regarded as a being set apart from the world of ordinary men, it followed that his aloofness would be increasingly emphasized. The world would more and more diminish in the eyes of the artist, and the artist would be self-magnified at the expense of the world. These tendencies, in turn, implied still others. Art would come to be treated as a self-sustaining entity, an essence neither produced by the world nor reacting upon it: art would be *purposeless*. No longer having to communicate with a public, it would become more opaque, difficult, *obscure*. It would be freed from all elements extraneous to itself, and particularly from logic and meaning, statistics and exhortation: it would become *pure poetry*. The independence of the artist would be asserted in always more vehement language: he would be proud, disdainful toward family duties and the laws of the tribe; he would end by assuming one of God's attributes and becoming a *creator*.

But this privileged function is also a limitation. The creator

cannot be a copyist: he must not content himself with reproducing nature, must not utilize the creations of other artists,
must not even copy his own creations. As soon as anything has
been reduced to a principle—by no matter whom—it must be
abandoned to the mere disciples. The "artists proper" must
always prophesy, explore, lead the way into new countries of
emotion; and they cannot turn back: they are confined to the
frontier, to the ever-receding land beyond the boundary of the
last formula. They are first authorized and then as it were condemned to go forward, to make discoveries and leave them
behind, to advance in all directions, faster, faster, till their headlong charge can scarcely be distinguished from headlong retreat.

And yet these diverse tendencies, these paths continually
diverging toward the four horizons, all set forth in the beginning from one easily apprehended principle. *Art is separate from
life; the artist is independent of the world and superior to the
lifelings.* From this principle, the hostile schools were born,
and the manifestoes that canceled one another, and the wholly
unintelligible poems they called forth. By this principle were
guided the careers of great poets and novelists, and the ambitions
toward which their careers were directed—Huysmans' attempt
to build an artificial paradise, Mallarmé's to invent an algebra
of literature, Ezra Pound's frantic flight from his admirers,
Joyce's ambition to create a work of genius, Proust's attempt
to recapture his own past in the longest novel ever written—
all these belonged to the religion of art; and even Valéry's
forsaking of art was a development out of that religion.
There is a sort of law that governs such developments, at least
for the lifetime of the particular culture in which they occur.
The law is that no aspiration or tendency of the human mind
that has once revealed itself in the culture is permitted to disappear until all the paths it suggests have been followed to the

end, nor until the ends have proved futile and conflicting, nor even until the whole search has been turned to ridicule by the searchers. Seen from a perspective of years, the process is as logical as the growth of a tree; one might say that the Dada movement and its ending were both foreshadowed in the letters of Gustave Flaubert.

Edmund Wilson believes that the Symbolist way of life leads naturally toward two extremes. "There are, as I have said, in our contemporary society, for writers who are unable to interest themselves in it either by studying it scientifically, by attempting to reform it or by satirizing it, only two alternative courses to follow, Axel's or Rimbaud's."—He has just been describing the hero idealized in a novel by Villiérs de l'Isle-Adam. Lord of a lonely castle in the Black Forest, Count Axel of Auersburg is a young man with a "paleness almost radiant" and "an expression mysterious from thought." He penetrates the Rosicrucian mysteries, he discovers a vast hoard of gold and jewels, he meets a young woman who equals him in beauty, learning, pride, who begs him to enjoy with her all the world's splendors, or at least to spend with her one enraptured night—Axel refuses: he convinces her that mere living is futile, and both of them commit suicide out of pure disdain for life.

If one chooses the first of these [Wilson continues], the way of Axel, one shuts oneself up in one's own private world, cultivating one's private fantasies, encouraging one's private manias, ultimately preferring one's absurdest chimeras to the most astonishing contemporary realities, ultimately mistaking one's chimeras for realities. If one chooses the second, the way of Rimbaud, one tries to leave the twentieth century behind—to find the good life in some country where modern manufacturing methods and modern democratic institutions do not present any problems to the artist because they haven't yet arrived.

Here, briefly and eloquently described, are the two courses adopted by what is perhaps a majority of the "pure poets" and "artists proper." But they are not the only alternatives. There is, moreover, a serious error in Wilson's formulation of the problem. What he calls the way of Rimbaud is not the one Rimbaud actually chose: instead it is the path followed by Paul Gauguin (or at least the path that Gauguin was described as following in *The Moon and Sixpence,* a novel enormously popular just after the war, and one that was until recently propelling the tourists of art toward Tahiti, Bali, Majorca and other islands still unspoiled by modern methods of production). It is the course generally described as that of "escape"—we have all met people who spoke of "running away" from New York, London or Paris, of "finding a refuge" from skyscrapers, cocktail parties and neuroses.

Rimbaud himself had no desire to escape into an artist's paradise. His temperament was adventurous, aggressive, and in three brief years he had made astonishing conquests in the world of art. Now he wished to leave that world behind, either because his achievements there seemed easy and unexciting, or else because he had confused literature in general with the homosexuality of his friend Paul Verlaine and had decided that "all that" was bad. Very clear in his mind was the idea that by obstinate patience, by pure will, he could make equal conquests in the more difficult world of life. When he finally reached Abyssinia, after a dozen wild attempts, he did not sit dozing or making verses in the shade of a banyan tree: he bought coffee from the natives and sold them modern rifles. Even a gangrened leg did not keep him from making long journeys on horseback, so great was his energy, so bitter his determination. . . . Rimbaud in the end was as tragically defeated by life as he had been triumphant in art. Yet his, too, was a possible course, and a heroic one, and there have been "artists proper" who tried to follow his example.

Still another extreme was that depicted by Paul Valéry in his imaginary portrait of M. Teste and his two essays on Leonardo (as indeed in his own career). He suggests that a great poet might abandon literature, not to embrace life, but in order to retreat still farther from it. Literature is regarded as something impure, tainted with action, and the "man of the greatest mind" will avoid all forms of action and, by dint of rigorous thought, will end by reducing himself to a state of practical hebetude in which he stares at his consciousness like an Oriental mystic staring at his navel. And there are other extremes to which the religion of art has led or might possibly lead. Valéry in one place speaks of "the chess game that we play with knowledge." There happens to be a highly talented artist who abandoned painting in order to play chess. When he found that he could not become the greatest chess player in the world, he half abandoned that also, and spent his time carving bits of marble into lumps of sugar; he kept a bowl of stone-sugar on his table for the amusement of his guests. And this, too, is a possible extreme. If carried beyond a certain point, the religion of art imperceptibly merges into the irreligion of art, into a state of mind in which the artist deliberately fritters away his talents through contempt for the idiot-public that can never understand.

But what I am trying to make clear is that all these extremes—Teste's, Rimbaud's, Axel's, the way of escape and the retreat into futility—existed side by side in the Dada movement. They were mingled there with an infusion of youth, vigor, Paris after the war and a not unnatural taste for novelty and scandal.

2: Discourse over a Grave

But what was Dada anyway? . . . Not many people have seriously tried to answer this question, and the Dadaists themselves took pains to avoid it. So great was their disdain for the public, and for the idols of clarity and logic worshiped by the public in France, that they could scarcely bring themselves to offer explanations. "I am by principle against manifestoes," said Tristan Tzara, "as I am also against principles. . . . To explain is the amusement of redbellied numbskulls. DADA HAS NO MEANING." And yet this meaningless movement published its manifesto, offered its explanations, and propounded its philosophy in the same breath as its hatred of philosophers. It had reached a point beyond the bounds of logic, but had reached it by a perfectly logical process. In every direction it was a carrying to extremes of the tendencies inherent in what I have called the religion of art.

It was, for example, the extreme of obscurity. That was a tendency that had been growing for half a century, and soon James Joyce would carry it to a point at which the reader was expected to master several languages, and the mythology of all races, and the geography of Dublin, in order to unravel his meaning. Gertrude Stein carried it still farther. She seemed, indeed, to be writing pure nonsense, and yet it was not quite pure: one felt uneasily that much of it could be deciphered if only one had the key. But in reading a Dada poem it was often useless to search for clues: even the poet himself might not possess them. The door of meaning was closed and double-locked; the key was thrown away.

Dada was also the extreme point reached in the long search for "absolute art" and "pure poetry." In discussing that topic the Dada Manifesto was serious and eloquent:

The new painter creates a world. . . . The new artist protests: he no longer paints (*i.e.* reproduces symbolically and illusionistically), but creates directly, in stone, in wood, in iron and tin, rocks and loco-motive organisms that can be turned in every direction by the limpid winds of his momentary sensation. Every pictorial or plastic work is useless. . . . Order = disorder; ego = non-ego; affirmation = nega-tion: all are supreme radiations of an absolute art. Absolute in the purity of cosmic and ordered chaos, eternal in the globule-second without duration, without respiration, without light, without control. . . . Art is a private matter; the artist does it for himself; any work of art that can be understood is the product of a journalist.

Dada, in art and life, was the extreme of individualism. It denied that there was any psychic basis common to all humanity. There was no emotion shared by all men, no law to which all were subject; there was not even a sure means of communica-tion between one man and another. Morality was a snare, "a plague produced by the intelligence."—"Thought is a fine thing for philosophy, but it is relative. There is no final Truth."— "Logic is a complication. Logic is always false."—"Everything one looks at is false." In a word, nothing is real or true except the individual pursuing his individual whims, the artist riding his hobbyhorse, his *dada*.

But the world could not be abolished merely by denying its reality. The world—and specifically the French public—re-mained as a hostile force to be fought, insulted or mystified. As for writers who tried to please the public, they were utterly beneath contempt: mere floor-walkers of the literary business, they did not realize that they were betraying an ideal. . . . This high disdain for the public and for popular writers had always

been a tradition in the religion of art, but it had lately been
emphasized by the revulsion that followed the war, and the
Dadaists pushed it forward to extremes of anti-human feeling.
The world, they said, "left in the hands of bandits, is in a state
of madness, aggressive and complete madness."—"Let each
man cry: there is a great labor of destruction and negation to
perform. We must sweep and clean."—"What there is within
us of the divine is the awakening of anti-human action." So
deep was their disgust that they no longer trusted in words to
express it: manifestoes must give place to manifestations and
poems to deeds, to "significant gestures." Thus, "I proclaim the
opposition of all the cosmic faculties to this gonorrhea of a
putrid sun produced by the factories of philosophic thought;
I proclaim a pitiless struggle with all the weapons of *Dadaist
Disgust*. Every product of disgust capable of becoming a nega-
tion of the family is *dada;* to protest with all the fists of one's
being in destructive action: DADA."

In passages like this it is impossible not to recognize the
presence of the crusading spirit. Dada, though it despised
morality, was animated by moral fervor—and in this respect
also it was the extreme of a long process. For nearly a century
artists had been fighting against the necessity of making their
works conform to the laws of the tribe. They had adapted from
various German Romantic philosophers the principle that
aesthetics was entirely separate from ethics—"Art has nothing
to do with morality." As a result of famous trials involving the
censorship of novels and pictures, they had succeeded in having
this principle partly admitted by the courts and wholly accepted
by a portion of the public. Then, having won this victory, they
began to proclaim that the laws of aesthetics were superior to
the moral laws enforced by Church and State. But the Dadaists
went farther: they went to the point of believing that public
morality ought to be abolished. The only laws that the artist

should be forced to observe were private ones, the laws of art. Those laws, however, applied not only to his books or paintings: they also should govern his career and his judgments of the world. *To be adventurous*—to explore and discover in life as in art—was the Categorical Imperative. Actions like pictures should be *dada*. "The good life," if it was ever achieved, would be surprising, novel, picturesque, purposeless, abstract, incomprehensible to the public—it would merit all the adjectives that applied to a Dadaist masterpiece.

But there was one other tendency that helps to explain the otherwise inexplicable works of art produced by the Dada movement. Those who took part in it were not only guided by a rigorous code of morals or anti-morals: they were also buoyed up by a feeling of liberty, which again was carried to the extreme. They believed that the new artist had freed himself from the limitations of the old artistic mediums. He was no longer confined to paint or words or marble: he was at liberty to utilize any methods or materials that might strike his fancy. He might, for example, make an arrangement of watch springs, ball bearings and kitchen matches, and photograph it (like Man Ray); he might clip illustrations out of old mail-order catalogues, shuffle them into an ingenious design and exhibit them as a painting (like Max Ernst, who later sold such pictures at a stiff price); he might devote himself to sculptures modeled from sealing wax and pipe cleaners (like Hidalgo); he might have his poems printed in the typography of advertisements for nerve tonics and cancer cures (like Tristan Tzara), or invent a new system of punctuation (like E. E. Cummings); he might even forsake all forms of plastic or verbal art and apply the same principles of self-expression to business, politics or, if he chose, to practical joking. Nobody in any case had the right to criticize.

It veritably seemed that Dada was opening a whole new world to writers. They had felt vaguely that everything was said, everything written, that all the great subjects of poetry and fiction had been seized upon by others, exploited and rendered unusable. Now they could take heart again. Here were new subjects waiting to be described, machinery, massacre, skyscrapers, urinals, sexual orgies, revolution—for Dada nothing could be too commonplace or novel, too cruel or shocking, to be celebrated by the writer in his own fashion. Or he might, if the notion struck him, desert the subject entirely—he might enter the stage of his drama and sweep all his puppets into the corner; or again he was privileged to disregard the limits of possibility —if he was writing a novel about modern Paris, he need not hesitate to introduce a tribe of Redskins, an octopus, a unicorn, Napoleon or the Virgin Mary. It suddenly seemed that all the writers of the past had been enslaved by reality: they had been limited to the task of copying the world, whereas the new writer could disregard it and create a world of his own in which he was master. He was at last free! . . . He was at liberty to indulge his whims, to marshal his characters and lead them ahead like an Alexander marching into unknown countries. But in practice his freedom proved illusory, his creations were inhuman, were monsters that never came to life. He could at best lead an army of ghosts into a kingdom of shadows.

Nobody can read about the Dada movement without being impressed by the absurd and half-tragic disproportion between its rich, complicated background and its poor achievements. Here was a group of young men, probably the most talented in Europe: there was not one of them who lacked the ability to become a good writer or, if he so decided, a very popular writer. They had behind them the long traditions of French literature (and knew them perfectly); they had the examples of living masters (and had pondered them); they had a burning love of their art and a fury to excel. And what, after all, did they accomplish? . . . They wrote a few interesting books, influenced a few others, launched and inspired half a dozen good artists, created scandals and gossip, had a good time. Nobody can help wondering why, in spite of their ability and moral fervor and battles over principle, they did nothing more.

Always Dada was bustling into action. There were the early meetings already described, the chief purpose of which was to mystify and insult the public; there was the later demonstration in a churchyard against religion (it rained and nobody listened to the speakers); there was the Dada trial of Maurice Barrès, which called forth angry headlines in all the daily papers; there were theatrical performances like one I attended that was given for the benefit of Tristan Tzara, in this case ending with fights on the stage and the police called in. Years later there was the famous incident of Louis Aragon and *Les Nouvelles Littéraires*—he promised that if his name was once more mentioned in the paper, he would wreck the editorial offices; his name was mentioned; the offices were wrecked. After that Aragon threatened to give a beating to any critic who reviewed his new book, which incidentally was a good one. No critic dared to review it —and what then? The Dada manifestations were ineffectual in spite of their violence, because they were directed against no social class and supported by no social class. All their significant gestures were gestures in the air.

There were Dadaists who spent weeks or months in polishing and consciously perfecting a few lines of verse; those were the ones who most fervently praised the Subconscious. Others abused criticism and the critics in majestic essays that abounded in the keenest sort of critical observations. Still others devoted themselves to automatic writing and published the results of their experiments without, so they said, changing a word of it. There were many who deliberately cultivated the fine art of always being in bad taste. For a time it was also the fashion to

be very busy à l'américaine: I remember the example of a
Dadaist who simultaneously wrote novels, conducted four love
affairs and a marriage, plunged into the wildest business ventures—he spent the next year recuperating in a sanitarium. I
believe there was one who set sail for Tahiti, following in
Gauguin's footsteps; another took ship for Rio de Janeiro. One
very talented poet wrote nothing but postcards to his friends.
There was a Dadaist who collected paper matches: he had the
largest collection of them in the world. He was a very ingenious
and elegant young man and determined to seek his fortune
in America. Having borrowed his passage money, he landed
in New York with a boiled shirt and two suitcases filled with
letters of introduction. He presented some of the letters, tried
bootlegging for a while, found the profession overcrowded, collected comic strips from the Hearst newspapers, married an
American wife, took drugs, committed suicide—he was Jacques
Rigaut, and after his death he became a sort of Dada saint. I am
confusing my dates: in reality Jacques lived long enough to become a Surrealist saint, but the two schools had so many doctrines and members in common that they are often hard to
distinguish. Shortly before he died, a whole squad of former
Dadaists announced that they were abandoning poetry for communism, and were very serious about it, but not quite serious
enough to be accepted by the Communist Party, which suspected
that they might soon veer off in a different direction. A very few
of them long afterwards became Communists in earnest; that is a
different story. Mostly, while waiting for the revolution, for any
revolution, it didn't matter, they spent their time in quarreling
with one another.

But the interesting feature of the quarrels is precisely that
they could not have been avoided: they were conflicts of principle inherent in the movement from the first. I have said that
the Dadaists were animated by fierce moral convictions. They

believed that life should be rash and adventurous, that literature should be freed from all impure motives, and especially from the commercial motive—thus, writing an article for a commercial magazine (like Tzara's piece for *Vanity Fair,* from which I quoted) was almost a sin against the Holy Ghost. But in practice they could not do what they preached. They did not live in a free society, nor did they belong among the rulers of the society that exists. For the most part they were poor young men of middle-class families with their way to make. They sooner or later had to betray their high principles; not many of them chose to starve. The uncompromising ones abused and excoriated the others—and then were forced to compromise in turn, and be excoriated. Dada began to split into smaller and smaller fractions. One of these, the largest that remained, issued the Surrealist Manifesto, became famous for a while, gained many adherents, but the process of fractioning continued—after a few years almost the only writers of talent left in the movement were Louis Aragon, who had been the most active and brilliant of the Dadaists, and André Breton, the most forceful in character. The two had been friends since childhood, but in the end they quarreled like the others, on a matter of principle. One might say that Dada died by principle: it committed suicide.

As for the religion of art, that broader tendency of which Dada was the extreme manifestation, it seemed to be growing more popular even while Dada was dying. It was gaining more adherents every year. Its foremost writers, its saints, were not widely read, since their books were too difficult for the public; but they exerted a wide influence and enjoyed a tremendous underground prestige.

Edmund Wilson explains that the postwar reputation of writers in this tradition "was due largely to extra-literary accidents":

When the prodigious concerted efforts of the war ended only in impoverishment and exhaustion for all the European peoples concerned, and in a general feeling of hopelessness about politics . . . the Western mind became peculiarly hospitable to a literature indifferent to action and unconcerned with the group. Many of the socially minded writers, besides, had been intellectually demoralized by the war and had irreparably lost credit in consequence; whereas these others—Yeats, Valéry, Joyce, Proust—had maintained an unassailable integrity.

It ought to be added that the intellectual world of the 1920s was repeating an old pattern. The art-for-art's-sake tradition had first been established in the middle of the nineteenth century, at a time when the intellectual atmosphere of France was not unlike that prevailing in postwar Europe. Many French writers had become emotionally or physically involved in the Revolution of 1848—Baudelaire, for example, fought on the workingmen's side of the barricades—and when the Revolution was defeated, some of them lost faith in social causes and began to seek in art the ideals they no longer hoped to see realized in life. Rimbaud and others had the same experience in 1871, during and after the Paris Commune: the great poet of individualism at one time tried to draw up an ideal constitution for a socialist state. After the war of 1914 and the betrayal at Versailles, the process was repeated more rapidly on an international scale.

And there was another reason, too, for the popularity at that time of a literature hostile to society. The religion of art is not at all a poor man's religion: a degree of economic freedom is essential to those embarking on a search for aesthetic absolutes. In the decade before 1930 more writers and painters than ever before, and especially more Americans, had leisure to meditate the problems of art and the self, to express themselves, to be creative. And the artists were now surrounded by a cultured mob of dilettantes, people without convictions of their own who fed upon them emotionally, adopted their beliefs and encouraged their vices. In a world where everybody felt lost and directionless, the artists were forced often in spite of themselves to become priests.

Yet the religion of art was approaching its end. For nearly a century now it had played an important role in literature, first in France, then in all the Western world. It had inspired men of talent wholly to consecrate themselves, to produce great works at a sacrifice and to refine the methods of poetry and fiction— even to embark on a search for the absolute that threatened to carry them beyond the frontiers of art. The search had been continued more frantically by their successors. After Dada, however, it became evident that all the diverging paths had been followed to the end, which was always the same—each path seemed to lead toward an infinitely bustling futility, a dance of fireflies in the twilight. After Dada, the historical role of the movement was completed and only the busy ghost of it was left. And so when Dada died it did not perish alone. This fact is enough to explain its importance. In a sense, the whole religion of art died with it and was buried in the same grave.[1]

3: Case Record

But Dada still was strenuously alive in the winter and spring of 1923, when I was learning to know the movement at first hand. The quarrels by which it was already divided did not seem to be fatal ones. Its adherents had begun to look back a little wistfully

[1] That's what I thought in 1934. I didn't foresee that the religion of art would be revived in another postwar (or interwar) period and would flourish again as in the 1920s; nor did I foresee that the writers of a new age would profit so little from the mistakes of their predecessors.

toward the days of the great early manifestations—when, as Aragon said more than once, they were too busy and excited even to sleep with their mistresses—but they also looked forward to a future still busier and more significant.

I was now seeing the Dadaists often, both factions of them, not only on my Wednesdays in Paris but also during the long weeks in Giverny. Aragon spent two months there, working on his new book: in the afternoons we tramped through the meadows fresh with primroses and English daisies while he recited poems from memory hour after hour or expounded his theories of writing. Often on week-ends Tzara came to visit us with a very pretty American girl who smoked sixty cigarettes a day to the great profit of the French government tobacco monopoly, while Tzara made puns, invented games and innocently changed the rules for fear of losing. And sometimes, but not when Tzara was there, all of André Breton's friends arrived on Sundays, a whole performing troupe of Dadaists with their mistresses or wives, or both. They were very serious, angry young men, on principle, but they laughed a great deal and enjoyed themselves and it would have been hard not to like them.

I didn't regard myself as one of the Dadaists. I tried to judge them dispassionately and take no part in their quarrels; I was a foreigner after all and would soon be returning to my own country. Still, I could not help absorbing their notions of literary conduct, as if from the atmosphere. One evening when my wife was away, Dos Passos and Cummings came down from Paris. With Aragon we went to a restaurant and had a gay dinner with several bottles of wine; then we returned to my studio over the blacksmith shop. I made a speech against book fetishism. The burden of it was that wherever I lived books seemed to accumulate; some were bought, some were gifts, some came by mail and others appeared one didn't know how; they moved in like relatives and soon the house was crowded. I sympathized with De Quincey, who used to rent a room, wait until it was full of books and then move away, leaving the books behind him. Here in France my American books couldn't be sold and nobody wanted them as presents, yet I felt an unreasoning and almost Chinese respect for the printed word that kept me from destroying them. We all had that weakness and should take violent steps to overcome it. . . . I went over to the shelves and pulled down an assortment of bad review books and French university texts that I wouldn't need again. After tearing some of them apart I piled them all on the asbestos mat in front of the stove; then I put a match to the pile. It was a gesture in the Dada manner, but not a successful one, for the books merely smoldered. We talked about bad writers while the smoke grew thicker; then Cummings proved that he was a better Dadaist—at least in someone else's studio—by walking over and urinating on the fire.

Jack Wheelwright arrived for a longer visit, with a lot of expensive luggage. Jack, whose father had been the architect of the *Lampoon* building in Cambridge, had already achieved a distinction of his own: he was the only student ever expelled from Harvard for misspelling a word. The word was "nausea" and he shouldn't have used it when he was in a fix already. After a series of minor misdeeds Jack had been put on probation for simply forgetting to take the final examination in one of his courses. Students on probation had to attend all their classes or offer an excuse that was convincing to the dean, who was hard to convince. Jack missed a class and then appeared in the dean's office with his excuse in writing: "I was absent yesterday from English 14"—or whatever the course was—"because I had acute *nausia* after seeing the moving picture, *Broken Blossoms*." He had been sent home to the family house in Back Bay. Now he appeared at Giverny with a sheaf of his own poems, full of fresh images and original spellings, and another sheaf of manuscripts that Gorham Munson had assembled for the next two issues of *Secession;* Jack was to have them printed in Italy, where prices at the time were even lower than in Vienna. I wondered what the issues would look like after being set in type by Italian printers who couldn't speak English and then proofread by the worst speller who ever failed to graduate from Harvard (though he might have run a dead heat in a spelling bee with F. Scott Fitzgerald of Princeton). I felt like sending a cable to Munson: "Make Jack submit proof," but then I reflected that if he didn't send proof the result would at least be arbitrary, surprising and utterly *dada*.

Reading over the letters I wrote that spring and early summer, and the entries in my notebook, I can see the extent to which my thinking had been influenced by my new friends. "The famous two years are ending," I told Kenneth Burke on July 5, in my last letter from Normandy, "with little accomplished and much learned. Yet it seems to me that their value was not so much the knowledge of books and writing they helped me to acquire as the aid they gave me in reaching a personal philosophy." I was using a big word. My philosophy was really an attitude, or at best a collection of beliefs, some of them evolved by myself and others merely adapted from my French friends. Let us try to set them down as a case record.

I believed, first of all, that the only respectable ambition for a man of letters was to be a man of letters—not exclusively a novelist, an essayist, a dramatist, but rather one who adopts the whole of literature as his province, "who devotes himself to literature," I wrote with fervor, "as one might devote a life to God or the Poor."

I believed that the man of letters, while retaining his own point of view, which was primarily that of the poet, should concern himself with every department of human activity, including science, sociology and revolution.

I believed that more writers were ruined by early success

than by the lack of it, and was therefore willing to make a fool of myself in order to avoid being successful.

I was violently opposed to what I called "the fallacy of contraction." "Writers," I observed in my notebook, "often speak of 'saving their energy,' as if each man were given a nickel's worth of it, which he is at liberty to spend—one cent on Love, one cent on Livelihood, two cents on Art or other wasteful activities, and the remainder on a big red apple. . . . To me, the mind of a poet resembles Fortunatus's purse: the more spent, the more it supplies.

"There are many writers who deliberately contract the circle of their interests. They refuse to participate in the public life of their time, or even in the discussion of social questions. They avoid general ideas, are 'bored' by this, 'not concerned' with that. They confine themselves to literary matters—in the end, to literary gossip. And they neglect the work of expanding the human mind to its extremest limits of thought and feeling—which, as I take it, is the aim of literature."

I was grandiloquent in those days; I was also highly moral, but in a fashion acquired from my Dada friends. A writer could steal, murder, drink or be sober, lie to his friends or with their wives: all this, I said, was none of my concern; but my tolerance did not extend to his writing, from which I demanded high courage, absolute integrity and a sort of intelligence that was in itself a moral quality. And I was romantic, too, in the strict sense of the word. After a period of admiring French classicism, I had taken to reading and praising the writers of the Romantic era, from Monk Lewis and Byron to Gérard de Nerval and Pétrus Borel. At the same time I was interested in applying their methods to new material drawn from the age of technology and high-pressure selling. I was determined to be humorless, having developed a furious contempt for "those beaten people who regard their own weakness with a deprecatory smile." And I had catchwords that reappeared in everything I wrote: "disinterestedness," "indiscretion" (I considered it a high virtue), "disdain," "significant" or "arbitrary gestures," "violence," "manifestoes," "courage."

My letters were filled with impractical projects:

"Yesterday, Kenneth," I wrote on June 29, "it struck me with the force of revelation that the time has come for us to write some political manifestoes. We are not critics or short-story writers; we are poets: in other words, we are interested in every form of human activity. To be ticketed and dismissed as such-and-such a sort of writer gives me a pain behind the ears. Also, I am eaten with the desire to do something significant and indiscreet. An Open Letter to President Harding. An Open Letter to the Postmaster General on the Censorship, in which I admit the right to censor, point out how dangerous my opinions are, even in book reviews, and demand why I am not suppressed. And other manifestations: for example, a call to voters to cease voting, an attack on the liberals, an attack on the Socialists and Communists. Imagine all these documents appearing together in a political issue of *Broom*. What a stink. But the stink would mean something. In a country as hypocritical as the United States, merely to enumerate the number of laws one has broken would be a significant gesture. And if all the literary forces of law and order rose up against us, we could always retire to farming or reading proofs. Think it over. The step is not to be taken tomorrow. And I have the feeling, Kenneth, that some such courageous and indiscreet step is required of us, if we are not going to resign ourselves to petty literary wars with Ezra Pound, Robert McAlmon, even Floyd Dell."

And so I was planning to carry literary ideals into the political world; I was contemplating a crusade and was prepared to be one of the leaders. But I was also a disciple: for the first and last time in my life I admitted to having a master.

"I have been intending to write you a letter about Louis Aragon," I said on June 4, "for his is a character which demands a long explanation. . . . Imagine this elegant young man, from a family whose social position is above reproach: a young man so gifted that the word 'genius' must have been applied to him ever since he was four years old and wrote his first novel. A brilliant career stretches in front of him. He has read everything and mastered it. Suddenly, at a given age, he rejects his family and social connections and, with a splendid disdain acquired from his early successes, begins to tell everybody exactly what he thinks. And he continues to be successful. He has so much charm, when he wishes to use it, that it takes him years to make an enemy; but by force of repeated insults he succeeds in this aim also. He retains all that hatred of compromise which is the attribute of youth—and of a type of youth we never wholly possessed. He disapproves of *La Nouvelle Revue Française;* therefore he refuses to write for it, although all other channels of publication are closed to him already.

"He lives literature. If I told him that a poem of Baudelaire's was badly written, he would be capable of slapping my face. He judges a writer largely by his moral qualities, such as courage, vigor of feeling, the refusal to compromise. He proclaims himself a romantic. In practice this means that his attitude toward women is abominable: he is either reciting poetry, which soon ceases to interest them, or trying to sleep with them, which they say becomes equally monotonous. He is always seriously in love; he never philanders. Often he is a terrible bore. He is an egoist and vain, but faithful to his friends. . . . I have met other people whose work is interesting, but Aragon is the only one to impose himself by force of character. I ought to add that he has a doglike affection for André Breton.

"My apologies for this long digression, but I think it will explain a good deal." Aragon, indeed, was affecting me more than I liked to admit. Under his influence I was becoming a Dadaist in spite of myself, was adopting many of the Dada standards, and was even preparing to put them into action.

4: Significant Gesture

During the last three weeks before sailing for America, I wrote no letters. I was much too excited to write letters; I had never, in fact, spent prouder, busier or more amusing days. I was being arrested and tried for punching a café proprietor in the jaw.

He deserved to be punched, though not especially by me; I had no personal grudge against him. His café, the Rotonde, had long been patronized by revolutionists of every nation. Lenin used to sit there, I was told; and proletarian revolts were still being planned, over coffee in the evening, by quiet men who paid no attention to the hilarious arguments of Swedish and Rumanian artists at the surrounding tables. The proprietor —whose name I forget—used to listen unobtrusively. It was believed, on more or less convincing evidence, that he was a paid informer. It was said that he had betrayed several anarchists to the French police. Moreover, it was known that he had insulted American girls, treating them with the cold brutality that French café proprietors reserve for prostitutes. He was a thoroughly disagreeable character and should, we felt, be called to account.

We were at the Dôme, ten or twelve of us packed together at a table in the midst of the crowd that swirled in the Boulevard Montparnasse. It was July 14, 1923, the national holiday. Chinese lanterns hung in rows among the trees; bands played at every corner; everywhere people were dancing in the streets. Paris, deserted for the summer by its aristocrats, bankers and politicians, forgetting its hordes of tourists, was given over to a vast plebeian carnival, a general madness in which we had eagerly joined. Now, tired of dancing, we sipped our drinks and talked in loud voices to make ourselves heard above the music, the rattle of saucers, the shuffle of feet along the sidewalk.. I was trying, with my two hands on the table, to imitate the ridiculous efforts of Tristan Tzara to hop a moving train. "Let's go over," said Laurence Vail, tossing back his long yellow hair from his forehead, "and assault the proprietor of the Rotonde."

"Let's," I said.

We crossed the street together, some of the girls in bright evening gowns and some in tweeds, Louis Aragon slim and dignified in a dinner jacket, Laurence bareheaded and wearing a raincoat which he never removed in the course of the hot starlit night, myself coatless, dressed in a workman's blue shirt, worn trousers and rope-soled shoes. Delayed and separated by the crowd on the pavement, we made our way singly into the bar, which I was the last to enter. Aragon, in periodic sentences pronounced in a beautifully modulated voice, was expressing his opinion of all stool pigeons—*mouchards*—and was asking why such a wholly contemptible character as the proprietor of the Rotonde presumed to solicit the patronage of respectable people. The waiters, smelling a fight, were forming a wall of shirt fronts around their employer. Laurence Vail pushed through the wall; he made an angry speech in such rapid French that I could catch only a few phrases, all of them insults. The proprietor backed away; his eyes shifted uneasily; his face was a dirty white behind his black mustache. Harold Loeb, looking on, was a pair of spectacles, a chin, a jutting pipe and an embarrassed smile.

I was angry at my friends, who were allowing the situation to resolve into a series of useless gestures; but even more I was seized with a physical revulsion for the proprietor, with his look of a dog caught stealing chickens and trying to sneak off. Pushing past the waiters, I struck him a glancing blow in the jaw. Then, before I could strike again, I was caught up in an excited crowd and forced to the door.

Five minutes later our band had once more assembled on the terrace of the Dôme. I had forgotten the affair already: nothing remained but a vague exhilaration and the desire for further activity. I was obsessed with the idea that we should *changer de quartier:* that instead of spending the rest of the night in Montparnasse, we should visit other sections of Paris. Though no one else seemed enthusiastic, I managed by force of argument to assemble five hesitant couples, and the ten of us went strolling southeastward along the Boulevard Montparnasse.

On reaching the first café we stopped for a drink of beer and a waltz under the chestnut trees. One couple decided to return to the Dôme. Eight of us walked on to another café, where, after a bock, two other couples became deserters. "Let's change our quarter," I said once more. At the next café, Bob Coates consulted his companion. "We're going back to the Dôme," he said. Two of us walked on sadly. We caught sight of Montrouge —more Chinese lanterns and wailing accordions and workmen dancing with shopgirls in the streets—then we too returned to Montparnasse.

It was long after midnight, but the streets were as crowded as before and I was eager for adventure. At the Dôme I met Tristan Tzara, seized him by the arm and insisted that we go for a stroll. We argued the question whether the Dada movement could be revived. Under the chestnut trees we met a high-brown woman dressed in barbaric clothes; she was thought to be a princess from Senegal. I addressed her extravagant compliments in English and French; Tzara added others in French, German and his three words of Rumanian. "Go 'way, white boys," she said in a Harlem voice. We turned back, passing the crowded terrace of the Rotonde. The proprietor was standing there with his arms folded. At the sight of him a fresh rage surged over me.

"*Quel salaud!*" I roared for the benefit of his six hundred customers. "*Ah, quel petit mouchard!*"

Then we crossed the street once more toward the Dôme, slowly. But when I reached the middle of the tracks I felt each of my arms seized by a little blue policeman. "Come along with us," they said. And they marched me toward the station house, while Tzara rushed off to get the identification papers left behind in my coat. The crowds disappeared behind us; we were alone—I and the two *flics* and the proprietor of the Rotonde.

One of the two policemen was determined to amuse himself. "You're lucky," he said, "to be arrested in Paris. If you were arrested by those brutal policemen of New York, they would cuff you on the ear—like this," he snarled, cuffing me on the ear, "but in Paris we pat you gently on the shoulder."

I knew I was in trouble. I said nothing and walked peacefully beside him.

"Ah, the police of Paris are incomparably gentle. If you were arrested in New York, they would crack you in the jaw—like this," he said, cracking me in the jaw, "but here we do nothing; we take you with us calmly."

He rubbed his hands, then thrust his face toward mine. His breath stank of brandy.

"You like the police of Paris, *hein?*"

"Assuredly," I answered. The proprietor of the Rotonde walked on beside us, letting his red tongue play over the ends of his mustache. The other *flic* said nothing.

"I won't punch you in the nose like the New York policemen," said the drunken man, punching me in the nose. "I will merely

ask you to walk on in front of me. . . . Walk in front of me,
pig!"

I walked in front of him, looking back suspiciously under
my armpit. His hand was on his holster, loosening the flap. I
had read about people shot "while trying to escape" and began
walking so very slowly that he had to kick me in the heels to
urge me up the steps of the police station. When we stood at
the desk before the sergeant, he charged me with an unprovoked
assault on the proprietor of the Rotonde—and also with forcibly
resisting an officer. "Why," he said, "he kicked me in the shins,
leaving a scar. Look here!"

He rolled up his trouser leg, showing a scratch half an inch
long. It was useless for me to object that my rope-soled shoes
wouldn't have scratched a baby. Police courts in France, like
police courts everywhere, operate on the theory that a policeman's word is always to be taken against that of an accused
criminal.

Things looked black for me until my friends arrived—Laurence and Louis and Jacques Rigaut and my wife—bearing
with them my identification papers and a supply of money.
Consulting together, we agreed that the drunken policeman
must be bribed, and bribed he was: in the general confusion he
was bribed twice over. He received in all a hundred and thirty
francs, at least four times as much as was necessary. Standing
pigeon-toed before the sergeant at the desk and wearing an air
of bashful benevolence, he announced that I was a pretty good
fellow after all, even though I had kicked him in the shins.
He wished to withdraw the charge of resisting an officer.

My prospects brightened perceptibly. Everyone agreed that
the false charge was the more serious of the two. For merely
punching a stool-pigeon, the heaviest sentence I could receive
would be a month in jail. Perhaps I would escape with a
week.

A preliminary hearing was held on the following evening, after a night in jail and a day spent vainly trying to sleep between visits from the police and telephone calls from anxious friends. I stopped at the Dôme to collect my witnesses; fortunately there was a party that evening and they were easy to find. They consisted of nine young ladies in evening gowns. None of them had been present at the scene in the Rotonde the night before, but that didn't matter: all of them testified in halting French that I hadn't been present either; the whole affair was an imposition on a writer known for his serious character; it was a hoax invented by a café proprietor who was a pig and very impolite to American young women.

The examining magistrate was impressed. He confided later to André Salmon that the proprietor of the Rotonde had only his waiters to support the story he told, whereas I had nine witnesses, all of them very respectable people, *des gens très bien*. That helped Salmon to get me out of the scrape, although he also brought his own influence to bear. He was a poet and novelist who was also a star reporter and covered all the important murder trials for *Le Matin*. Since magistrates liked to be on good terms with him, he managed to have my trial postponed from day to day and finally abandoned.

But the most amusing feature of the affair, and my justification for dealing with it at length, was the effect it produced on my French acquaintances. They looked at me with an admiration I could not understand, even when I reflected that French writers rarely came to blows and that they placed a high value on my unusual action. Years later I realized that by punching a café proprietor in the jaw I had performed an act to which all their favorite catchwords could be applied. First of all, I had acted for reasons of public morality; bearing no private grudge against my victim, I had been *disinterested*. I had committed an *indiscretion*, acted with *violence* and *disdain* for the

law, performed an *arbitrary* and *significant gesture,* uttered a
manifesto; in their opinion I had shown *courage.* . . . For the
first time in my life I became a public character. I was entertained at dinners and cocktail parties, interviewed for the
newspapers, asked to contribute to reviews published by the
Dadaists in Amsterdam, Brussels, Lyon and Belgrade. My stories
were translated into Hungarian and German. A party of Russian writers then visiting Paris returned to Moscow with several
of my poems, to be printed in their own magazines.

The poems were not at all revolutionary in tone, but they
dealt with a subject that, in those briefly liberal days of the
New Economic Policy in Russia, had been arousing the enthusiasm of Soviet writers. They were poems about America, poems
that spoke of movies and skyscrapers and machines, dwelling
upon them with all the nostalgia derived from two long years of
exile. I, too, was enthusiastic over America; I had learned from
a distance to admire its picturesque qualities. And I was returning to New York with a set of values that bore no relation to
American life, with convictions that could not fail to be misunderstood in a country where Dada was hardly a name, and
moral judgments on literary matters were thought to be in
questionable taste—in a city where writers had only three justifi-
cations for their acts: they did them to make money, or to get
their name in the papers, or because they were drunk.

VI: The City of Anger

1: The French Line Pier, 1923

When the exiles of art came straggling home by twos and threes, year after year, there were no official committees to welcome them. No cameramen invited them to pose against the ship's rail with the Statue of Liberty in the background; no reporters asked what they thought of economic conditions in Europe and wasn't it true that America had the most beautiful girls in the world. The police launch lay moored to its dock when they arrived and pigeons fed undisturbed in City Hall Park. Broadway was empty of tickertape. At best, as they drove toward their anonymous lodgings, a dozen old newspapers flapped like banners of greeting in the tired summer wind.

It was early in August 1923, just before my twenty-fifth birthday, that I landed in New York after a sultry night at anchor in the Lower Bay. The boat was crowded with Good Will Girls returning after a tour of the battlefields that had resulted from the success of Ray Johnson's latest venture in money-raising. That last night they gathered on deck to give a sort of college yell:

> One, two, three, four,
> Who are we for?
> *America, America, America!*
> Two, four, six, eight,

Who do we appreciate?
France! France!

The bar was closed and the Cowleys went down to Ramon
Guthrie's cabin to drink the last of the prunelle that he had carried with him from his brother-in-law's farm near Nancy.
Ramon had been an ambulance driver, then a flyer and then a
student; he was a tall, angular, square-shouldered man who
made abrupt gestures, as if he had been put together with metal
plates and wires. The surgeons had done something like that
after his plane crashed in 1918; it was a lumbering biplane of a
type that Germans shot down like pen-raised pheasants. Once
a new major, eager to distinguish himself, had ordered the
squadron to make a mass flight over the German lines, and
Ramon was the only survivor. He had studied in France after
the war and now he was coming home with a dark-eyed wife
from Lorraine and a doctorate from the University of Toulouse;
he wanted to write novels just as I wanted to write essays and
poems. We knew a great deal more about France than did the
Good Will Girls, but we were just as hopeful and innocent.

We said good-by to the Guthries at the French Line pier.
There was nobody to meet us, and I didn't even know where to
send our big trunk, for I had only five dollars in my pocket and
couldn't afford a hotel. While the customs man was hastily
glancing through our baggage—it hadn't the look of containing
anything dutiable—I made several telephone calls, as a result of
which our difficulties were solved for the moment. Our two
trunks would go to the house of a friend far downtown, almost
in the shadow of the Woolworth Building. We ourselves would
spend the morning in the apartment of Matthew Josephson,
who had recently come home from Berlin and was trying to
publish *Broom* in Greenwich Village.

We took a taxicab and rode east on Fourteenth Street, passing a row of wholesale meat markets in front of which a few torn newspapers fluttered weakly, passing the Elevated station at Ninth Avenue, with its look of being a Chinese pagoda, passing two rows of high brownstone houses, and the Convent of Our Lady of Guadalupe, marked only by a cross, and the Ninth Regiment Armory, and turning south on Sixth Avenue under the El pillars. Everything was strange to me: the exhausting and dispiriting heat, the colors of the houses, the straightaway vistas, the girls on the sidewalk in their bright frocks, so different from the drab ones that French shopgirls wore, and most of all the lack of anything green to break the monotony of the square streets, the glass, brick and iron. The next year—the next three years, in fact—would be spent in readjusting myself to this once familiar environment.

The first problem I had to face was how to earn a living. Before me was a choice that in those days, when jobs and literary markets both were plentiful, had to be made by every apprentice writer without an independent income—the choice between free-lance authorship and working in an office. In the first case, I should be living by my own profession, yet everything I wrote would inevitably be molded by the need for carrying it to market. In the second case, four-fifths of my time would be wasted, yet the remaining fifth could be devoted to writing for its own sake, to the disinterested practice of the art of letters. That was my justification for taking a job—that and the fact that a job was offered me. Not until two years later did I realize that when one's writing ceases to have a functional relationship to one's life, when it becomes a way of spending otherwise idle evenings, it loses a part of its substance. At best it has an unreality that can usually be recognized, an after-hours atmosphere of rhetoric, fantasy and melodrama to be explained by the situation that produced it: the writer is seeking compensation for the qualities missing in his business career. More often there

are no idle evenings; writing disappears from his life, giving
way to the unhealthy feeling that he is better than his vocation,
by which he is frustrated, from which he must violently escape
to write a novel, a drama, an epic. But the fear persists that his
great work will be a failure: isn't it better to be paid each Saturday and talk drunkenly each Saturday night about the unwritten novel? . . .

I escaped that mood by falling into a different error, almost
as fatal: I assumed too many obligations. My job, for the first
month at least, meant working nine or ten hours a day under
pressure; but that was only the beginning of my duties. In addition to being proofreader, copywriter and general utility man
for *Sweet's Architectural Catalogue,* I also became an associate
editor of *Broom,* a position without pay or honor that involved
reading manuscripts and proofs, writing letters—and articles,
too, when I had an hour to spare—pacifying subscribers, insult-
ing contributors and raising money. With my wife I tried to
redecorate our flat in Dominick Street, the most battered and
primitive lodging to be found in New York. I attended literary
teas that lasted all night. I composed an open letter to the Postmaster General and another to the editor of the *Dial,* both very
insolent in tone. I intrigued for a higher salary. I wrote book
reviews for Dr. Canby's *Literary Review* and poems for nobody
in particular.

Meanwhile, with Josephson, Guthrie and a few others, I tried
to solve a second problem, that of reproducing in New York
the conditions that had seemed so congenial to us abroad, and
of continuing to appreciate and praise the picturesque American qualities of the Machine Age and the New Economic Era
while living under their shadow.

Coolidge was President now; the New Era was beginning.
On August 2, the day I left Paris, Harding had died in San

Francisco, and his place in history had already been assigned to him by the newspapers before my voyage ended: he was to be known throughout the ages as the great apostle of peace. French troops were bivouacked in the Ruhr. Hugo Stinnes, said to be richer than Rockefeller, was treating with France as an independent monarch. Lenin was living in seclusion: some asserted that his brain was drying up and others that he was being eaten by worms as God's punishment. The New Economic Policy was reported to be partly effective in Russia—to the degree, that is, in which it represented a departure from the strict monstrosities of communism. People were getting tired of hearing "Yes, We Have No Bananas." Prohibition and the Ku Klux Klan were now the commonest front-page topics of American newspapers, though some attention was being paid to the bumper wheat harvest and the low prices resulting from it. Factories were busy again, except in New England; construction was booming everywhere. The stock market, after declining in the spring, was slowly rising toward dizzier heights; and American literature, too, was entering a period of excitement and inflation. It was possible for young writers, myself included, to disregard the Ruhr, *fascismo,* reparations, the New Economic Policy, the birth of prosperity, as they bedazzled themselves with the future of their art.

New geniuses were being discovered every week in the leading critical reviews, usually a different one by each review: there was an appalling overproduction of genius. Old writers had suddenly become old fogies, querulous and absurd. The modern novel, the essay, the drama, all seemed incomparably rich, and lyric poetry was about to enter its golden age. "Coming out in the train," wrote Burton Rascoe, "I had been counting up our lyric poets of the first order since Poe"; and he compiled a list that the Elizabethan or the Romantic period could scarcely equal—certainly not in lyric poets of the first order:

Emily Dickinson, yes, on the evidence of two or three lyrics alone
—Sara Teasdale, darn near it, darn near first rank anyhow. . . .
Edna St. Vincent Millay, absolutely, because she is one of the few
poets who have been able to breathe life into the sonnet since Shakespeare; Arthur Davison Ficke is another, and Cummings! But we'll
come to him—Wallace Stevens for a certainty . . . and there's Conrad Aiken, ecstatically and imperishably lyrical when you excavate—
and T. S. Eliot, poet laureate and elegist of the jazz age . . . Ezra
Pound; now Pound's a talent, but has he written more than one lyric?
. . . Put him down anyway— Comes then who? Sandburg? Bodenheim, Lindsay, Masters, Lowell (Amy), Kreymborg?—let's keep
Kreymborg in . . . Robinson, Wheelock. . . .

Who remains? Who indeed, but the chap we're to meet this afternoon. If there is a finer lyricist since Keats and Swinburne (I include
them both), forgetting Yeats, in the English language, I wish you
would introduce me to him. Uneven? Yes, I grant you! So was God.

E. E. Cummings, the subject of this paragraph, is an extremely
gifted poet, and Rascoe showed perspicuity in recognizing his
talent at a time when most critics were merely ridiculing his
use of the lower-case "i." But Cummings must have been
embarrassed at being glorified like Miss Universe, placed on a
level with Keats and Swinburne, and practically left standing
at the right hand of God.

If I quote from Burton Rascoe, it is because his weekly book
page in the *New York Herald Tribune*—selected passages from
which were later reprinted, without textual changes, as *A Bookman's Daybook*—gave a better picture of that frenzied age
than any historian could hope to equal. He was distinguished
among literary journalists by really loving his profession, by
speaking with hasty candor and being absolutely unself-protec-
tive in his hates and enthusiasms. He attacked the men of
swollen reputation, in spite of the pain to them and danger to
himself (and eventually at the cost of his job). He tried to dis-

cover and glorify the work of writers and artists then unknown to the public—the good, bad and indifferent ones, Cabell and Proust, Eliot, Mencken, Szymanowski ("the greatest musical apparition that has arisen since Wagner"), Henry Blake Fuller ("certainly more readable" than Stendhal, "more carefully constructed, richer in overtones of suaver irony"). Like any good journalist, he saw everything bigger than life size. Meeting the new and incomparable celebrities who appeared from week to week at the Coffee House Club or at the round table in the Hotel Algonquin, he lived in an atmosphere of feverish glamour and reported their conversations as if he were describing a banquet at which Plato had jested with Alcibiades.

"Only very young writers," he said, "or writers who talk a great deal more (and better) than they write, discuss Art and Style and Culture; the others give themselves over in conversation to gossip and anecdote (if art and artists form the topic of conversation)." He might have reflected that people usually talk about whatever interests them most. If the celebrities he met rarely discussed art or style, perhaps it was because those subjects had ceased to concern them; writing had become a job like any other. Gossip and anecdote—who ran off with whose wife, and who served good cocktails, and who got the biggest royalties—were the topics closest to their hearts.

Carl Sandburg [he continued] plays a jew's-harp and a guitar and sings barroom songs. Robert Nathan plays a cello; Ben Hecht plays the violin; H. L. Mencken plays the bass in four-handed arrangements for piano and small orchestra; Edmund Wilson is a sleight-of-hand performer; George Jean Nathan is an expert clog-dancer, having taken innumerable first prizes (incognito) on amateur nights at the burlesque houses; John Dos Passos is a juggler; Alfred Kreymborg plays the mandolute; Maxwell Bodenheim is an exhibition dancer; Carl Van Vechten is a spirit medium; Ernest Boyd is very deft with the musical glasses; Elinor Wylie can throw her thumbs out of joint; Scott Fitzgerald is a high diver and sometimes leaps from great heights into a bathtub only partially filled with water; Samuel Hoffenstein is a ventriloquist; F. P. Adams plays the harmonica; Robert Benchley is good at charades and impersonations; Percy Hammond does the sailor's hornpipe; Wallace Smith and Achmed Abdullah are sword swallowers; Florence Kiper Frank is a toe dancer; Will Cuppy plays "The Maiden's Prayer" on the piano; Floyd Dell can do a Russian Cossack dance; James Branch Cabell gives a fascinating exhibition in shadow swordsmanship; Rupert Hughes is a yodeler; Joseph Hergesheimer likes pillow and post office; Charles Hanson Towne and George Chappell are a perfect scream in a burlesque of the opera. . . .

The literary business was booming like General Motors, like the better night clubs in the Roaring Forties, like the subdivision racket, and yet. . . . In this distinguished vaudeville there wasn't much place for angry young men without parlor tricks, who talked seriously about the problems of their craft and boasted of having no sense of humor. They were laying plans for new ventures to entertain themselves and advance the cause of fine letters. But their only real hope, not of success, but merely of keeping their heads above water, depended on their remaining united among themselves and quarreling only with the public.

About the first of October, *Sweet's Architectural Catalogue* went to press and tension at the office instantly slackened; instead of working ten or twelve hours a day under pressure, I had merely to preserve the appearance of vague industry for six or seven. There was time to think of literary matters, and particularly of my connection with *Broom*. Matty Josephson had just assembled the October issue, originally planned as a collection of political manifestoes: it was a sad affair and proved, if nothing else, that we and the writers we published were

innocent of political ideas. Slater Brown, our colleague, planned
to spend the winter in somebody's summer studio near Woodstock. Gilbert Seldes had returned from Paris to resume the
managing editorship of the *Dial,* and Kenneth Burke, who
had taken his place during the summer, was living in his New
Jersey farmhouse, to which I soon addressed an urgent letter:

"Can you come into town next Friday (October 19)? Me, I
place great importance on your coming. *Broom* is perhaps near
its end, which must not be ignoble. To die gently on an ebb
tide is not my idea of death. Munson is meditating new plans
for *Secession.* When they are ripe, I suppose he will present
them to us and ask us to contribute to his magazine. Everybody
else seems content to settle down to a winter of occasional
drunks and conversation about living conditions. The greatest
American writers are George Moore and Arthur Schnitzler.
. . . The situation would be less discouraging if anybody retained the capacity for indignation. But if you hate a person
violently, the strongest expression you are permitted to employ
is, 'I take no interest in him.'

"Kenneth, I decided with Matty to call a meeting of everybody who has worked for *Broom* or *Secession,* a catholic meeting with Brown, Burke, Coates, Cowley, Crane, Frank, Guthrie,
Josephson, Munson, Sanborn, Schneider, Toomer, Wescott, Williams, or such of them as are beyond taking-no-interest-in the
immediate future. If we can get together in one room, we can
at least define our separate positions, whether or not we can
make plans to go ahead. Eternal Jesus. The people who can be
content with art-for-art, three issues of a harmless little magazine and an occasional glass of synthetic gin will continue to
be content. For God's sake let's brew some stronger liquor."

The liquor we planned to brew was not dangerously potent
stuff. We planned, for example, to hire a theater some afternoon
and give a literary entertainment, with violent and profane

attacks on the most famous contemporary writers, courts-martial of the more prominent critics, burlesques of Sherwood Anderson, Floyd Dell, Paul Rosenfeld and others—all this interspersed with card tricks, solos on the jew's-harp, meaningless dialogues and whatever else would show our contempt for the audience and the sanctity of American letters. We planned to pass out handbills in the theatrical district and make defamatory soapbox orations in Union Square. We planned to continue *Broom* as long as its capital or credit lasted; we hoped to make it an organ for good prose, experimental verse and violent polemics. We were willing to plan anything that would add to the excitement of living or writing. And, as a beginning, we had convoked this meeting in an Italian restaurant on Prince Street, under the shadow of the Elevated.

Most of the writers mentioned in my letter were present, as were the wives of some and a few non-literary acquaintances; in all there must have been thirty persons. Waldo Frank, Jean Toomer and William Carlos Williams did not appear. Gorham B. Munson was in the Catskills recuperating from an illness. At my request he sent a statement to be read at the meeting; it surprised me by consisting largely of a vehement attack on Josephson. I had known of a quarrel between them, based on a conflict of personalities: Munson was wax-mustached and a little solemn, while Josephson was addicted to practical jokes that weren't always funny to the victim. When they were editing *Secession* in uneasy collaboration, Munson had accepted a very long and bad romantic poem for the fourth issue. Josephson, who was having the issue printed in Berlin, had omitted all but the last two lines of the poem:

> To me you are no more than Chinese, O moon,
> Are no more than Chinese.

—"I think the two lines standing alone have a certain value in themselves," he explained unwinkingly. Munson was a friend of the author and didn't see the joke. Moreover, Josephson and I were friends of Jack Wheelwright and it may be that Munson held us partly to blame for the fantastic errors in the two issues of *Secession* that Wheelwright had had printed in Italy. Other grievances accumulated between the two editiors; I hadn't known how many, nor had I realized that they were leading Munson to extremes of feeling.

Unfortunately I have lost his statement, but the burden of it is easy to remember. Matthew Josephson, it said in effect, was self-seeking, irresponsible, inconsistent, apt to exhibit (I quote from another letter) "the fallacious mental mechanisms of Paul Rosenfeld, Upton Sinclair and F.P.A." His writings did not lead toward "a more passionate apprehension of life." In short he was "an intellectual faker" and therefore the magazine he helped to edit and the literary activities he proposed were unworthy of cooperation from all respectable authors and critics, including the undersigned Gorham B. Munson.

Because his feelings were intense, Munson was betrayed into using a pompous style. His rhetoric was as noble as Cicero's; his phrases scanned; I have the impression that his statement was written more in blank verse than in prose. I began to read it seriously to my audience, but halfway through I was overcome by a sense of absurdity and began to declaim it like a blue-jawed actor reciting Hamlet's soliloquy. The effect was unfortunate. Munson's friends, of whom several were present, declared that I was doing him an injustice (and they were right about it). His opponents retorted that the statement deserved less respectful treatment than it was receiving. Fifteen minutes after the meeting began it had already dissolved in monologues and squabbles.

I tried to start a general discussion of our problems; nobody would listen. Jimmy Light, fresh from a cocktail party, had a thesis of his own, which he expounded in a passionate low voice to his neighbor. "They're treading us under their heels," he said. "They're stamping us down. They're pressing us into the dirt. They're walking on us." Hart Crane, shaking his finger like an angry lawyer, was exploding into argument with Josephson on the subject of Munson's letter. Bottles appeared; somebody spilled a glass of red wine on the tablecloth. Burke, with his shock of blue-black hair standing on end, was telling a hilarious story about his neighbor's dog. Hannah Josephson rapped vainly for order. "We've come here to talk business," she murmured hopelessly. Somebody told Jimmy Light to change his tune. The general hubbub increased. Isidor Schneider, the most amiable and pacific of rebel poets, sat overwhelmed by the thought that people could be so disagreeable to one another. Glenway Wescott rose from the table, very pale and stern. "How can you people expect to accomplish anything," he said precisely, "when you can't even preserve ordinary parlor decorum?" He swept out of the restaurant with the air of one gathering an invisible cloak about him. I was too depressed to laugh at him; indeed, I was tempted to follow his example. For the first time I realized the pathos and absurdity of the fierce individualism preserved by American writers in the midst of the most unified civilization now existing. "Politicians unite to share the boodle," I thought, "and businessmen to plan a sales campaign: why can't we come together for ten minutes in the cause of literature?" Hart Crane, with red face and bristling hair, stamped up and down the room, repeating "Parlor, hell, parlor." More bottles appeared on the table. "They're pressing us into the dirt," Jimmy Light said with conviction.

"Aw, shut up," yelled half a dozen apprentice gangsters, natives of Prince Street, emerging suddenly from the rear door that led into a dirt-paved bowling alley. A moment later they reappeared at the front door and cried more loudly, "Aw, shut up."

Our long table grew quiet, not in obedience or fear, but simply from the consciousness that its proceedings were being watched by people from another world. Hart Crane poured himself a glass of wine and drank it rapidly. "The question," Josephson said, "is what we are going to print in the next issue of *Broom*." We discussed the question dispiritedly, having received a tacit answer to the other question, whether we should engage in more flamboyant activities. Somebody recited a limerick. About half-past eleven the meeting dispersed.

Our departure was attended by our friends the apprentice gangsters; by now they must have numbered twenty or thirty. They offered to get us taxicabs for a quarter or fight us at the drop of a hat. In harried silence we plodded homeward, feeling like Napoleon's grenadiers on the retreat from Moscow. In the struggle we had lately undertaken we were beaten almost before we began. We should have realized that there was no chance of imposing our ideas on others when we couldn't agree among ourselves, or even preserve the decorum customary in an Italian speakeasy.

A different sort of fight resulted from the meeting in Prince Street; it happened ten days later and a hundred miles from New York. Josephson made a flying trip to Woodstock, ostensibly to enjoy the October weather and confer with his editorial colleague, Slater Brown. Munson was spending the autumn with his friend Murrell Fisher, the art historian, whose cabin was only a mile away. Josephson paid him a visit one afternoon and suggested that their differences, being personal, could best be settled with their fists. Munson demurred. Finally his host entered the discussion, voted for fisticuffs and led both warriors to a marshy pasture, where, as Fisher afterward explained, he thought that neither of them would be damaged much by falling. The battle began.

It continued in an autumn drizzle. Nobody would talk much about it, but I gathered that it was a dull spectacle, a war fought horizontally more than vertically, a series of slips and wallows that ended when both heroes were too stiff with mud and bruises to battle on; separately they limped away from the battlefield. It was not until eight months later that the war of *Secession* was celebrated in song and story. Then, on Independence Day, Slater Brown, Jack Wheelwright and I determined to follow the great example set by Abraham Lincoln sixty years before and dedicate a battlefield monument. It consisted of a heap of stones tumbled together in the pasture lot. We marched around it in procession, chanting an Introit that Wheelwright, a high churchman, had composed for the occasion. Brown gave the Gettysburg speech in doubletalk. My contribution was an ode that began, as all such odes should do, with an invocation to the Muse of history:

> O Muse, that Homer's wingèd quill,
> Plucked from an eagle's wing, invoked—
> Clio, I think, whose spirit still
> Is that which Pindarus unyoked
> For flights beyond our mortal seeing—
> Bright Clio, virgin, obsolescent being,
>
> Seize me, soar up with me inspired
> To thine heroic melancholy
> That I may sing of mortals fired
> To deeds of more than mortal folly
> Whom worship of the Muse is leading
> To fields where Munson bleeds and Fame lies bleeding.

Know, Muse, that heroes yet exist
 Whose anger brooks no intercession,
And tooth meets tooth and fist meets fist
And "Up," cries Munson, "with *Secession!*
Down *Broom,*" he snarls, and warriors pant
Each to defend his literary slant.

All afternoon the battle wavers;
Now fortune smiles on Josephson,
Now frowns, and now stout Munson quavers,
"*Broom* is unswept. I've almost won."
The other sneers, "Almost how splendid!"
As deep in mud both heroes lie up-ended,

Yet battling on, till strength and light
Together failed. Then Fisher rose,
Grimly dividing weary wight
From bleary knight and fist from nose:
So, on another fateful day,
Half-dead Achilles by half-living Hector lay.

 Stout Hector like a featherbed,
Stuffed with the down from geese's tails,
Is leaking feathers dyed with red;
Achilles' gore fills waterpails,
The while he gasps, "I blacked his eye."
Sighs Hector, " 'Twas a moral victory."

And now, the furious carnage ending,
Darkness has veiled the wallowed fields
And Stygian rays of night descending:
 Where heroes would not yield, day yields,
And all is quiet on the hill
And vale and copse forevermore are still.

2: Women Have One Breast

The November 1923 issue of *Broom,* the one assembled after the disastrous meeting in Prince Street, was the best of the five published in New York, the nearest to our elastic ideal of what a magazine should be. Together with poems by E. E. Cummings, Wallace Stevens and William Carlos Williams, translations from the French of Roger Vitrac and Louis Aragon, and a Wall Street fantasy by Slater Brown, it contained an extraordinary story entitled "An Awful Storming Fire, or Her and I on a Journey to the Secret of the Sun, by the author who solved the mysterious riddle." The author was Charles L. Durboraw, a Chicago paper-hanger whose gifts included a talent for writing in the vernacular and a vast ingenuousness. With more admirers, he might have reached a place in literature approaching that of le Douanier Rousseau in painting. "An Awful Storming Fire" is the story of a street-corner pickup. "Standing on a busy corner waiting for a street car and smoking a cigarette in one of the world's largest cities," the hero is accosted by a woman who soon confesses that "I used to be kind of sporty, but cut it out." She takes him to her empty apartment, explains that she "can read men like a book," shows him the parlor, the kitchen, the bedroom; and the story abruptly transforms itself into an enormous dream, an account of black shining forms like alligators and storms of fire into which the woman is engulfed. It ends with a moral: "I do know that man's laws punish us for our sins and that man gets these laws of his from the principle of nature's laws, and so it stands to reason that nature punishes us in different ways for our sins the same as man's laws." Unfortunately for the editors of *Broom,* the story, moral and all, was extremely readable. The postal censorship was rigorous toward little magazines, but often their mild indecency was too abstract or involved to be understood by the authorities. "An Awful Storming Fire" was simple enough to be exactly on the level of the censor's comprehension. He warned us indirectly that we had better mend our ways.

In those days the acting post-office censor was known in New York magazine offices as "Mr. Smith"; I have forgotten his real name. He received a comfortable salary from the government and a larger one from several of the sex magazines then at the height of their popularity. His duty toward them consisted in reading each issue before publication and making changes to meet the postal standards. The chief standard, perhaps, was anatomical. That every woman has one breast was Mr. Smith's professional conviction: he was willing to permit any number of seductions in print as long as the willing victim was not a two-breasted woman. Naturally he was most considerate of the magazines that paid him the largest retainers. He barred occasional issues from the mails, as a matter of form, but was always careful to see that the suppression was not financially harmful—that it did not take place until the issue had been distributed to subscribers. For this obligingness he atoned by his severity toward little unpopular magazines. He was very angry about "An Awful Storming Fire," even though it complied with the single-breasted standard. He discussed it with a sex-magazine editor of our acquaintance, explaining that he hadn't read the story until it was too late to take action. "But those guys better watch out. I'll read the next issue before it's mailed, and if I find anything the least bit off-color, I'll stop it like that—"

The threat disturbed us. We were experienced enough to know that postal censorship, though it sometimes helps the powerful magazines with money enough to publicize the event and thereby increase their circulation, is disastrous for periodicals that must struggle from month to month without resources. The total resources of *Broom* had lately vanished. They had consisted, since August, of a printer sufficiently interested in modern art to stand a loss on each successive issue. But the loss had proved greater than his literary enthusiasm: he had just informed us that the November number of *Broom* was the last he would print, except for cash paid in advance.

In the life of every magazine published for art's sake, there is a moment when the subvention is definitely withdrawn. The editors assemble dolefully; they review their exploits in the cause of letters; they assure one another that a place and a public undoubtedly exist for a magazine such as theirs; they decide whether to struggle on or expire gently in the parched wind. Usually they decide to struggle on. They issue appeals to which their readers are infallibly deaf. They search for new benefactors, for those with thousands to give, for those with hundreds, for any kind soul, at last, who will contribute five or ten dollars toward the printer's bill. They begin subscription campaigns that are doomed to failure; successful campaigns cost money. They reduce costs by ceasing to pay their contributors, by printing smaller issues.

Usually the history of a little magazine is summarized in its format. The first issue consists, let us say, of sixty-four pages, with half-tone illustrations printed on coated paper. The second issue has sixty-four pages, illustrated with line cuts. The third has only forty-eight pages; the fourth has thirty-two, without illustrations; the fifth never appears. *Broom* had surpassed this formula: it could boast of twenty issues, extending over three years; after being published in Rome (under the editorship of Harold Loeb and Alfred Kreymborg), it had reappeared in Berlin (under Loeb and Matthew Josephson); it had been reborn in New York; but in dying it followed the established pattern. Its size was of course reduced; its contributors were to go unpaid. Josephson, who had been receiving a small salary for his editorial work, took a job in Wall Street, pimping, as I expressed it, for a brokerage house. The two of us agreed to edit the magazine in our spare time, with such help as Slater Brown could give us from Woodstock. We found a new printer, cheaper if less charitably inclined: our next issue of thirty-two pages would cost only two hundred and fifty dollars. All that remained was to raise two hundred and fifty dollars.

Part of this sum we contributed ourselves. The rest had to be begged from acquaintances none of whom was wealthy. I can remember the month of December as a series of luncheons with this man or that, a continued exposition of our plans, a long plea that resulted sometimes in a check for five or ten dollars, sometimes in an embarrassed refusal. There was no time for reflection. We consoled ourselves, as we neared the goal, by saying that the next month would be easier, that new subscriptions would be received and money from bookshops, that the deficit would be no greater than we could cover from our white-collar salaries.

In the mornings I sometimes dozed at my desk, but the idle season had ended and office duties were rapidly piling up. In the evenings, working till we fell asleep over unread manuscripts, Josephson and I prepared the January issue, that for December having been tacitly omitted. The issue wouldn't be one of our best, but we set great store by a philosophical narrative that Kenneth Burke had just completed, an "ethical masque" into which he had ingeniously condensed all his theories of art and living. "Prince Llan," it is true, was in places too outspoken to meet the requirements of the postal authorities, but it was the sort of thing that *Broom* existed to publish—and if we couldn't publish it, what was the use of our continuing the

struggle? We reassured ourselves by saying that it was too ab-
struse for Mr. Smith. In our weariness we failed to notice that,
on the first page, in the third paragraph, it referred to plural-
breasted women.

As we continued raising money, writing letters, editing manuscripts, our minds grew weary and our nerves uncertain. We
quarreled with each other, with the world in general. Crowds,
whistles, skidding taxicabs, all the discomforts of the city were
a personal affront. In my uneasy sleep I trembled when a subway local passed underneath me, gathering speed as it left the
Canal Street station. I had nightmares in which I suffered from
the malice directed against contemporary art. Was there a general conspiracy of slander? Emerson Hough, in a statement
issued just after his death, had accused the young intellectuals
of being unpatriotic by conviction, East European by descent,
unclean morally and physically, adenoidal, garlicky and syphi-
litic. All this was too violent to be dangerous, but other critics
adopted subtler methods of attack. I came to believe that a general offensive was about to be made against modern art, an
offensive based on the theory that all modern writers, painters
and musicians were homosexual. The *Broom* offices at 45 King
Street received letters that mentioned Oscar Wilde. Envelopes
were addressed to *Broom* at "45 Queer Street." I began to feel
harried and combative, like Aubrey Beardsley forced to defend
his masculinity against whispers. When the first issue of the
American Mercury appeared, with Ernest Boyd's portrait of a
modern aesthete, I was prepared to find in it slanders that the
article did not set forth.

Slanders it really contained, but of a different type. "Aesthete:
Model 1924" was a composite portrait, based on the early careers
of Gilbert Seldes, Kenneth Burke, Edmund Wilson and Matthew Josephson, with touches borrowed, I should say, from

John Dos Passos, E. E. Cummings, myself, Gorham B. Munson and John Farrar. The resulting hero, a spraddling, disproportionate creature, was endowed by his author with a name, a history and several pansylike gestures. His associates were those who avowed their "intention of not being he-men"; his dreams were "haunted by fears of Sodom and Gomorrah"; but I can see, on rereading the article after ten years, that Mr. Boyd made these remarks with innocence; he did not mean to descend beneath the standards of ordinary pamphleteering.

The ordinary methods of pamphleteering are not at all lofty: they chiefly involve an appeal to the settled prejudices of the reader. Thus, to say that your opponent carries a cane, went to Harvard and is of dubiously Nordic ancestry is a means of attacking his literary standing, at least in the minds of those who are prejudiced against Harvard men, cane carriers and Jews. Mr. Boyd's Aesthete had all those unpopular characteristics, and, in addition, he had been a slacker during the war, one who "by luck or cunning . . . succeeded in getting out of the actual trenches." He now lived in Greenwich Village, wrote free verse, drank synthetic gin, edited a little magazine and was obsessed with sex. Moreover—and here we approach a more serious accusation, offered as no sop to the groundlings, but sincerely as a heartfelt plaint—"the Aesthete seeks to monopolize the field of contemporary foreign art."

It was in developing this theme that Mr. Boyd invented real slanders, which were, it should be added, of a purely commercial type. As critic, translator and editorial adviser, he himself had prospered in the field of contemporary foreign art. He was faced with competition from new sources. The best defense of his economic position would be to attack the scholarship of his competitors. This he did by citing their real or imaginary mistranslations, by exaggerating the errors they actually committed, by creating others where none existed—in brief, by a series of petty and exasperating misrepresentations. He was like a cigarette manufacturer spreading the rumor that another cigarette manufacturer mixed alfalfa with his product.

So the article impresses me as I read it today with some curiosity and an occasional yawn. But when it first appeared I failed to perceive these economic issues, in my absorption with the moral-artistic standards I had carried with me from Paris. It seemed to me, simply, that a critic of some distinction was taking sides with the philistines against his natural allies, was appealing to dangerous forms of prejudice, was making implications about the personal lives of people many of whom were my friends. "He ought to be punched in the jaw," I said. And the remark, being overheard, was repeated to Mr. Boyd with elaborations that concerned my character as a gangster and triggerman of letters: I was not merely going to punch his jaw, with my own horny and bloodstained fist; I was going to kneel on his chest and one by one pluck out the hairs of his beard. Mr. Boyd, who describes his character as timid and bookish, did not attempt to conceal his apprehension.

Knowing that "Aesthete: Model 1924" was directed against others, that my own part in the composite portrait was negligible, a matter of two or three details, I had a feeling of noble disinterestedness in my anger. I regarded myself as a sort of West Texas sheriff sworn to uphold a code of literary conduct. I determined, in ignorance of the bloodthirsty rumors carried toward Gramercy Park from the Lower West Side, to see Mr. Boyd, explain my objections to his article, and request a private apology for certain passages. I telephoned to ask for an appointment. Mr. Boyd, after some hesitation, said that he could see no occasion for the visit I suggested. There was a note of terror in his voice that puzzled and amazed me. I assured him that the interview would be entirely peaceful; still he demurred. "Then you won't see me?" I said.

"No, I can only repeat that really; I mean we have nothing whatever to discuss."

His voice was shrill and unsteady: it somehow suggested my last evening at the Rotonde, the scurrying waiters, the proprietor with his dirty white face and frightened eyes. Seized with the same quick rage that swept over me before, I cursed over the telephone, delivering three round oaths before hanging up the receiver. The next day, still furious, I wrote Mr. Boyd a note in which I apologized for my profanity, saying that I had merely wished to imply that he was a sneak, a liar and a coward.

This incident, reflecting little glory on either side, was the beginning of the Battle of the Aesthetes and, simultaneously, of Mr. Boyd's well-advertised martyrdom. For a time he must really have suffered discomfort, although his opponents were only partially responsible. They sent him a telegram which they thought to be funny; once, in the midst of a party, they telephoned his residence and held a pompous, leg-pulling conversation in which they found that he was their master at repartee. I rather discouraged those activities, holding that there was nothing more to be said; indeed, for my own part, I said nothing more. But Mr. Boyd's malicious friends refused to let the battle die so abruptly: it was too precious a subject for gossip. Trading on his known timidity, they assured him that his person was really endangered by hard-boiled, furious, blackjack-toting aesthetes; they advised him to ask for police protection, then went about saying that he had followed their advice. He hesitated to leave his apartment. Burton Rascoe, in an amusing and hyperbolic attack on Boyd's enemies, pictured him as "barricaded behind his books, subsisting on depleted rations and grown wan and weary under the assaults and harassments." Once, in the street, he encountered Gilbert Seldes, a writer whose features were included in the portrait of the imaginary Aesthete. Seldes harbored no grudge and raised his walking stick in friendly greeting. Mr. Boyd, however, interpreted this gesture as a threat and walked hurriedly away. Seldes followed him, having a message to deliver. Mr. Boyd walked faster. Seldes shouted and quickened his pace. It is easy to imagine the spectacle of these two prominent critics, both of them sedentary and peaceful by disposition, one fleeing with terror dogging his footsteps, the other pursuing with an uplifted cane and the most amicable intentions.

Mr. Boyd doubtless retired into his book-barricaded study, there to fulminate against the two-fisted, hairy-chested aesthetes who were threatening his days. He wrote vehemently; he abounded in diatribes against Greenwich Village and little magazines and myself; he poured forth abuse and ridicule in the best eighteenth-century manner; he was Voltaire at Ferney annihilating his rivals with sledgehammer blows of wit. Like Voltaire, he sometimes presented the truth in a revised version. He announced, with a who-is-this-person air adopted from his great models, that he had never even heard of his opponents until they came bursting into his life. This purely tactical misstatement led him fatally into making another: how else could he explain his terror? He therefore asserted that I, over the telephone, had explicitly offered to beat him up.

Both these misstatements, I think, were tactical blunders. There is no use misrepresenting your opponents if the truth in itself is sufficiently damaging; and the truth in this case was damaging enough. I had made myself ridiculous by applying standards of ethics to a situation that called for standards of salesmanship. I had behaved much as I did on July 14, in Paris, but all my favorite catchwords could now be turned against me. New York had catchwords of its own, which I had deliberately forgotten. My *disinterestedness* was interpreted there as a meddlesome effort to push myself forward, to break the front page.

My *significant gesture* was a silly touchinesss, an offense taken where none was intended. My *manifestation* was a flop. I had been *violent, arbitrary, indiscreet:* what more need be said to cover me with confusion? My witnesses and allies were no longer *des gens très bien;* they could be dismissed as Greenwich Village rowdies. And my opponents, cultivating their advantage, were about to flourish exceedingly.

Mr. Boyd, that year, was a literary hero and a commercial success. There was no list of distinguished critics that did not mention his name. No magazine was complete without one of his imaginary portraits.[1] The *American Mercury,* having published the first of these, was launched on a profitable career: copies of the January issue, exhausted on the newsstands, were already selling at a premium. The Battle of the Aesthetes was monopolizing literary gossip; the aesthetes themselves were covered with ridicule, and silent. Even had they wished to fight back, they no longer possessed a magazine in which to print their rejoinders. For, on January 14, in the midst of the tumult aroused by the battle, another blow had fallen. *Broom* had been suppressed under Section 480 of the Postal Laws, which prohibits the mailing of contraceptives and other obscene matter.

I learned of the event that morning before setting out for the office. A mail truck stopped in front of the house on Dominick Street; two postal employees jumped from the seat, asked for me by name, held a short consultation, and struggled into the cellar with six heavy bags containing our January issue. I telephoned Josephson, who had already been notified of the suppression. We conferred hastily with a lawyer; he gave us

[1] Boyd, who had more than his share of Dublin wit and Dublin bitterness, was still a prominent literary figure when I wrote this narrative. In his later years we became friends in a distant fashion. He died in 1946 at the age of fifty-nine.

no encouragement whatever. Coming when it did, the blow was fatal. Had we possessed the money with which to continue, it would have meant no more than the loss of a single issue; at present it meant the loss of all the resources on which we depended for the future. We might of course repeat our labors of the preceding month; we might somehow assemble money enough to pay the printer and publish another number under the hostile supervision of Mr. Smith, but we were utterly tired and discouraged. We did what we could under the circumstances. We tried for the first time to get newspaper publicity, thinking it might help the magazine; we telephoned prominent people to ask for statements; we examined our files of accepted manuscripts, planned statements and editorials; but this was done almost mechanically; the spirit had gone out of it; we were tired and beaten.

We had tried on Manhattan Island to re-create the atmosphere of intellectual excitement and moral indignation that had stimulated us in Paris among the Dadaists. We had tried to prove that it was worth while fighting and making oneself ridiculous and getting one's head broken for purely aesthetic motives. We had tried to write and publish a new sort of literature celebrating the picturesque qualities of American machinery and our business civilization, and we found that American businessmen in the age of machines were not interested in reading poems about them. The *American Mercury,* with its easy incredulity, its middle-agedness, its belligerent philistinism, was the expression of a prevailing mood. *Broom* was dead, with all the activities planned to surround it. "We'll stick it out," I said. But five months after my return from Europe I was dispirited, exhausted, licked—by Mr. Smith and Mr. Boyd and the quarrels among my friends, but most of all by myself, by my efforts to apply in one country the standards I had brought from another.

3: Manhattan Melody

Washington's birthday would fall on a Friday. Work was
slackening again at the office; there was no need to punch the
time clock Saturday morning. On Thursday afternoon I left
for Woodstock to spend the rest of the week in the Catskills,
carrying with me a sheaf of blank paper, a bottle of gin and a
little bundle of manuscripts which would compose a new issue
of *Broom,* if we ever got round to printing it.

William Slater Brown was to be my host. He was living alone,
in a shack built hastily as a summer studio, with a high ceiling
and porous walls and a vast north window that rattled in the
wind. Bill had practically abandoned the attempt to keep it
warm. He made the gesture of having a fire in the stove, a
smoldering heap of chestnut branches, but he had learned to
work when the temperature in the room was well below freez-
ing, and work he did, twelve hours a day, writing stories, tearing
them up and beginning them over again, addressing a long
monologue to his typewriter. He ate his meals with a copy of
Tristram Shandy or a translation of Aeschylus propped against
the coffee pot. Once a week he trudged to Woodstock through
the snow to buy whatever provisions he could afford and exchange a few words with the grocer. About as often he entertained a guest—Henry Billings the painter or Murrell Fisher
the art critic; one or the other would come stumbling through
the woods at dusk, bearing a jug of cider and a lantern. Both
of them appeared during my visit. Bill saw more people that
week-end than he would see again till the snow melted and

the summer artists began to blossom on the landscape like mullein stalks.

On Thursday night we drank most of the gin, mixed with cider. On Friday morning we ran hastily through the manuscripts assembled for the new issue of *Broom,* and decided that most of them were undistinguished. We were appalled at the expense involved in printing them and, though we talked bravely of plans for the future, both of us felt that nothing would be done. In the afternoon, after lunching on salt pork and stewed lentils, we each sat down with three pencils and thirty sheets of blank paper, to try our hand at automatic writing, a tiring exercise. One simply writes at top speed, for three hours by the clock, on any subject that pops into the head. The first hour is generally wasted; but during the second and third hours, when the conscious mind is thoroughly fatigued, one is likely to produce interesting phrases and fancies, and sometimes whole stories in the manner of our Dada friends, with whom the exercise was popular. Bill and I had never tried it before, and we were disappointed with the results, which would be of interest only to a psychologist. The sun was setting as the three hours ended; it was time for our dinner of salt pork and lentils.

In the evening we walked along the Bearsville road between high banks of snow. Bill was bent on expounding a theory of aesthetics that he had derived from staring at a pine tree outside his studio window. Art, he said, should resemble a tree rather than a machine. The perfect machine is one to which any added part is useless and from which no part can be subtracted without impairing its efficiency. Trees, on the other hand, have any number of excess branches; and art should resemble them, should have a higher factor of safety than the machine. Art is the superfluous. . . . I disagreed with him so vehemently that I slipped and plunged head foremost into a snowbank.

The nights were still and cold, with skies the color of oiled steel. We slept under blankets, overcoats, rugs pulled from the floor, and rose in the morning stiffly, as if stones had been piled on our chests. All day the yellow sun shone in a blue sky, melting the snow on the roof until two-foot icicles hung from the eaves. We cooked, chopped wood, went for long walks and talked incessantly, without ever mentioning office work, or magazines (after the first unhappy morning) or the world of literary quarrels. On Saturday night Josh Billings came, and Murrell Fisher, each with a jug of hard cider. On Sunday afternoon, after carrying my valise through the deep snow to Woodstock, I caught the bus that would take me to the Kingston station, from which a train would take me to the terminal at Weehawken, from which in its turn a ferry would take me to snowless Manhattan.

It was ten o'clock when I reached the house in Dominick Street. I dropped my valise and looked at the windows under the roof, where we occupied three rooms. There was no light visible in the house, or in the house next door; the street slept in shadow between the arc lights. My latchkey was upstairs in the bureau drawer: would I have to spend the night in a hotel? I rang the bell twice and waited; there was no answer. I pounded my fists on the door and waited again; there was no sound of footsteps on the stairs. I put my ear to the keyhole. Faintly, from the rear of the house, I thought I could distinguish voices; they died away. I pounded on the door again, waited, lost patience and threw my weight against it; the lock yielded and let me go plunging forward into the hall.

"Here we are, Frances," said a voice from the darkness. "Come on upstairs and have a drink."

On the second story, in a back room furnished with a cot, a bureau and one chair, I found Jimmy Dwyer, a classmate of mine who worked intermittently in Wall Street, and Terry Carlin, a hobo philosopher and mystic who boasted of never having worked at all. Jimmy was twenty-six and Terry was sixty-nine. That evening they looked alike, both being singularly pale and both wearing a vague expression that was not so much unfriendly as inaccessible: after three days of steady drinking they had entered a cosmos of their own. The air of it was warm and moist and dead, the air of a closed room in which a gas stove has burned steadily since morning. There were little drops of water on the green-painted walls. On the bureau were eight empty bottles, one bottle half-full of gin and three empty glasses. The blinds, tightly drawn that morning against the sun, continued to be drawn against the night.

"Have a drink, Frances," said Jimmy Dwyer. "Oh, you're not Frances, are you? That's funny. Well, have a drink."

"Thanks, I've had one. Where's Peggy?"

"Oh"—with a broad gesture—"she went out. Frances insulted Peggy and went out, too. She went out last Monday."

"How long ago was that?" I asked curiously.

"Let me see . . . Monday, Tuesday . . . it's Wednesday night now, isn't it, Terry?"

Terry finished rolling a cigarette with long muscular fingers that hardly shook with age. He swept the flakes of Bull Durham from the blanket beside him and put them neatly back into the bag. "Time is relative," he said. "Time in the abstract doesn't exist. On Mars it may be Wednesday, on Venus Thursday, on Jupiter Friday. I live in a world beyond time, that embraces all time. On the earth, I think it is Tuesday morning."

"It's Wednesday night," said Jimmy Dwyer positively.

I left them, climbed another flight of stairs and lit the gaslight over my desk. The room was cold, not like Bill's shack in the country, but like a sealed tomb. To kindle a fire in the grate would be a waste of time: in ten minutes I would be in bed. I found my notebook, filled a fountain pen, and began to write a letter:

"My dear Malcolm," I wrote, addressing myself as a distant acquaintance, "it would be wise to admit that you were mistaken, and that you cannot, while working for Sweet's Catalogue Service, Inc., be editor, free lance, boon companion, literary polemist. Instead you must confine yourself to essentials: thinking, reading, conversation, writing, livelihood, in about the order named. At this moment you must strip yourself of everything inessential to these aims; and especially of the functions of editor, free lance, drinking companion and literary polemist. You must arrange your life against interruptions; you must sleep, exercise, earn your living and pass the other moments beneath a lamp or talking. Too many excitements: at this moment you are tired and discouraged. . . . You have left the stage and you did not even bow."

New York, inhabited by six million strangers, is the metropolis of curiosity and suspicion. It is the city without landmarks, the home of lasting impermanence, of dynamic immobility. It is the seat of violent emotions, hate, desire, envy, contempt, all changing from moment to moment, all existing at the tips of the nerves. It is the city of anger . . . but underneath the anger is another mood, a feeling of timeless melancholy, dry, reckless, defeated and perverse.

New York, to one returning from Paris or London, seems the least human of all the babylons. Its life is expressed in terms of geometry and mechanics: the height and cubical content of its buildings, the pressure that squeezes them upward like clay squeezed out between the fingers, the suction that empties one district to overcrowd another, the lines of force radiating from subway stations, the density of traffic. Its people have a purely numerical function: they are counted as units that daily pass a given point. Their emotions are coefficients used in calculating the probability of trade. Thus, by applying the coefficient of

thirst to the numbered crowds on Broadway, one decides where
to place a tavern or an orange-drink stand. The coefficient of
vanity determines the location of beauty parlors. Just what is
the coefficient of art? How many geniuses should we compute
to each million shares of stock or billion dollars of assessable
real estate?

When the exiles returned from Europe, their normal instinct
was to remake the environment, to substitute moral for mechanical values, to create a background that would render their own
lives more exciting or rewarding. Having failed in this attempt,
they sought to adjust themselves to the existing environment as
best they could. Some were already trying to escape from it by
moving to farms in Connecticut or New Jersey; among these
country dwellers was Kenneth Burke. From the letters I wrote
him during the winter of 1923–24, it is easy to reconstruct my
own state of mind:

"I live by clocks that mislead me. I rise at 8:45 and reach
the office at 8:45. I rise at 9:05 and reach the office at 9:20. I
rise at 8:00 and reach the office at 9:30. I never keep engage-
ments, but on no principle. I have time for nothing." And again:
"It frightens me how my life is episodic. What I lay down is
never picked up again. To find any personality for myself, I
have to reread my own letters. . . . Let us estimate that I can
think for a maximum of two hours per day. Every day the topic
changes, my interests change, I am less downhearted, or more,
I plan different futures. To read seriously. To construct an
aesthetic. To write a novel. To be financially independent. One
aim conflicts with another, and our lives are held together only
by the calendar, the daily papers, the chain of Saturdays, the
Sundays like empty brackets. People who live in cities have
bright eyes like squirrels. . . . Mr. Cowley you write don't you
question mark. No comma Mrs. Smith comma I can take it or
leave it alone. The function of poetry is to make the world

inhabitable period. Three dots. Suddenly I had a hysterical desire to read Plato and rushed to the library."

Plato was a symbol of escape: to read him was not to understand the innateness of the Idea, but merely to place oneself
at a distance of four thousand miles and half as many years
from Broadway. I felt, for the only time and for reasons in-
acceptable to them, a curious sympathy for the American Humanists. "From Paul Elmer More," I wrote to Kenneth, "one
derives a statement of the great truth that the aim of philosophy
is to attain ataraxy, which the Oxford Concise Dictionary de-
fines as free security or, more vulgarly, stoical indifference, from
a, not, and *tarasso,* disturb. Philosophy is the power of not being
disturbed. After six months in New York, one takes refuge in
such preoccupations, and the atmosphere of New York is a
hysterical classicism, to be distinguished from the classicism
of the Mediterranean, which results from sympathy with one's
environment instead of rebellion against it. Let us repeat that
I am not disturbed, am not disturbed, not disturbed."

Sometimes there were outbursts of moral indignation. "I
utterly hate and despise the trade and the tradesmen of letters.
Your typical writer—beg pardon, your creator, for hacks have
usurped the principal attribute of God—is a child spoiled by
his audience, a vanity parading before comic mirrors, a soloist
begging for another curtain call. . . ." I sometimes had pleasant nightmares in which I fancied that New York was being
destroyed by an earthquake: its towers snapped like pine trees
in a storm, a tidal wave poured through its streets and swept
them clean of lice. But slowly, in spite of these rebellions, I was
adjusting myself to an old situation.

"One afternoon last week," I wrote, "there was a party at
the office, much dancing, pretty stenographers; my head still
buzzes with jazz (rings with rag?). Afterward I went to Ridge-
field with Gene O'Neill and Agnes and Hart Crane. I wrote

a jazz poem in jazzy prose and swore I should write no more verse. Matty is publishing *The Poet Assassinated* to clear off some of the *Broom* deficit or pile it on—one becomes so confused. Apparently Munson has Broken Off Relations with me. Mr. Eugene O'Neill speaks a language so different from ours that we seem to converse from distant worlds. Cummings' book has appeared. The beer is getting poorer. New York has enveloped itself in a haze of ragtime tunes, a sort of poetry that leads to a melancholy happiness."

Ten days later I returned to the same theme. "The function of poetry is to make life tolerable. New York was becoming more than I could bear. During my few moments alone I found myself miserable to a degree that you would never credit. The dance at our office was a partial salvation: it filled my head with jazz, impossibilities and pretty girls, all of which is the strong and vulgar poetry peculiar to Manhattan. Afterward the irregular red-brick landscapes took on a different meaning. . . ." I was relearning a forgotten lesson, that New York had its folklore, its proper music, that the city was less inhuman than it seemed.

In fact, once the returning exiles had been stripped of their ambitions, once they surrendered to the city and lived the common life of its peasants, they found abundant compensations in their lot. During the winter there were dancing parties in Harlem, drinking parties in the Village, invasions of Second Avenue to sip white wine and applaud Mr. Moscowitz's interpretation of "Hearts and Flowers" on the cymbalon, perhaps after a visit to the National Winter Garden Burlesque; there were concerts and bridge and incursions into the Roaring Forties. In summer there were trips to Coney Island, extended weekends in the country; and at all seasons there were the speakeasies where the returning exiles congregated, always in larger numbers—where, over a Tom Collins, they exchanged news

from Montparnasse and impressions of the Tyrol; where even
the bartender had spent his Paris year; he said, "How'd you
like to be up in Montmartre tonight, at Zelli's?"—and Flossie
Martin answered, "Or just sitting outside the Select with a good
long drink and nothing to do but drink it"—all this had a sort
of reminiscent charm, but it seemed, to the returning exiles,
farther and farther away. They were learning that New York
had another life, too—subterranean, like almost everything that
was human in the city—a life of writers meeting in restaurants
at lunchtime or in coffeehouses after business hours to talk of
work just started or magazines unpublished, and even to lay
modest plans for the future. Modestly they were beginning to
write poems worth the trouble of reading to their friends over
the coffee cups. Modestly they were rebelling once more. They
hadn't time to be very unhappy; most of their hours were given
over to the simple business of earning a livelihood; yet there grew
on them the desire to escape and the hope of living somewhere
under more favorable conditions, perhaps in their own countryside, of which they still dreamed, perhaps on a Connecticut
farm.

VII: The Age of Islands

1: Connecticut Valley

In the preceding chapters I have been describing a process that first impressed me as being geographical. A whole generation of American writers—and how many others, architects, painters, bond salesmen, professors and their wives, all the more studious and impressionable section of the middle-class youth—had been uprooted, schooled away, almost wrenched away, I said, from their attachment to any locality or local tradition. For years the process continued, through school and college and the war; always they were moving farther from home. At last hundreds and thousands of them became veritable exiles, living in Paris or the South of France and adhering to a theory of art which held that the creative artist is absolutely independent of all localities, nations or classes. But most of them didn't remain exiled forever. One by one they came lingering back to New York, even though they came there as aliens, many of them holding ideas that would cause them a difficult period of re-adjustment. . . . And what happened then? Once the process had reversed itself, did it carry them homeward at an accelerating speed, till they had returned in body and spirit to their own townships?

Something of the sort might actually have happened if the repatriated exiles had retained their freedom of movement. But most of them had ceased to be free. They were poor and married; they had livings to earn, professional careers to think about and not much time to pursue ideas toward their logical limits. At this point the clear process I have been describing becomes confused: the lives of the literary exiles lose their individual outline and become merged with the lives of a whole class in American society.

At this point, too, the author begins to disappear from his book. In the preceding chapters, although I was trying to tell the story of a generation of writers, I felt justified in recounting my own adventures because they were in some ways representative of what was happening to others. That partly ceased to be true in the following years. After the suppression of *Broom* I had no energy for new undertakings and for a time I was simply another advertising copywriter who hated his job. I saved a little money, enough to buy furniture and garden tools, and in the summer of 1926 we moved to the country, near our friends Slater Brown and Hart Crane. There I supported the family by doing translations from the French and writing for magazines, and eventually I bought a back-road farmhouse, making the down payment of seventy-five dollars with part of a prize of a hundred dollars that I had received from *Poetry* (and keeping out the rest for groceries). My adventures were interesting to me, even absorbing, but many of them had lost the element of freedom or novelty and most of them had ceased to be representative; instead they were merely typical. As I think back on the period it seems to me that I am looking at a class or crowd photograph in which my face is lost in a mass of faces.

New York was beginning to be crowded with people like ourselves. As American business entered the boom era, it needed more and more propagandists to aid in the increasingly difficult task of selling more commodities each year to families that were given no higher wages to buy them with, and therefore had to be tempted with all the devices of art, literature and science into bartering their future earnings for an automobile or a bedroom suite. Business needed public-relations counselors, it needed advertising artists and copywriters, it needed romancers to fill the pages of the magazines in which its products were advertised and illustrators to make the romance visible (and psychologists to explain how the whole process could be intensified); it needed designers, stylists, editors, and all these professions came flocking to Manhattan. Soon it became evident that all the younger members of this class had had about the same experiences, the Midwestern background, the year in the army if they were men, the unhappy love affair that took its place if they were women, the long voyage to France; and it was evident, too, that most of them were lost in their new environment and discontented.

That was the class into which the exiles were being merged. All its members were individualists by theory, yet they lived the life of their social order as strictly as Prussian officers, and had to cultivate meaningless affectations and real vices in order to possess even the appearance of individuality. "All of them have Watkins, Algonquin or Stuyvesant telephone numbers and live in the Village. . . . I know so well what they are doing. There will be greetings and ringings of the telephone, cocktails will be poured and drunk, cigarettes held in nervous fingers. Toward eight o'clock or later, women will be crowding before the mirror in the bathroom, men will be hunting out overcoats from the tangle of clothes on the bed in the alcove and shoving their arms into the sleeves; people will be going trailing laughter down the stairs. We shall all gather on the sidewalk in a little noisy cluster, deep down among the silent unfriendly houses. . . ."

The life they led was molding people into such strict patterns that when my friend Robert M. Coates wrote a novel about them, in 1933, he chose as his hero a man of the crowd. The book was *Yesterday's Burdens;* the hero's name was Henderson. "When I saw him," Coates said, "I had always the sense that he was several: that like the crowd that has not yet chosen its leader and begun its movement toward an elected goal, he had not yet compacted himself, not taken his ultimate direction." Henderson, in the afternoon, "is to be seen in the apartments of the more recherché commercial artists; of writers who are either just going to, or just returning from, Hollywood; of stockbrokers who collect, with a tempered enthusiasm, lalique glass and finance, every second year or so, an unsuccessful musical comedy. He is poised, alert, insouciant; he goes well with modernique furniture." And Henderson, like most of the other characters in Coates's novel, is profoundly unhappy.

All these people with whom the exiles were beginning to mingle as the years passed by, as their incomes rose a little, articles were sold to magazines and publishers' contracts signed —all these people were living a series of contradictions. They prided themselves chiefly on their professional competence, their skill with words or lines or colors, their ability to gauge the public taste, and yet their skill was devoted to aims in which none of them believed. Their function as a class was to be the guardians of intellectual things, and yet they were acting as propagandists for a way of life in which the intellect played a minor part. They were selling their talents, often at a stiff price, and yet they didn't know what to do with the money they received, except spend it for automobiles and gin and the house beautiful, exactly like the gulled public for which they were writing and drawing. They had satisfied a childhood ambition by moving to the metropolis and becoming more or less successful there, yet most of them wanted to be somewhere else:

they wanted to leave it all and go back to something, perhaps to their childhoods.

Of course they couldn't go back: their own countrysides or Midwestern towns would offer no scope to their talents, no opportunity for earning the sort of living to which they had grown accustomed. They were inexorably tied to New York —but perhaps they could make a compromise, could enjoy the advantages of two worlds by purchasing a farm somewhere within a hundred miles of Manhattan and spending their summers in the country without separating themselves from their urban sources of income. About the year 1924 there began a great exodus toward Connecticut, the Catskills, northern New Jersey and Bucks County, Pennsylvania. Many of the former expatriates took part in it; and soon the long process of exile-and-return was resumed almost in the form of a mass migration.

The emotional effects of it are suggested in Robert Coates's book. "My present occupation," the narrator begins, "is that of a book reviewer, but I live in the country." He goes on to describe his daily life, his memories of Henderson; then, "There is, of course, the great problem of whether or not I belong here. On all sides one sees writers, painters, fashion designers buying acres of tillable land or pasture and dedicating them to the cultivation of sumac, goldenrod and blackberry brambles. Is it for revenge? The artist's tendencies, it would seem, are always atavistic: he would raze cities, he would remake New England into a wilderness. But what of the land itself?

"I sometimes feel a strange uneasiness: the trees look hostile, the very grass seems to regard me with a venomous air. I have bought these fields and doomed them to sterility. Can you tell me if there is anything in common law concerning the rights of the soil to expect careful husbandry on the part of its owner?" . . . Perhaps such a law exists, though still unwritten; perhaps it levies its quiet penalties against the man that holds even stony acres without plowing them, or lives in a community without taking part in its life.

At any rate, the Connecticut migration failed to produce the great effects that were hoped of it. I can report this from experience, having lived for years in a valley near the one that Coates described. During the long winters it was almost deserted. No more than thirty voters attended the town meeting in November, where formerly there would have been two hundred. In December the snow fell, blocking all but the main-traveled roads until April; the valley hibernated. Then, late in spring when the arbutus buds were half-open, the city people came trooping back. There was the sound of banging shutters, of rugs beaten in the yard, and the first smoke rose from a dozen chimneys, to mingle with the spring haze sleeping over the hill.

In May the housewives laid plans for a rock garden here, a terrace there, a pergola where the outhouse used to stand. It would be nice to remodel the dairy barn into a studio—or perhaps they should tear it down in order to have an unobstructed view into the valley. They walked along the hillside, their faces pink with the spring wind, and lamented because the old tobacco fields were growing up in sumac and sweetfern. A little flock of sheep would keep them clean—but who would care for the sheep in the winter, with so few natives left and most of them unreliable? Then, looking toward the crest of the hill where the rock-oak buds were a smoky green, they said, "Isn't all this beautiful! Aren't you glad we live in this lovely valley?"

During July and August, the summer people traveled incessantly over the valley roads. They drove to the last remaining dairy farms for milk and eggs; they drove to the Moffats for croquet, to the Denisons for a highball, to Green Pond for a swim. They had social functions of their own, gin parties, ping-pong parties, barn parties, musical evenings, which they attended in force. Over the week-end their houses were crowded with guests from the city, who exclaimed between two drinks, "Oh, how I envy you this lovely old farmhouse!"—"Yes, isn't the valley beautiful," the summer people agreed. And, if they wandered outside into the moonlight, they saw that the valley had lost its ravaged daytime look: the roofless barns seemed whole; the goldenrod on the hillside might be a ripe field of wheat.

In autumn, when the neglected orchards are heavy with apples and fields are dotted with gentians almost the color of the autumn haze, the summer people prepare to go. They sprinkle mothballs in the closets, they lock the shutters, they store their bright lawn furniture in the empty barns. Their cars, waiting at the front gate, are piled with suitcases, unfinished manuscripts or paintings, vaseline glass and the two Hitchcock chairs they bought at a real bargain. For a moment they wait before starting the motor. They look at the hilltops, where the oaks are red-brown, and at the steep pastures with their pools of wine-colored sumac; they look down at the blazing maples in the swamp. Somewhere in the fields a hound is baying on a cold scent; the sound of an ax comes drifting down from the hill. "Isn't the valley beautiful in October," the summer people repeat as if they were dutifully admiring a masterpiece. "Aren't you glad we live here," they say as they drive off.

There have always been summer people—and as time went on there were more of them—who stayed through the winter, who voted in town meetings and sent their children to the local school; they were partially absorbed into the life of the countryside.[1] There were others who acquired a real taste for gardening

[1] This has been particularly true of Sherman, Connecticut, the town—

or fishing, and even the most insensitive were somewhat affected by their new residence. It remained true, however, that most of them lived in their country homes as they might live in a summer hotel. The ownership of an old house full of Boston rockers and Hitchcock chairs did not endow them with a past. The land for which they were overassessed was not really theirs; it did not stain their hands or color their thoughts. They had no functional relation to it: they did not clear new fields, plant crops, depend on its seasons or live by its fruits; in a Connecticut valley, as in Manhattan, there remained the problem "of whether or not I belong here."

They might have traveled farther without ceasing to be faced by the same answer. Modern transportation makes everything easy: there are airplanes, buses, railroads and concrete highways leading everywhere, and even to one's birthplace. Driving westward from New York, a writer might suddenly find himself in his own country, the village where he went to school, the woods where he gathered hickory nuts and listened to the red squirrels that sang as they cut down hemlock cones from the trees crowding the slopes of dark ravines. He might pass the house where his grandmother used to live, and stop at the roadside, wondering what would happen if he bought the house from strangers and planted a new garden on the site of the old. He could live and die there like his ancestors—but no, the door was double-locked against him; the house would not take him back.

---

or township—where the narrator of Coates's novel lived. Sherman had more than a hundred farms in 1920; by 1950 it had just twenty-one, and yet it was not a dying community. Sherman people had shown more interest in local affairs than most residents of the week-end belt and beginning in the late 1930s there was a rebirth of community life. More and more of the newcomers took to spending the winter in Sherman. Many of the displaced farmers were supporting themselves by building houses for the summer people.

He was seeking for something that was no longer there. It wasn't so much his childhood, which of course was irrecapturable; it was rather a quality remembered from childhood, a sense of belonging to something, of living in a country whose people spoke his language and shared his interests. Now he had ceased to belong—the country had changed since the new concrete highway was put through; the woods were gone, the thick-growing hemlocks cut down, and there were only stumps, dried tops, branches and fireweed where the woods had been. The people had changed—he could write about them now, but not write for them, not resume his part in the common life. And he himself had changed, so that wherever he lived he would be a stranger. It was no use regretting the past; he might as well drive on.

For the long process I have been describing was not so simple as it seemed to me at first. The sense of uneasiness and isolation that oppressed American writers was not the result of a purely geographical process and could not be cured by retracing their steps—they could go back to Iowa, but only as alien observers, and back to Wisconsin, but only as Glenway Wescott did, to say good-by. They had been uprooted from something more than a birthplace, a county or a town. Their real exile was from society itself, from any society to which they could honestly contribute and from which they could draw the strength that lies in shared convictions.

2: Charlestown Prison

All during the 1920s many, and perhaps most, of the serious American writers felt like strangers in their own land. They were deeply attached to it, no matter what pretense they made of being indifferent and cosmopolitan, but they felt obscurely that it had rejected them. The country in those days was being managed by persons for whom they felt a professional hostility. It was the age when directors' meetings were more important than cabinet meetings and when the national destiny was being decided by middle-aged bankers and corporation executives. One saw their pictures week after week in the slick-paper magazines; they wore high collars and white-piped waistcoats beautifully tailored over little round paunches. Sometimes they assumed a commanding look, sometimes they tried to smile, but their eyes were like stones in their soft, gray, wrinkled cheeks.

These rulers of America, as they were called in magazine articles, showed little interest in books or ideas. The few statements they made to the press were empty and pompous, yet the statements announced one doctrine that was almost universally held. Americans should work longer and harder, produce always more, consume always more, save always more and invest in the future of the country, which was in safe hands.

Apparently the doctrine was the secret of American prosperity. Year after year there were more factories employing more workers to produce more goods per man-hour; year after year there were more automobiles on the highways, bigger crowds and brighter lights on the main stem, and in the suburbs more and more houses completely equipped with radios, mechanical refrigerators, vacuum cleaners and pop-up toasters. Year after year the advertising pages were becoming more shameless; they cajoled, tempted, flattered, bullied or frightened people into trading in or throwing away everything they had bought the year before, in order to win the envy of their neighbors by acquiring, on easy monthly terms, the latest super-heterodyne or super-powered, super-attractive model. Installment buying had plunged more and more people into debt; trying hard to earn a higher salary with special bonuses, they had less and less leisure to enjoy their new possessions. Stocks rose from year to year; their prices were based not so much on past earnings as on faith in the future. There seemed to be no reason why the whole process of making, selling, servicing and discarding could not continue indefinitely at an always increasing speed. But writers had begun to complain that the process left very little time for reading or gardening or family evenings together, and very little scope for virtues like independence or integrity.

Writers also complained—in dozens of books and hundreds of articles published in the less popular magazines—that except for the mass industries producing honest products almost the whole of American culture was becoming false or flimsy. The stage dealt with problems that had no meaning in terms of daily life; the movies offered dreams of impossible luxury to shop-girls; the popular magazines were merely vehicles for advertising and the popular newspapers effectively disfranchised their readers by failing to give them the information they needed as voters, while doping them with always bigger and brighter scandals. Worst of all, many writers said, was the hypocrisy that had come to pervade the whole system, with businessmen talking about service when they meant profits, with statesmen proclaiming their love for the common man while taking orders from Wall Street (and sometimes money from oil operators, in little black bags) and with prohibition agents raiding one gang of bootleggers so they could sell the seized liquor to another gang.

In those days hardly anyone seemed to believe in what he was doing—not the workman on the production line, or the dealer forced to sell more units each month to more and more unwilling customers, on threat of losing his sales agency, or the salesman with his foot stuck in the door while he repeated an argument learned by rote, or the underpaid newspaperman kidding his stories, hating his managing editor and despising his readers—not even the people at the head of the system, the bankers and stock promoters and politicians in the little green house on K Street; everybody was in it for the money, everybody was hoping to make a killing and get away. The advertising men who served as priests and poets of American prosperity were the biggest cynics of all. Often on Saturday nights one heard them saying drunkenly that they were only misleading the public, that they wanted to chuck it all up—everything, job, wife, children—and escape to some island where they could paint or write a book or just loaf in the sun.

"Why don't you then?" the writers asked them, feeling superior because they had once worked in offices and had managed to break away. Like the advertising men, however, they suffered from a feeling of real discomfort. Something oppressed them, some force was preventing them from doing their best work. They did not understand its nature, but they tried to exorcise it by giving it names—it was the stupidity of the crowd, it was hurry and haste, it was Mass Production, Babbittry, Our Business Civilization; or perhaps it was the Machine, which had been developed to satisfy men's needs, but which was now controlling those needs and forcing its standardized products upon us by means of omnipresent advertising and omnipresent vulgarity—the Voice of the Machine, the Tyranny of the Mob. The same social mechanism that fed and clothed the body was starving the emotions, was closing every path toward creativeness and self-expression.

There was no political theory that seemed to promise a haven to the individual spirit. All the moderate reformers, including the right-wing Socialists, had been discredited by the war and the Treaty of Versailles; all the radicals were impractical and silly. Guild socialists, anarchists and syndicalists belonged to a forgotten age of innocent aspirations. The Communists were shrill futile voices crying out that we should imitate Russia —and to what purpose? The Russian experiment was interesting to watch, but it would probably fail. If it succeeded, writers liked to say that it would merely combine the mechanical efficiency of the West with a terrifying system of mob control; it would lead toward a utopia of identical human ants, a dullard's paradise, and the liberty of the individual would wither from within. Russia was like America: they were two formidable giants marching against the old European culture to which writers clung, and Europe was weakening before their onslaughts.

It seemed in those days that nobody could hasten or direct the heavy march of history or hope for any political solution of his problems: the individual would have to solve them for himself. He could either adjust himself to society by yielding to its standards, or else, if he was too proud to accept that course, he could escape society by seeking new places, new ideals, new ways of living. He could either surrender or else assert his independence by running away.

Yet there was one political event of the later 1920s that brought a great many writers together for a common purpose. It did more than that, for it aroused and unified a larger group with which writers are more or less closely affiliated. At this point I am not referring to the group composed of editors, commercial artists and advertising men that writers were meeting socially if they lived in Manhattan or Connecticut. I am thinking about another group scattered over the country and united by its manner of thinking more than by its economic interests; the best name for it is "the intellectuals."

Nobody likes the name, but there is nothing else that will take its place, "the intelligentsia" being too foreign, "the elite" too flattering, "the highbrows" and "the longhairs" too un-friendly, while "the liberals" is too contentious and confusing. The intellectuals can be defined as the part of the population that tries to think independently and to value ideas without regard to personal interests or popular prejudice. They are now fairly numerous, to judge by the sales of their favorite books and magazines, yet the history of their class has been surprisingly brief in this country. It began to be conscious of itself in the years after 1900; it played a large part in the cultural renaissance that preceded the war; it was terrified and rendered politically sterile by the postwar reaction. During the early 1920s it appeared to be chiefly interested in moral revolt, progressive education and Freudian psychology. But the Sacco-Vanzetti case, in 1927, was another crisis in its development.

There were several features of the case that stirred the intellectuals profoundly. First of all there was the situation of two men tried unjustly and sentenced to death, the old story of innocence endangered. There was the fact that these men were radicals and had been arrested during the Palmer Raids, when the intellectuals had also been threatened. There was the high smugness of the Massachusetts officials, some of whom turned themselves into caricatures of everything that artists hate in the bourgeoisie. There were the international echoes of the case: the riots in Paris, Berlin and London, the general strikes in Rosario and Montevideo, the bombs exploded in Sofia, Nice, Basel and Buenos Aires. Then, overshadowing all other issues, there were the personalities of two men who had spent seven years between life and death, seven years of being threatened, praised, lied about and continually tortured with hope. Most prisoners would have broken down or developed illusions of grandeur. These two—little, impulsive, confiding Sacco and big, mustachioed Vanzetti—managed in their different fashions to remain skeptical and human, thanking their good friends, contriving presents for their lawyers and, incidentally, writing more eloquently than all the bigwigs who made speeches for and against them—the artists for, the politicians against. It is no wonder that they aroused a blind hatred and a fanatical loyalty.

It was the intellectuals rather than the labor unions who conducted their defense. Some of the unions struck and demonstrated; the radical parties held literally thousands of meetings (although they regarded Sacco and Vanzetti merely as two more victims in the class war); but the intellectuals for once assumed most of the responsibility: they raised funds, issued statements, suggested new appeals to new courts. "Artists and Writers Appeal for Sacco," the newspapers would announce. "Intellectuals Ask New Sacco Respite" — "Appeal Signed by Hundreds of Professional Men and Women Is Sent to Fuller." At the very end the intellectuals even came out into the streets and got themselves arrested, like workers on the picket line of a strike that is being broken.

Boston on the night of the execution was a city beleaguered by its own fears of violent revolt. The public buildings were guarded; the streets were heavily patrolled. In the vicinity of Charlestown Prison, people were warned not to leave their houses. The prison itself was armed and garrisoned as if to beat off an attacking army. Five hundred special patrolmen, detectives and state constables had been summoned to reinforce the prison guards. Riot guns and tear-gas bombs were stacked inside the gate. The top of the prison wall was lined with machine guns and searchlights in clusters of three. An advance guard of mounted police was posted at some distance from the prison to hold back the crowd. On the other side, facing the river, the prison was guarded by marine patrol boats, bright with searchlights and flares. And all this armament by land and water, all this infantry, cavalry and artillery, was posted there to defend the prison—against just whom, just what? It is a question that the Massachusetts authorities could hardly answer. The only movement they could possibly interpret as aggressive was a protest parade of three hundred intellectuals, led by Ruth Hale, that started toward Charlestown late in the evening. They were unarmed and pacific and they scattered at the first charge by the mounted police.

Afterward I talked with some of the people who joined in that strange nocturnal march. They knew that it was absolutely futile, that everything had been done that could be done, yet as long as Sacco and Vanzetti were alive they could not sit in a hall and talk and wait; they had to make a last united protest. Then came the execution, the catastrophe that nobody had really believed could happen. Suddenly they wept or fell silent, they separated, and many of them walked the streets alone, all night. Just as the fight for a common cause had brought the intellectuals together, so the defeat drove them apart, each back into his personal isolation.

For a time it seemed that Sacco and Vanzetti would be forgotten, in the midst of the stock-market boom and the exhilaration of easy money. Yet the effects of the case continued to operate, in a subterranean way, and after a few years they would once more appear on the surface.

3: The Roaring Boy

Writing about the late 1920s and remembering how disastrously they ended, one is tempted to dwell on everything in those years that now seems ominous or frantic or merely ill directed. One says too little about other qualities of the period: its high spirits, its industriousness, its candor and its reckless freedom. One talks about the big parties—especially the later ones that broke up in hysterical quarrels—and forgets to mention the long mornings at one's desk, the afternoons in the garden, the after-supper hours of reading by a kerosene lamp while embers glowed through the cracks in the kitchen stove.

We stayed in the country till very late in the autumn—I am speaking now of my immediate friends—but most of our winters were spent in New York, in furnished rooms or cold-water flats. I remember the good winter when we used to meet two or three times a week at Squarcialupi's Restaurant on Perry Street. We were all writing poems then, and, sitting after dinner around the long table in the back room, we used to read them without self-consciousness, knowing that nobody there would either be bored by them or gush over them ignorantly. Kenneth Burke would wipe his spectacles with a napkin and give an affirmative "Mhmmm." — "That's good enough to read again," Allen Tate might say; "I'd like to catch the rhyme scheme." John Squarcialupi would stand in the kitchen doorway listening, with a bottle of red wine in each hand. He was an operatic baritone who had missed his career, and he used to sing for us late at night after the other guests had gone home; if we applauded wildly enough the wine was free. We were all about twenty-six, a good age, and looked no older; we were interested only in writing and in keeping alive while we wrote, and we had the feeling of being invulnerable—we didn't see how anything in the world could ever touch us, certainly not the crazy desire to earn and spend more money and be pointed out as prominent people. There was only Hart Crane who complained of being "caught like a rat in a trap" and displayed angers and enthusiasms out of proportion to the objects that aroused them, a first foreshadowing of hysteria and suicide.[2]

[2] On his way home from Mexico in April 1932, Hart committed suicide by diving from the stern of the steamship *Orizaba*.

A few of the early meetings to plan and organize the *New Masses* were held in the same restaurant, with different people attending them: Mike Gold, John Dos Passos, Joe Freeman. One evening Dos Passos called over to our table self-derisively, "Intellectual workers of the world unite, you have nothing to lose but your brains." The others glanced up at us without much interest, feeling that we weren't serious about politics. Usually the radical writers met at another Italian restaurant, on East Tenth Street, with an upstairs room that was big enough to accommodate a fund-raising party of fifty or a hundred. In those prohibition days every group had its favorite Italian restaurants and Irish or German saloons; everyone's wallet was stuffed with cards that were supposed to be shown at the locked doors. . . . I remember being taken to an unfamiliar saloon —it was in the winter of 1925-26—and finding that the back room was full of young writers and their wives just home from Paris. They were all telling stories about Hemingway, whose first book had just appeared, and they were talking in what I afterward came to recognize as the Hemingway dialect—tough, matter-of-fact and confidential. In the middle of the evening one of them rose, took off his jacket and used it to show how he would dominate a bull.

About that time it became possible for young men of promise to support themselves by writing novels and biographies. The book trade was prospering, new publishers were competing for new authors, and suddenly it seemed that everybody you knew was living on publishers' advances—sometimes a hundred dollars a month for an extended period, sometimes three hundred or five hundred in a flat sum—toward the writing of a book that might or might not be finished. Most of the books financed by publishers were not worth writing at all, but some of them were good and a few were enormously successful—the man you had seen night after night eating spaghetti at the next table in

a cheap Italian restaurant and counting his money before he
ordered dessert or a glass of red wine would suddenly disappear,
would be snatched away into a floodlighted world of press
interviews, trips by airplane to Hollywood, sunbasking on the
Riviera, well-advertised books that regularly appeared on the
best-seller lists. In those days writing could be a profitable business, but it was a perilous business, too, and the ordeal by success was fatal to almost as many talents as was the ordeal by
failure.

I remember the time—it must have been the winter of
1927–28—when it seemed that New York had been suddenly
inundated with pretty girls from Smith and Vassar and
wherever, all of them determined to lead their own lives and
have a lot of interesting love affairs—they wore leather jackets
like commissars and had bright natural-pink cheeks and were
so full of vitality that the young men they allowed to escort them
seemed colorless and dry. They had been very young flappers
during the war; now they were learning to talk about "our
own" generation, which they contrasted with "your lost" generation, and it was hard for us to get used to the idea that there
were rebels younger than ourselves, who regarded us as relics
of an age that was passing. But the relics managed to enjoy
themselves almost as much as did the Smith College girls. When
we put together an issue of a little magazine we did the work
gaily and in common, as if we were taking part in a husking
bee.

Since the disappearance of *Broom* and *Secession* my friends
hadn't had any magazine of their own, although once as a lark
we got out the first number of something called *Aesthete 1925*,
which was intended as a bundle of squibs to be tossed in the
direction of Ernest Boyd and his friends; the squibs went off
without making much noise. We never scraped together money
enough to print a second number of *Aesthete*, but later we were

asked to furnish material for special issues of the *Little Review* and *transition*. The procedure was the same in all these undertakings: we hired a suite of rooms in an old-fashioned hotel and appeared there at nine in the morning, each with his portable typewriter and a manuscript or two. By working together all day—rewriting, arguing, jotting down new ideas and exploding into laughter—we would have the issue finished at four or five in the afternoon, and then we set out together for new adventures. After one of the magazine-writing bees we took our wives to the Savoy Ballroom in Harlem; after another we all attended a publisher's tea to which only one of us had been invited. It was being held to celebrate the publication of a book by a bewildered English nobleman. There were hundreds of guests and gallons of punch, and the nobleman's book, after being mentioned briefly, was forgotten for the afternoon and forever.

That was the great era of publishers' teas, so called, at which the usual beverage was Fish House punch. Year after year there seemed to be more teas, more guests at each of them and stronger punch for the guests to drink. The biggest tea was for Peggy Hopkins Joyce, who had written or let her name be signed to a book about her four successive million-dollar marriages. It was held in the ballroom of the Ritz-Carlton and an adjoining suite of rooms. There were three punch bowls, with a mob around each of them, and music was furnished by two orchestras. I wandered into one of the smaller rooms and managed to keep two strangers from coming to blows about Ernest Hemingway. By that time Hemingway's influence had spread far beyond the circle of those who had known him in Paris. The Smith College girls in New York were modeling themselves after Lady Brett in *The Sun Also Rises*. Hundreds of bright young men from the Middle West were trying to be Hemingway heroes, talking in tough understatements from the sides of their mouths—"but just cut them open," I said, "and you'll find that their souls are little white flowers."

It doesn't seem to me now that we had any right to be scornful. We had our own affectations, which we failed to recognize, and our innocent notions about leading the good life. In those days I shared with some of my friends—not all of them—the notion that we could retain our personal independence by reducing our needs to a minimum, that is, to the plainest sort of food, shelter, clothing and transportation; everything else was free. If we tried to earn more we should spend more, and thereby raise our standard of living to a level which we could maintain only by writing best-sellers or by finding best-paying jobs, which one is always afraid of losing; we should be caught in the squirrel cage. On the other hand, if we spent most of the year in the country; if we lived in old farmhouses without conveniences [3] —they were easy to find in those days and rented for ten dollars a month; if we grew our own vegetables, made our own cider, dressed in denim or khaki and traveled the back roads on foot or in the oldest Model T that would hold together; if we associated with others who lived in the same fashion, then we could pick our jobs, take our time over them, do our best work and live as it were on a private island, while profiting from the surplus wealth of a culture enslaved by commodities:

> The merchant serves the purse,
> The eater serves his meat;
> 'Tis the day of the chattel,
> Web to weave and corn to grind;
> Things are in the saddle,
> And ride mankind.

[3] Some of the year-round country dwellers mentioned in this narrative held out for a long time against modern conveniences, although most of them yielded in the end. Robert Coates wired his house for electricity and installed a bathroom in 1938. Kenneth Burke had no electricity in his New

In those days hardly anyone read Emerson, but we all admired Thoreau in a distant fashion; the trouble was that we didn't carry his doctrine to the same extreme of self-dependence. Some of us accepted too much from publishers and Wall Street plungers—too many invitations to parties and week-ends, too many commissions for work we didn't really want to do but it paid well; we took our little portion of the easy money that seemed to be everywhere, and we thereby engaged or committed ourselves without meaning to do so. We became part of the system we were trying to evade, and it defeated us from within, not from without; our hearts beat to its tempo. We laughed too much, sang too much, changed the record and danced too hard, drank more than we intended (for wasn't the liquor free?)—we fell in love unwisely, quarreled without knowing why, and after a few years we were, in Zelda Fitzgerald's phrase, "lost and driven now like the rest."

From earlier days I remember how Hart Crane used to write his poems. There would be a Sunday-afternoon party on Tory Hill, near Patterson, New York, just across the state line from Sherman, Connecticut. Besides Hart there might be eight or ten of us present: the Tates, the Josephsons, the Cowleys, the Browns—or perhaps Bob Coates and Peter Blume, both curly redheads, the novelist Nathan Asch [4] and Jack Wheelwright with his white week-end shoes and kempt and ruly hair; at one time or another all of them lived in the neighborhood. The

Jersey farmhouse until 1949, even with a power line thirty feet from the front door. His excuse for yielding at last was that he couldn't buy good kerosene any longer. Philip Hillyer Smith, the author of *Perennial Harvest,* still spends his winters in Sherman without conveniences of any sort, except a pump in the kitchen across from the wood-burning stove.

[4] Asch wrote a cycle of stories about life in the Tory Hill neighborhood (*The Valley,* 1935), and Slater Brown wrote a novel about it (*The Burning Wheel,* 1942).

party would be held, like others, in the repaired but unpainted and unremodeled farmhouse that Bill Brown had bought shortly after his marriage. When Bill was making the repairs, with Hart as his carpenter's helper, they had received a visit from Uncle Charlie Jennings, the former owner, an old-fashioned, cider-drinking New Englander who lived across the line in Sherman. Uncle Charlie had the plans explained to him and said, "I'm glad to see you an't putting in one of those bathrooms. I always said they was a passing fad." That was one of the stories told on a Sunday afternoon. I can't remember the other stories or why we laughed at them so hard; I can remember only the general atmosphere of youth and poverty and good humor.

We would play croquet, wrangling, laughing, shouting over every wicket, with a pitcher of cider half hidden in the tall grass beside the court; or else we would sit beside the fireplace in the big, low-ceilinged kitchen, while a spring rain soaped the windowpanes. Hart—we sometimes called him the Roaring Boy—would laugh twice as hard as the rest of us and drink at least twice as much hard cider, while contributing more than his share of the crazy metaphors and overblown epithets. Gradually he would fall silent, and a little later he disappeared. In lulls that began to interrupt the laughter, now Hart was gone, we would hear a new hubbub through the walls of his room —the phonograph playing a Cuban rumba, the typewriter clacking simultaneously; then the phonograph would run down and the typewriter stop while Hart changed the record, perhaps to a torch song, perhaps to Ravel's *Bolero*. Sometimes he stamped across the room, declaiming to the four walls and the slow spring rain.

An hour later, after the rain had stopped, he would appear in the kitchen or on the croquet court, his face brick-red, his eyes burning, his already iron-gray hair bristling straight up from his skull. He would be chewing a five-cent cigar which he had forgotten to light. In his hands would be two or three sheets of typewritten manuscript, with words crossed out and new lines scrawled in. "R-read that," he would say. "Isn't that the grreatest poem ever written?"

We would read it dutifully, Allen Tate perhaps making a profound comment. The rest of us would get practically nothing out of it except the rhythm like that of a tom-tom and a few startling images. But we would all agree that it was absolutely superb. In Hart's state of exultation there was nothing else we could say without driving him to rage or tears.

But that is neither the beginning nor the real end of the story. Hart, as I later discovered, would have been meditating over that particular poem for months or even years, scribbling lines on pieces of paper that he carried in his pockets and meanwhile waiting for the moment of genuine inspiration when he could put it all together. In that respect he reminded me of another friend, Jim Butler, a painter and a famous killer of woodchucks, who instead of shooting at them from a distance with a high-powered rifle and probably missing them, used to frighten them into their holes and wait until they came out again. Sometimes, he said, when they were slow about it he used to charm them out by playing a mouth organ. In the same way Hart tried to charm his inspiration out of its hiding place with a Cuban rumba and a pitcher of hard cider.

As for the end of the story, it might be delayed for a week or a month. Painfully, persistently—and dead sober—Hart would revise his new poem, clarifying the images, correcting the meter and searching for the right word hour after hour. "The seal's wide spindrift gaze toward paradise," in the second of his "Voyages," was the result of a search that lasted for several days. At first he had written, "The seal's *findrinny* gaze toward paradise," but someone had objected that he was using a nonexistent word. Hart and I worked in the same office that year, and I remember his frantic searches through *Webster's Unabridged* and the big *Standard,* his trips to the library—on office time—and his reports of consultations with old sailors in South Street speakeasies. "Findrinny" he could never find,[5] but after paging through the dictionary again he decided that "spindrift" was almost as good and he declaimed the new line exultantly. Even after one of his manuscripts had been sent to *Poetry* or the *Dial* and perhaps had been accepted, he would still have changes to make. There were many poets of the 1920s who worked hard to be obscure, veiling a simple idea in phrases that grew more labored and opaque with each revision of a poem. With Crane it was the original meaning that was complicated and difficult; his revisions brought it out more clearly. He said, making fun of himself, "I practice invention to the brink of intelligibility." The truth was that he had something to say and wanted to be understood, but not at the cost of weakening or simplifying his original vision.

Just what were these "meanings" and these "visions"? They were different, of course, in each new poem, but it seems to me that most of them expressed a purpose that was also revealed in his method of composition. Essentially Crane was a poet of ecstasy or frenzy or intoxication; you can choose your word depending on how much you like his work. Essentially he was using rhyme and meter and fantastic images to convey the emotional states that were induced in him by alcohol, jazz, machinery, laughter, intellectual stimulation, the shape and sound of words and the madness of New York in the late Coolidge era. At their worst his poems are ineffective unless read in something approximating the same atmosphere, with a drink at your elbow, the phonograph blaring and somebody shouting into your ear,

[5] After Hart's death Bill Brown found the word in *Moby Dick,* where Hart must have seen it originally.

"Isn't that grreat!" At their best, however, the poems do their work unaided except by their proper glitter and violence. At their very best, as in "The River," they have an emotional force that has not been equaled by any other American poet of our century.

Hart drank to write: he drank to invoke the visions that his poems are intended to convey. But the recipe could be followed for a few years at the most, and it was completely effective only for two periods of about a month each, in 1926 and 1927, when working at top speed he finished most of the poems included in *The Bridge.* After that more and more alcohol was needed, so much of it that when the visions came he was incapable of putting them on paper. He drank in Village speakeasies and Brooklyn waterfront dives; he insulted everyone within hearing or shouted that he was Christopher Marlowe; then waking after a night spent with a drunken sailor, he drank again to forget his sense of guilt. He really forgot it, for the moment. By the following afternoon all the outrageous things he had done at night became merely funny, became an epic misadventure to be embroidered—"And then I began throwing furniture out the window," he would say with an enormous chuckle. Everybody would laugh and Hart would pound the table, calling for another bottle of wine. At a certain stage in drunkenness he gave himself and others the illusion of completely painless brilliance; words poured out of him, puns, metaphors, epigrams, visions; but soon the high spirits would be mingled with obsessions—"See that man staring at us, I think he's a detective" —and then the violence would start all over again, to be followed next day by the repentance that became a form of boasting. In this repeated process there was no longer a free hour for writing down his poems, or a week or a month in which to revise them.

Even before his disastrous trips to Southern California—
which he called "this Pollyanna greasepaint pinkpoodle paradise"—to France and to Mexico, Hart's adventures had become
a many-chaptered saga. There was, for example, his quarrel
with Bill and Sue Brown, when he swept out of their house
at midnight, vowing never to come back. But the Browns lived
alone on a hillside, and the path to Mrs. Addie Turner's gaunt
barn of a house, where Hart was living, twisted through a second-
growth woodland in which even a sober man might have lost
his way. About three o'clock the Browns were wakened by the
noise of Hart crashing through the bushes and then stamping
on their front porch. Soon they heard him mutter, "Brrowns,
Brrowns, you can't get away from them," as if he were penned
and circumscribed by Browns. On another evening that started
in much the same fashion, he had been talking excitedly about
Mexico. He got home safely this time, and he began furiously
typing a letter to the Mexican President in Spanish, of which
he knew only a few words. He blamed his typewriter for not
being a linguist and threw it out the window without bothering
to open the sash. When we passed the house next morning we
saw it lying in a tangle of black ribbon. In it was a sheet of paper
on which we could read the words, *"Mi caro Presidente Calles"*
—in Spanish that was all the typewriter could say.

I suppose that no other American poet, not even Poe, heaped
so many troubles on his friends or had his transgressions so long
endured. Scenes, shouts, obscenities, broken furniture were the
commonplaces of an evening with Hart, and for a long time
nobody did anything about it, except to complain in a humorous
way. The 1920s had their moral principles, one of which was
not to pass moral judgments on other people, especially if they
were creative artists. We should have been violating the principle if we had condemned Hart for his dissipations on the waterfront or had even scolded him for his behavior in company. But

the real reason he was forgiven was that he had an abounding warmth of affection for the people around him. To hear him roar with laughter, to receive his clumsy, kind attentions when ill, to hear his honest and discerning evaluations of other people's work, offered without a trace of malice, and to realize that he always praised his friends except to their faces was enough to cancel out his misdeeds, even though they were renewed weekly and at the end almost daily. It was Hart himself who took to avoiding his friends, largely, I think, through a sense of guilt. During the last three years of his life he was always seeking new companions, being spoiled by them for a time and then avoiding them in turn.

One of my last serious talks with him must have taken place in November 1929. Hart had come back from Paris early that summer after getting into a fight with the police and spending a week in prison; his rich friend Harry Crosby had hired a lawyer for him, paid his fine and given him money for the passage home. The Crosbys' little publishing house, the Black Sun Press, had undertaken to issue a limited edition of *The Bridge,* and Hart had spent the summer and fall trying to finish the group of poems he had started five years before. He had worked desperately in his sober weeks, although they had been interspersed with drinking bouts. One afternoon I arrived at the Turner house to find Peter Blume sitting on Hart's chest and Bill Brown sitting on his feet; he had been smashing the furniture and throwing his books out the window and there was no other way to stop him. Hart was gasping between his clenched teeth, "You can kill me—but you can't—destroy—*The Bridge.* It's finished—it's on the *Bremen*—on its way—to Paris."

For the rest of the week he was sober and busy cleaning up the wreckage of his room. I called one day to take him for a walk. Hart began telling me about the Crosbys: Caresse was beautiful and gay; Harry was mad in a genial fashion; he would do anything and everything that entered his mind. They were coming to New York in December and Hart was eager for me to meet them. . . . We stumbled in the frozen ruts of the road that led up Hardscrabble Hill. I had always refrained from interfering with Hart's life, but at last I was making the effort to give him good advice. I said, bringing the words out haltingly, that he had been devoting himself to the literature of ecstasy and that it involved more of a psychological strain than most writers could stand. Now, having finished *The Bridge,* perhaps he might shift over to the literature of experience, as Goethe had done (I was trying to persuade him by using great examples). It might be years before he was ready to undertake another group of poems as ambitious as those he had just completed. In the meantime he might cultivate his talent for writing quiet and thoughtful prose.

Hart cut me short. "Oh, you mean that I shouldn't drink so much."

Yes, I said after an uncomfortable pause, I had meant that partly and I had also meant that his drinking was, among other things, the result of a special attitude toward living and writing. If he changed the attitude and tried to write something different he would feel less need of intoxication. Hart looked at me sullenly and did not answer; he had gone so far on the path toward self-destruction that none of his friends could touch him any longer. He was more lost and driven than the others, and although he kept fleeing toward distant havens of refuge he felt in his heart that he could not escape himself. That night I dreamed of him and woke in the darkness feeling that he was already doomed, already dead.

4: No Escape

The late 1920s were an age of islands, real and metaphorical.
They were an age when Americans by thousands and tens of
thousands were scheming to take the next boat for the South
Seas or the West Indies, or better still for Paris, from which they
could scatter to Majorca, Corsica, Capri or the isles of Greece.
Paris itself was a modern city that seemed islanded in the past,
and there were island countries, like Mexico, where Americans
could feel that they had escaped from everything that oppressed
them in a business civilization. Or without leaving home they
could build themselves private islands of art or philosophy; or
else—and this was a frequent solution—they could create social
islands in the shadow of the skyscrapers, groups of close friends
among whom they could live as unconstrainedly as in a Poly-
nesian valley, live without moral scruples or modern conveniences, live in the pure moment, live gaily on gin and love and
two lamb chops broiled over a coal fire in the grate. That was
part of the Greenwich Village idea, and soon it was being
copied in Boston, San Francisco, everywhere.

The late 1920s were an age of coteries. They were a time when
many of the larger social groups, especially those based on residence in a good suburb or membership in a country club, were
losing their cohesiveness. Always at dances there were smaller
groups that gathered with a confidential air—"Let's get together
after the crowd goes home," one heard them say. Prosperous
Americans, especially the younger married people, but some of
the older ones too, had begun to form cliques or sets that dis-
regarded the conventions. Each of the little sets had its gin

parties and private jokes, each had its illusion of being free, sophisticated and set apart from the mass that believed in Rotarian ideals—till slowly each group discovered that it had dozens of counterparts in every big American city. In those days almost everyone seemed to be looking for an island, and escape from the mass was becoming a mass movement.

There is a danger in using the word "escape." It carries with it an overtone of moral disapproval; it suggests evasion and cowardice and flight from something that ought to be faced. Yet there is no real shame in retreating from an impossible situation or in fleeing from an enemy that seems too powerful to attack. Many writers of the 1920s regarded our commercial society as an enemy of that sort and believed that their only hope lay in finding a refuge from it. Escape was the central theme of poems, essays, novels by the hundred; it was the motive underlying many types of action that seemed impulsive and contradictory. Most of its manifestations, however, could be grouped under three general headings.

There was first the *escape into art,* a tendency discussed at some length in the chapter on the Dadaists, and second there was the *escape toward the primitive*. People felt vaguely that the most oppressive feature of modern civilization was its binding and falsifying of the natural instincts. To achieve happiness they should seek a life in which their instincts would have full play —perhaps they could plow the rich earth and plant and harvest; perhaps they could sail off on a three-masted schooner into the South Seas; or perhaps they could revolt against the falsity of urban standards without leaving the city streets. Indeed, it was in New York and other large cities that this escape into primitivism was carried farthest and assumed a dozen different forms. It was expressed, for example, in the enthusiasm of tired intellectuals for Negro dances and music, the spirituals, the blues, Black Bottom and *Emperor Jones;* time and again one was told that the Negroes had retained a direct virility that the whites had lost through being overeducated. It was similarly expressed in the omnipresent cult of youth, which seemed to depend on the notion that very young people are more simple, physical and instinctive. It was expressed in the sort of body worship that would be codified into Nudism, and again it was expressed in an intense preoccupation with sex and with the overcoming of sexual inhibitions—wives deceived their husbands joylessly, out of a sense of duty, and husbands tried so hard to be natural that they developed into monsters. The search for the primitive was becoming confused with the hysteria of civilized frustration. Meanwhile, by those with money enough to get away, the same tendency was being expressed in a search for adventure, for natural dangers met face to face, lions shot with bow and arrows, sharks harpooned, mountains conquered on skis, the five oceans braved in an open boat.

Some of the methods of escape falling under the first two categories of Art and the Primitive were described by Nathanael West in a tender and recklessly imaginative novel that had few readers.[6] *Miss Lonelyhearts* (1933) has for its hero a young newspaperman who is hired to write a column of advice to the lovelorn. "The job," he says, explaining his own predicament, "is a circulation stunt and the whole staff considers it a joke. . . . He too considers the job a joke, but after several months at it, the joke begins to escape him. He sees that the majority of the letters are profoundly humble pleas for moral and spiritual advice, that they are inarticulate expressions of

[6] When it was reissued after the author's death, *Miss Lonelyhearts* had a somewhat larger public. West, born in 1904, spent the last five years of his life working for various moving-picture studios, but he found time to write what is still the best of the Hollywood novels, *The Day of the Locust* (1939). He was driving back from a hunting trip when he was killed in an automobile accident on December 22, 1940, the day after his Hollywood neighbor F. Scott Fitzgerald died of a heart attack.

genuine suffering. He also discovers that his correspondents take him seriously. For the first time in his life he is forced to examine the values by which he lives. This examination shows him that he is the victim of the joke and not its perpetrator."

Miss Lonelyhearts—that is how he signs his column—has a nervous breakdown and takes to his bed. Into his room bursts Shrike, the managing editor. Shrike is an obviously unhappy man who has adjusted himself to his world by becoming completely cynical; his one joy is to shatter the illusions of those about him, and particularly of Miss Lonelyhearts, who is his favorite target. Overhearing a snatch of conversation, he bursts out:

"My friend, I agree with Betty, you're an escapist. But I do not agree that the soil is the proper method for you to use. There are other methods, and for your edification I shall describe them. But first let us do the escape to the soil, as recommended by Betty:

"You are fed up with the city and its teeming millions. . . . So what do you do? So you buy a farm and walk behind your horse's moist behind, no collar, or tie, plowing your broad swift acres. As you turn up the rich black soil, the wind carries the smell of pine and dung across the fields and the rhythm of an old, old work enters your soul. To this rhythm you sow and weep and chivy your kine, not kin or kind, between the pregnant rows of corn and taters. Your step becomes the heavy sexual step of a dance-drunk Indian and you tread the seed down into the female earth. . . ."

Miss Lonelyhearts turns his face to the wall and pulls the covers over his head. But Shrike raises his voice and talks on while the sick man tries not to hear him.

"Let us now consider the South Seas:

"You live in a thatch hut with the daughter of a king, a slim young maiden in whose eyes is an ancient wisdom. Her breasts are golden speckled pears, her belly a melon, and her odor is like nothing so much as a jungle fern. In the evening, on the blue lagoon, under the silvery moon, to your love you croon in the soft sylabelew and voca-belew of her languorous tongorour. Your body is golden brown like hers, and tourists have need of the indignant finger of the missionary to point you out. They envy you your breech clout and carefree laugh and little brown bride and fingers instead of forks. But you don't return their envy. . . . And so you dream away the days, fishing, hunting, dancing, swimming, kissing and picking flowers to twine in your hair. . . .

"Well, my friend, what do you think of the South Seas?"

Miss Lonelyhearts pretends to be asleep. But Shrike is not fooled; he talks on inescapably:

"Art! Be an artist or a writer. When you are cold, warm yourself before the flaming tints of Titian, when you are hungry nourish yourself with great spiritual foods by listening to the noble periods of Bach, the harmonies of Brahms and the thunder of Beethoven. . . . Tell them to keep their society whores and pressed duck with oranges. For you *l'art vivant,*.the living art, as you call it. Tell them that you know that your shoes are broken and that there are pimples on your face, yes, and that you have buck teeth and a club foot, but that you don't care, for tomorrow they are playing Beethoven's last quartets in Carnegie Hall and at home you have Shakespeare's plays in one volume."

And Shrike continues. He describes the escape by hedonism, not neglecting the pleasures of the mind—"You fornicate under pictures by Matisse and Picasso, you drink from Renaissance glassware, and often you spend an evening beside the fireplace with Proust and an apple"—he describes the escape by drugs, the escape by suicide, while Miss Lonelyhearts trembles beneath the covers; finally he describes the escape by religion, the escape to Christ, which Miss Lonelyhearts wants to choose. . . . But curiously enough he does not describe the commonest of the forms of escape adopted during that period, the escape by sea, by simply packing one's bags and announcing that one was going to the South of France to write—"and don't expect me home for Christmas, not this year or next, because I'm leaving this hell-hole forever."

Ever since 1920 there had been no break in the movement toward France. Artists and writers, art photographers, art salesmen, dancers, movie actors, Guggenheim fellows, divorcées dabbling in sculpture, unhappy ex-débutantes wondering whether a literary career wouldn't take the place of marriage —a whole world of people with and without talent but sharing the same ideals happily deserted the homeland. Each year some of them returned while others crowded into their places: the migration continued at a swifter rate. But after the middle of the decade the motives behind it underwent an imperceptible but real change in emphasis. The earlier exiles had been driven abroad by a hatred of American dullness and puritanism, yet primarily they had traveled *in search of* something—leisure, freedom, knowledge, some quality that was offered by an older culture. Their successors felt the same desires, but felt them a little less strongly. Instead of being drawn ahead, they were propelled from behind, pushed eastward by the need for *getting away from* something. They were not so much exiles as refugees.

They began to scatter over the earth like fragments of an eruption. F. Scott Fitzgerald said that Americans

. . . were wandering ever more widely—friends seemed eternally bound for Russia, Persia, Abyssinia and Central Africa. And by 1928, Paris had grown suffocating. With each new shipment of Americans spewed up by the boom the quality fell off, until toward the end there was something sinister about the crazy boatloads. They were no longer the simple pa and ma and son and daughter, infinitely superior in their qualities of kindness and curiosity to the corresponding class in Europe, but fantastic neanderthals who believed something, something vague, that you remembered from a very cheap novel. . . . There were citizens traveling in luxury in 1928 and 1929 who, in the distortion of their new condition, had the human value of pekinese, bivalves, cretins, goats.

But those weren't the people that made Paris seem suffocating to the refugees of art. Creatures like them were easy to avoid: one had merely to keep away from the big hotels, the banks and the night clubs in Montmartre. The refugees were also trying to escape something more subtle, some quality of American civilization that they carried within themselves. Wherever half a dozen of them gathered together, the quality reappeared and the same experience was re-enacted. There was a first glow of enthusiasm; friends were told about this marvelous untouched place and came hastening to enjoy it—as Fitzgerald said of life near the Cap d'Antibes in 1926, "whatever happened seemed to have something to do with art." Then, as the colony grew, there were jealousies, boredom, gossip, intrigues; some Americans became landlords and quarreled with their American tenants— but by this time there were Germans, too, and a broken-down English viscount and a handful of Russian émigrés, while the natives were grasping the opportunity of exploiting all these visitors by raising prices and installing a jazz band in the principal café. Artists complained that it was impossible to work here any longer with all these interruptions; writers again felt that something was constraining them, interfering with their thoughts—and the colony began to dissolve, a good half of it moving onward in search of a place that was still unspoiled by themselves.

All over the Mediterranean lands, but especially on the Riviera and in the Balearic Islands, colonies of the sort sprang up and flourished and eventually sent forth out-wanderers in search of a deeper solitude. It was only natural that the more energetic pilgrims should eventually reach the goal they had been pursuing. Some morning, inevitably, they woke and found themselves in a town that was virgin of tourists. It might be in the western isles of Greece; it might be at Lebda on the Tripolitanian coast, or in Dalmatia, or perhaps on the northern edge of the great desert, at Biskra in an off-season—at any rate they had finally escaped from all the things they hated. They sat in the one café looking out across the sun-hallucinated square and saw walls and crazy houses that must have been standing in the Middle Ages, with nowhere a sign of new construction, nowhere a Woolworth Building or a Chrysler Tower. There were no machines, not even a coffee mill or a Ford roadster; there was no false shame about the functions of the body. In the middle of the square a little Negro girl had lifted her skirts and was squatting oblivious of the village sheik who passed her in his black and white burnoose. No belfry marked the hours: tomorrow and yesterday had intermingled.

Here at last one was free to live and write in one's own fashion. Here one could lie abed all day and work through the night— or, if one chose, get roaring drunk, smoke hashish, sleep with the native girls, indulge in any sort of orgy without fearing the police or even public censure. Here again one could write without thought of editorial deadlines or critics asking what it meant; one could write exactly as one pleased. . . . But the days passed by and the great novel or poem was not even started. The refugees were undergoing a peculiar experience. In Paris or the South of France they had written stories about their childhood, about Michigan or Nebraska, stories the hero of which was a sensitive boy oppressed by his surroundings. Later, when this feeling of oppression faded in their minds, they had begun to write about their new friends in Europe, but without the same enthusiasm; they were easily interrupted. Here in this ultimate refuge there were no distractions whatever, nothing to keep them from working except the terrifying discovery that they had nothing now to say. Boredom and loneliness set in. They began to find that the food was bad, that there were fleas in the hotel, a dozen minor discomforts—and suddenly one morning they packed their bags and started north toward Paris, where for all the tourists like fantastic neanderthals, still there were people who spoke your own language.

Perhaps they even felt homesick for America, but unless they had run out of money there seemed to be no special reason for returning. New York, in the effort to overcome its native vices, had adopted those of Paris. Everywhere in the world of the arts, which had now allied itself with the world of cosmopolitan wealth, there existed the same atmosphere of frustration and purposeless tension; the laughter was keyed too high on both sides of the Atlantic. "By 1927 a widespread neurosis began to be evident, faintly signaled, like a nervous beating of the feet, by the popularity of crossword puzzles." Again the quotation is from F. Scott Fitzgerald, whose novels and stories are in some ways the best record of this whole period. He was living near the Cap d'Antibes, where "pretty much of anything went," but he kept in touch with his friends at home and was amused or disturbed at what he heard from them. "I remember," he says, "a fellow expatriate opening a letter from a mutual friend of ours, urging him to come home and be revitalized by the hardy, bracing qualities of the native soil. It was a strong letter and it affected us both deeply, until we noticed that it was headed from a nerve sanitarium in Pennsylvania."

There was no escape. Whatever the path they followed and the principle they chose to guide them—whether they drank gin cocktails in Manhattan, or retired into Connecticut to be close to the soil, or wandered from island to island in the Pacific, or tried to disregard their surroundings and live only in the bitter air of masterpieces—it did not matter; the refugees of art ended by reaching the same goal: they ended in an atmosphere of hysteria and bewilderment that was not unlike the atmosphere of the bourgeois society they were trying to evade. Fitzgerald said that by this time—it was in 1927—

. . . contemporaries of mine had begun to disappear into the dark maw of violence. A classmate killed his wife and himself on Long Island, another tumbled "accidentally" from a skyscraper in Philadelphia, another purposely from a skyscraper in New York. One was killed in a speakeasy in Chicago; another was beaten to death in a speakeasy in New York and crawled home to the Princeton Club to die; still another had his skull crushed by a maniac in an insane asylum where he was confined. These are not catastrophes that I went out of my way to look for—these were my friends; moreover, these things happened not during the depression but during the boom.

When he wrote that passage Fitzgerald may have been thinking about his own tragic decline, which was the result of events that took place "not during the depression but during the boom." All the emotional and intellectual foundations for what would follow were laid in the boom years. Thus, even under Harding and Coolidge the doctrine of individualism had already defeated itself. In spite of the universal praise it received from essayists, politicians and business apologists, it had ceased to flourish at the heart of the social system—the very millionaires were colorless indoor persons who tried to live up to the conception of themselves created by their press agents and who, in their private lives, were ruled by the public that enriched them. Individualism had deserted the forum, the marketplace, and was taking refuge in marginal doctrines, in the past, in exile or in dreams. And it found no safety there: on the contrary, it was being forced to acknowledge its failure. The individualistic way of life was even failing to produce individuals. In their flight from social uniformity, artists were likely to choose uniform paths of escape and obey the conventions of their own small groups; even their abnormalities of conduct belonged to fixed types; even in the neuroses from which more and more of them suffered they followed established patterns.

Every age has its representative failures of personality and acts of violence, and the late 1920s had more than their share of both. Let us examine the background of one such act, a double suicide that took place in the early winter of 1929, six weeks after the Wall Street crash. Perhaps we shall find that it casts a retrospective light on the literary history of the whole decade.

VIII: Echoes of a Suicide

1: Letter Left on a Dressing Table

Harry Crosby and his wife arrived in New York during the first week of December 1929 and Hart Crane gave a party for them in his room on Brooklyn Heights. It was a good party, too; Harry smiled a lot—you remembered his very white teeth—and had easy manners and, without talking a great deal, he charmed everyone. On the afternoon of December 10 he borrowed the keys to a friend's studio in the Hotel des Artistes. When he failed to answer the telephone or the doorbell that evening, the friend had the door broken down and found Harry's body with that of a young society woman, Mrs. Josephine Bigelow.

The double suicide was a front-page story, but the newspapers could find no reason for it and the police had no explanation to offer. Harry was young, just six months past his thirty-first birthday; he was rich, happily married and, except for a slight infection of the throat, in the best of health. All the usual motives were lacking. He had lost a little money in the stock market but did not brood about it; he had love affairs but spoke of breaking them off; he was not dissatisfied with his progress as a poet and a publisher. Nor did he suffer from any sense of inferiority: people had always liked him, all his life had moved in pleasant ways; and he lay there now beside a dead woman in a borrowed studio.

He left behind him no letter, not even a final scrawl.

This deliberate silence seemed strange to the police. They knew that suicides usually give some explanation, often in the shape of a long document addressed to wife, mother or husband, insisting that they had done the wisest thing, justifying themselves before and accusing society. Poets in particular, among whom suicide is almost an occupational disease, are likely to write final messages to the world that neglected them. They insist on this last word—and if Harry Crosby left none, he must have believed that his message was already written.

He had been keeping a diary—later published in three volumes by the Black Sun Press in Paris—and, in effect, it takes the place of a letter slipped into the frame of the mirror or left on the dressing table under a jar of cold cream. It does not explain the immediate occasion, does not tell why he chose to die on that particular afternoon after keeping a rendezvous and sharing a bottle of Scotch whisky. But the real causes of his deed can be clearly deciphered from this record of things done, books read and ideas seized upon for guidance.

And something more can be deciphered there. It happens that his brief and not particularly distinguished literary life of seven years included practically all the themes I have been trying to develop—the separation from home, the effects of service in the ambulance corps, the exile in France, then other themes, bohemianism, the religion of art, the escape from society, the effort to defend one's individuality even at the cost of sterility and madness, then the final period of demoralization when the whole philosophical structure crumbled from within, just at the moment when bourgeois society seemed about to crumble after its greatest outpouring of luxuries, its longest debauch—all this is suggested in Harry Crosby's life and is rendered fairly explicit in his diary. But it is not my only reason for writing about him. Harry was wealthier than the other pure poets and refugees of art: he had means and leisure to carry his ideas to their conclusion, while most of the others were being turned aside, partly by the homely skepticism that is instilled into the middle classes and partly by the daily business of earning a living. He was not more talented than his associates, but he was more single-minded, more literal, and was not held back by the fear of death or ridicule from carrying his principles to their extremes. As a result, his life had the quality of a logical structure. His suicide was the last term of a syllogism; it was like the signature to a second-rate but honest and exciting poem.

But there is one question raised by his life that his diary doesn't answer. How did he first become entangled in the chain of events and ambitions that ended in the Hotel des Artistes? His background seemed to promise an entirely different career.

Henry Grew Crosby was born in Boston on June 4, 1898; his parents lived toward the lower end of Beacon Street. His father, Stephen Van Rensselaer Crosby, was a banker; his mother, born Henrietta Grew, was the sister of Mrs. J. Pierpont Morgan. Harry attended St. Mark's, an Episcopalian preparatory school, where, being too light for football, he ran on the cross-country team. He graduated in June 1917. With several of his classmates he immediately volunteered for the American Ambulance Service in France. . . . Boys with this background had an easy path to follow. St. Mark's was popularly supposed to lead, after four years at Harvard, to Kidder, Peabody and Company, the Boston bankers (just as Groton School led to Lee, Higginson). Then, after a proper apprenticeship, the young man moved on to New York, where his parents bought him a seat on the Stock Exchange; he might end as a Morgan partner. Alternatively, he might study law and become the attorney for a big public utility; or he might enter the diplomatic service and rise to an ambassadorship, like Harry's cousin Joseph Grew; or he might retire at the age of thirty-five and live on his income and buy pictures. The American high bourgeoisie takes care of its sons, provided only that they make a proper marriage and don't drink too much. What was it that turned Harry aside from the smooth road in front of him?

I think the answer lies in what happened to him during the war, and particularly in one brief experience to which he alludes several times in his diary, but without explaining it fully. The whole story is told in his war letters, privately printed by his parents—incidentally they are exactly like the war letters of fifty other nice American boys of good families which were printed in the same pious fashion. On November 22, 1917, Harry was at a dressing station in the hills near Verdun. While he was waiting to drive an ambulance full of wounded men to the field hospital at Bras, a shell burst in the road; the boy standing next to him was seriously wounded. Harry helped to put him into the ambulance and drove back toward Bras through a German barrage. There was one especially bad moment when the road was blocked by a stalled truck and Harry had to wait for minute after minute while shells rained down on either side of the road.

The hills of Verdun [he noted in his diary on the tenth anniversary of the adventure] and the red sun setting back of the hills and the charred skeletons of trees and the river Meuse and the black shells spouting up in columns along the road to Bras and the thunder of the barrage and the wounded and the ride through red explosions and the violent metamorphose from boy into man.

There was indeed a violent metamorphosis, but not from boy into man: rather, it was from life into death. What really hap-

pened was that Harry died in those endless moments when he
was waiting for the road to be cleared. In his heart he felt that
he belonged with his good friends Aaron Davis Weld and Oliver
Ames, Jr., both killed in action. Bodily he survived, and with
a keener appetite for pleasure, but only to find that something
was dead inside him—his boyhood, Boston, St. Mark's, the
Myopia Hunt, a respectable marriage, an assured future as a
banker, everything that was supposed to lead him toward a responsible place in the world.

At first he didn't realize what had happened. He went back
to Boston after the war and tried to resume his old life. He
entered Harvard in the fall of 1919; he made the cross-country
squad and was almost automatically elected to the societies, waiting clubs and final clubs which a young man of good family
was supposed to join—Institute of 1770, D.K.E., Hasty Pudding,
S.K. Club, A.D. Club. But he wasn't much interested, he wasn't
a nice boy any longer, and after two years he seized the opportunity of being graduated with a wartime degree, *honoris
causa.* Under protest he took a position in a bank, but stayed
away from it as much as possible and drank enough to insure
himself against the danger of being promoted. He read, he fell
in love, he gambled, and on January 1, 1922, he began his diary.

"New York," the first brief entry reads, "New York and all
day in bed all arms around while the snow falls silently outside
and all night on the train alone to Boston." He went back to
his abhorrent desk—then, on February 7, "Mamma gave me a
hundred dollars for going a month without drinking. Wasn't
worth it." On March 12, "Have not been to the Bank for five
days." On March 14, "Resigned from the Bank," and on
March 21:

Mamma has secured for me a position in the Bank in Paris.
Happier— One of my wild days where I threw all care to the wind

and drank to excess with 405— Result of being happier. At midnight drove old Walrus's new automobile down the Arlington Street subway until we crashed slap-bang into an iron fence. A shower of broken glass, a crushed radiator, a bent axle, but no one hurt. Still another episode to add to my rotten reputation.

Shadows of the Sun—the title under which the diary was published—is better than these early notes suggest, but it won't ever be ranked as one of the great autobiographies. Such works have usually been distinguished either by the author's outward observation of people or else by his ability to look inward into his heart. Harry Crosby looked hard in neither direction. Like so many other poets of our age, he was self-centered without being at all introspective, and was devoted to his friends without being sympathetic—he did not feel with people or feel into them. The figures that recur in his diary—Joyce, D. H. Lawrence, Hart Crane, Archibald MacLeish, Caresse (his wife), his parents, the Fire Princess, the Sorceress, E. E. Cummings, Kay Boyle —all remain as wooden as marionettes: they *do* things, they move their arms, raise glasses to their lips, utter judgments about one another, but you cannot see the motives behind the actions and the words. Rather than the people, it is the background that finally comes alive.

But this rule has one exception. Harry Crosby himself, though at first he seems as mechanical as the other figures presented in his story, ends in an unexpected fashion by impressing his personality upon you and half-winning your affection. You begin with the conviction that he was a bad poet, a man who dramatized himself, and most of all a fool. Without ever abandoning those ideas you gradually revise them, and are glad to admit that he was an appealing fool, a gallant fool, a brave, candid, single-minded and fanatically generous fool who bore nobody malice. He was not a weakling. Indeed, you come to feel that his strength was what killed him: a weaker man would have been prudent enough to survive. He had gifts that would have made him an explorer, a soldier of fortune, a revolutionist: they were qualities fatal to a poet.

Yet even in this profession where he didn't belong he wasn't altogether a failure. It is true that his early poems were naïve, awkward, false, unspeakably flat; it is true that he never acquired, even at the end, a sense of the value of words. But he was beginning to develop something else, a quality of speed, intensity, crazy vigor—and a poem need not have all the virtues to survive; sometimes one virtue is enough. As for his diary, I think there is no doubt that it will continue to be read by those lucky enough to get hold of it. It isn't a great autobiography, no, but it is a valuable record of behavior and a great source document for the manners of the age that was ours.

And it is something else besides, an interesting story. It tells how a young man from Back Bay adjusted himself to another world—how he got married, went to Paris and threw up his job in an American bank there—how he traveled through southern Europe and northern Africa, observing the landscapes, if not the people, with a sure eye—how he lived in an old mill near Paris and entertained everybody, poets, Russian refugees, hopheads, pederasts, artists and princes royal—how he returned to New York, lived too feverishly, became completely demoralized. . . . But it is not the mere story of his life with which we are concerned. Let us see what his problems were, and how he tried to solve them, and how the answers that he found led him inevitably toward one conclusion.

2: City of the Sun

His boyhood and its easy aspirations being dead within him, Harry Crosby was left after the war with nothing to live for and no desires except an immoderate thirst for enjoyment, the sort of thirst that parches young men when they feel that any sip of pleasure may be their last. But his boyhood life, though dead, had not been buried. He was like a blackboard from which something had been partly erased: the old words had to be wiped clean before new ones could be written; all that Boston implied had to be eradicated. Then, too, he had to find a new home to take the place of the one he was bent on losing. His war experience had to be integrated into his life after the war. . . . Problems like these were difficult, but they could be solved *ambulando,* as he went along. His really urgent problem was to find immediately a new ideal, a reason for living.

He tried to find it in books. In the midst of banking, love-making and drinking, he read devotedly, with the sense of new vistas opening out before him. Almost all the books he admired were those belonging to the Symbolist tradition and to what I have called the religion of art.

He began by sampling the more popular works of this category: *The Picture of Dorian Gray,* Laurence Hope's *Songs of India,* then, rising to a higher level, *Les Fleurs du Mal,* which he read easily in the original, having improved his French while in the army. In all these books he found quotations that seemed to explain or ennoble his private misadventures. Thus, after smashing old Walrus's car in the Arlington Street subway, he wrote that his youth, "to quote Baudelaire, *n'est qu'un ténébreux orage, traversé ça et là par de brillants soleils."* After a love af-

fair, he quoted E. E. Cummings: "I like my body when it is with
your body, it is so quite new a thing." His knowledge of literature was widening. He read and approved T. S. Eliot until *The
Hollow Men* appeared; then he became indignant at the idea of
the world's ending "not with a bang but a whimper." He read
Rimbaud and was enraptured. He read Huysmans' *À Rebours,*
and was so impressed by the hero's making a trip to London
without leaving the Rue de Rivoli that he essayed an equally
imaginary voyage at sea. He read Van Gogh's letters. On reading *Ulysses,* he wrote, "I would rather have seen Joyce than
any man alive"; and again the following year:

Today I saw Joyce three times . . . he was walking slowly (felt
hat overcoat hands in pockets) lost in thought (Work in Progress)
entirely unaware of his surroundings. Somnambulist. And in me
the same emotion as when Lindbergh arrived. But what is the Atlantic to the oceans Joyce has crossed?

He was not only reading these men, and later meeting such of
them as survived in Paris, and even publishing their work; he
was also reading the books that critics had written about them to
expound their philosophies. Thus, from Arthur Symons' essay
on Villiers de l'Isle-Adam, he quoted with approval: "Become
the flower of Thyself. Thou art but what thou thinkest: therefore think thyself eternal. . . . Thou art the God thou art able
to become." Again, from another essay by the same critic: "And
the whole soul of Huysmans characterizes itself in the turn of a
single phrase, 'that art is the only clean thing on earth except
holiness.'" He looked up many of his favorite authors in the
Encyclopædia Britannica and went to the trouble of copying a
passage about Flaubert:

This ruddy giant was secretly gnawn by misanthropy and disgust
of life. This hatred of the bourgeois began in his childhood and de-

veloped into a kind of monomania. He despised his fellow men, their habits, their lack of intelligence, their contempt for beauty, with a passionate scorn which has been compared to that of an ascetic monk.

Gradually out of his favorite books the materials for a new ideal of life were being assembled: he wrote that he was beginning "to lay the foundation for my castle of philosophy (not to be confounded with my inner or *inmost* (to be exact) Castle of Beauty)":

Life is pathetic, futile save for the development of the soul; memories, passionate memories are the utmost gold; poetry is religion (for me); silence invariably has her compensation; thought-control is a necessity (but is disloyal in affairs of love); simplicity is strengthening (the strength of the Sun); fanatic faith in the Sun is essential (for the utmost Castle of Beauty).

Outside the ivory walls of this castle was a landscape devastated as if by a hostile army. "Machinery has stamped its heel of ugliness upon the unromantic world." America in particular was pustulant with "civic federations . . . boy-scout clubs . . . educational toys and its Y.M.C.A. and its congregational baptist churches and all this smug self-satisfaction. Horribly bleak, horribly depressing."—"This damn country" seemed to be run for children and "smelt, stank rather, of bananas and Coca Cola and ice cream." Even Europe was falling before the invader. "Industrialism is triumphant and ugliness, sordid ugliness, is everywhere destroying beauty, which has fled to the museums (dead) or into the dark forests of the soul (alive)." The only safety lay in strengthening one's defenses. "The gorgeous flame of poetry is the moat and beyond, the monstrous (and menstruous) world, the world that must be continually beaten back, the world that is always laying siege to the castle of the soul."

Whatever happened in the outside world (with the exception

of a few heroic and individual feats, like Lindbergh's flight and
Alain Gerbault's voyage in an open boat) was absolutely without interest to the soul inside its castle. Harry didn't even read
newspapers (sometimes he glanced at *Paris-Sport* to learn the
racing results). He was "bored by politics (full of sound and sig-
nifying nothing)." So strong were his defenses that not only
machinery and mediocrity but also the commonest human emotions were barred out. No living impulse, no creative force, could
cross his moat of fire. In his safe donjon where the larders were
stocked with golden memories and bank dividends, he threatened to be transformed into something not so much superhuman
as dehumanized.

"I hate children," he wrote. "Rose up in my wrath and fired
all three servants," he wrote. "Christ, how I hate servants." People in general were like vermin. "Depressing to consider the
ugly bodies that have washed in one's bathtub, to imagine the
people who have been born, who have made love, or who have
died in one's bed, or to know that myriad unclean fingers have
soiled the pages of one's favorite book." Again: "There are too
many people in the world and Mount Etna is erupting and
thousands of lives are lost. Let them be lost. Let them be lost."

People were tolerable only if they were of his own age and
belonged to his social class or to the world of letters. The others
threatened to arouse his pity and he tried to avoid them. "Bank
banquet," he wrote. "A dismal affair. Poor people trying to enjoy themselves are more pathetic than rich people trying to have
a good time, for the poor are utterly defenseless where the rich
are sheltered by their cynicism."—"The tragic sadness of the
pleasures of the poor!" he wrote on a Fourteenth of July after
watching them dance in the streets of Paris. "Glimpses of the
underworld, the restless, sweating underworld, the rabble seeking after happiness (O Jesu make it stop) and how much more
beautiful the full moon turning to silver the garden of the pa-

vilion."—"I hate the multitude," he wrote. *"Je suis royaliste* and to hell with democracy where the gross comforts of the majority are obtained by the sacrifice of a cultural minority." And again, more briefly and significantly, "I am glad that France has taken the Ruhr." The religion of art was not without having its political sequels.

It also had its sequels in action: of this there can be no doubt whatever. Long ago, in the course of the prolonged debate about life and literature and censorship, it used to be said that art and morality existed in different worlds, that nobody was ever improved or corrupted by reading a book. But Harry advanced a different idea in a bad sonnet to Baudelaire:

> Within my soul you've set your blackest flag
> And made my disillusioned heart your tomb,
> My mind which once was young and virginal
> Is now a swamp, a spleenfilled pregnant womb.

His disillusioned heart and spleen-filled mind were delighted with *The Picture of Dorian Gray,* which he read for a second time. He particularly enjoyed

. . . its sparkling cynicism, its color idealism and its undercurrent of dangerous philosophy. . . . "Every impulse that we strive to strangle broods in the mind and poisons us. The body sins once and is done with its sin, for action is a mode of purification. . . . The only way to get rid of a temptation is to yield to it" (tempest of applause).

This was written on July 19, 1924. On July 21 came the sequel:

The sun is streaming through the bedroom window, it is eleven o'clock and I know by my dirty hands, by the torn banknotes on the dressing table, by the clothes and matches and small change scattered over the floor that last night I was drunk. . . . This the result of reading Wilde. Blanche. Rhymes with Avalanche.

His reading of Baudelaire and Wilde was of course not the only or the principal cause of his wining and wenching and gambling for high stakes: the war had already given him a taste for strong pleasures. What his reading did was to supply him with moral justification for a course he might have followed in any case. It also supplied him with maxims: Live dangerously! Seize the day! Be in all things extravagant! Money troubles are never fatal, *une plaie d'argent ne tue jamais* (not even when starving? Harry wondered, but put his doubts aside). Finally his reading supplied him with a goal to be attained by debauches —ecstasy! "The human soul belongs to the spiritual world and is ever seeking to be reunited to its source (the Sun). Such union is hindered by the bodily senses, but though not permanently attainable until death, it can be enjoyed at times in the state called ecstasy when the veil of sensual perception is rent asunder and the soul is merged in God (in the Sun)." Stimulants were an aid in achieving that condition: alcohol, hashish, love and opium were successive rites that led toward a vast upsoaring of the spirit; they served as a Eucharist.

Such was the religion of art, not as it was found at its best in the books of a great writer like Joyce or Valéry or Proust, but as it existed more typically in the mind of a young man home from the war, whose education had been interrupted and whose talent was for action rather than contemplation. Even to Harry Crosby, it was not entirely harmful: it gave him a sort of discipline in his debaucheries; it even ended by teaching him to write. But it prevented his interests from expanding, his life from broadening; it protected him from any new, reinvigorating currents that might have come to him from any other social classes than his own tired class; it condemned him to move in only one direction, toward greater intensity, isolation, frenzy, and finally toward madness. For that, too, was imposed on him by the religion of art. "I believe," he wrote in the midst of a short credo, "in the half-sane half-insane madness and illuminism of the seer." He quoted from Symons and from a résumé of Schopenhauer: "Social rules are made by normal people for normal people, and the man of genius is fundamentally abnormal."— "The direct connection of madness and genius is established by the biographies of great men, such as Rousseau, Byron, Poe, etc. Yet in these semi-madmen, these geniuses, lies the true aristocracy of mankind."—"Applause," he added, "of Suns crashing against Suns." He had set himself the goal of going crazy in order to become a genius. He was the boy apprenticed to a lunatic.

So he had found his way of living, such as it was; he had found his two castles of philosophy and beauty, one within the other, like wooden eggs from Russia. It still remained for him to find a home, and to lose the dead traces of the old home that persisted in his mind.

More than anything else in Harry Crosby's diary, his attempt to eradicate Boston has the elements of high farce. To him Boston was "a dreary place (dreary, drearier, dreariest). . . . No concentration here, no stimulus, no inner centrality, no exploding into the Beyond, no Sun. It is the City of Dreadful Night, a Target for Disgust." He not only fled from the abominable city, and the ideals upheld by it, and the country containing it: he also resigned from the Paris bank because it reminded him of the one where he had worked in Boston. Often he congratulated himself on having evaded

. . . the horrors of Boston and particularly of Boston virgins who are brought up among sexless surroundings, who wear canvas drawers and flat-heeled shoes and tortoise-shell glasses and who, once they are married, bear a child punctually every nine months for five or six years and then retire to end their days at the Chilton Club. Christ, what a narrow escape, far narrower than the shells at Verdun.

And yet he couldn't get Massachusetts out of his blood. Particularly on mornings-after, the images of his childhood became vivid and desirable. Thus, on the day that followed the Quatz' Arts ball of 1923, there was "Bed," he wrote, "and no banking . . . and a vague *mal du pays* for Singing Beach and Myopia Links and the Apple Trees in the Fog." After *Dorian Gray* and the Blanche who rhymed with Avalanche, he bitterly longed

. . . for the sunbasking on Singing Beach, for the smell of the woods around Essex, for the sunset at Coffin's Beach, for the friendliness of the apple trees. . . . I would even like (for me tremendous admission) a small farm near Annisquam with a stone farmhouse looking out over flat stretches of sand toward the sea. The hell you say.

But he had only to meet a few of his fellow countrymen and this longing disappeared. "Two Americans for luncheon," he noted three months later:

One thought that every gentleman should knock down every Negro he meets (and every Negress? Knock up?) and the other considered love a form of indigestion—it certainly would be for him. Glad I am *déraciné. Ubi bene, ibi patria.*

In the search for that fatherland where everything was best, he traveled through Brittany, the Basque coast, Italy and Spain. At Biskra, on the northern edge of the African desert, it seemed to him that he had finally escaped from ugliness and industrialism:

There are Arabs coming into town on diminutive donkeys (not coming into town in diminutive Fords) and there is a tiny Tofla tending her goats in a deserted palm garden and there are crumbling walls and sun-baked houses and a certain sluggishness and it never rains and the sun gives health and all one needs are dried dates and bread and coffee (and of course hashish) and a straw mat in a bare room of stone ("a man's wealth should be estimated by what he can do without") and we walk to the Café Maure and smoke hashish (to the amusement of the *indigènes*) and we see the village sheik in a black and white burnous and a little Negress *accroupie* in his path (no self-consciousness here). . . .

That evening Harry and Caresse went to a house opening off a dark alleyway to watch a little naked Arab girl do a *danse du ventre:*

. . . little Zora removing layer after layer of the most voluminous garments, the last piece being a pair of vast cotton drawers such as clowns wear, and which was gathered about her slender waist by a huge halyard. Then she begins to dance, slowness at first with curious rhythms of her ventre and then convulsive shiverings (two match-less breasts like succulent fruit) and wilder the music and more serpentine her rhythms and her head moves forward and backward and her body weaves an invitation and we went home to the hotel and O God when shall we ever cast off the chains of New England?

The following morning he wrote, "And the chains of New England are broken and unbroken—the death of conscience is not the death of self-consciousness." Biskra had not produced the desired effect. Eight days later he was back in Paris—"Paris, and all other lands and cities dwindle into Nothingness. Paris the City of the Sun."

Here, he decided, he would spend his days; this Sun-City would be his spiritual home. In June he faithfully attended the races; in August he went driving off to Deauville to play baccarat and bask on the beach; in October, his favorite month, there was racing again near Paris; there were visits to booksellers and picture galleries, and long exhilarating walks in the Bois, and friends in for cocktails—he was entering into the life of the city and meeting not only exiles like himself, young writers like Hemingway, MacLeish, Kay Boyle and Hart Crane, but also French artists and noblemen. As the years passed by he saw less often the little stone farmhouse near Annisquam and heard less often "the sound of the Fog Horn booming through the Fog"; there was nothing to remind him of his dead boyhood. Yet he was beginning again to be restless and dissatisfied.

In truth the Paris in which he had chosen to live was not the only Paris. It was one among many cities that bore the same name and were built one inside the other like Harry's castles of philosophy and beauty. It was the Paris of the international revelers and refugees. It was the Paris symbolized by the famous House of All Nations, to which Harry paid a formal visit

. . . and saw the Persian and the Russian and the Turkish and the Japanese and the Spanish rooms . . . and the bathroom with mirrored walls and mirrored ceilings and a glimpse of the thirty harlots waiting in the salon and there was the flogging post where men came to flagellate young girls and where others (masochists) came to be flagellated.

It was the Paris of drugs and sexual perversions:

Z is busily preparing a pipe, deftly twisting the treacly substance over a little lamp while Y paler than I have ever seen her reaches out white hands like a child asking for its toy. . . .

A great drinking of cocktails in our bathroom—it was too cold in the other rooms—and there were eleven of us all drinking and shrieking and we went to eat oysters and then to the Jungle where there was a great drinking of whiskey and mad music and life is exciting nowadays with all the pederasts and the lesbians—no one knows who is flirting with whom.

It was the Paris of the Bal des Quatz' Arts, which Harry always attended:

At eight the Students begin to appear—more and more and more (many more people than last year) and the Punch Bowl is filled and the Party has begun and soon everyone is Gay and Noisy Noisier and Noisiest toward ten o'clock and seventy empty bottles of champagne rattle upon the floor and now straight gin Gin Gin Gin like the Russian refugees clamoring for bread and everyone clamored and the fire roared in the hearth (roared with the wine in my heart) and the room was hot and reeked with cigarette and cigar smoke with fard and sweat and smell of underarms and we were all in Khmer costume . . . and at eleven we formed in line in the courtyard (I with the sack full of snakes) and marched away on foot . . . and at last exhausted into the Salle Wagram (snarling of tigers at the gate snarling of tigers inside) and up the ladder to the loge and up another ladder to an attic and up an imaginary ladder to and into the Sun and here I undid the sack and turned it upside down and all the snakes dropped down among the dancers and there were shrieks and catcalls and there was a riot and I remember two strong young men stark naked wrestling on the floor for the honor of dancing with a young girl (silver paint conquered purple paint) and I remember a mad student drinking wine out of a skull which he had pilfered from my library as I had pilfered it a year ago from the Catacombs (O happy skull to be filled full of sparkling gold) and in a corner I watched two savages making love (stark naked wrestling on the floor) and beside me sitting on the floor a plump woman with bare breasts absorbed in the passion of giving milk to one of the snakes.

This was the crazy Paris which, to its own people, seemed the innermost city: in truth it was the outmost and the youngest. It was not the Paris of Villon or Cyrano or Rameau's famous nephew, who were wastrels too, but in a different fashion. It was a Paris that began to flourish under the Second Empire, when the landlords and suddenly enriched speculators of all

Europe came flocking toward a world capital where they could spend their profits and be ostentatious in their vice. From year to year this Paris became more feverish and gilded—but there was a time after Louis Napoleon fell when it suddenly ceased to exist.

"Wonderful indeed," wrote Karl Marx in 1871, "was the change the Commune had wrought!"

No longer any trace of the meretricious Paris of the Second Empire. No longer was Paris the rendezvous of British landlords, Irish absentees, American ex-slaveholders and shoddy men, Russian ex-serf-owners and Wallachian boyars. No more corpses at the Morgue, no nocturnal burglaries, scarcely any robberies; in fact, for the first time since the days of February 1848, the streets of Paris were safe, and that without any police of any kind. "We," said a member of the Commune, "hear no longer of assassination, theft and personal assault; it seems, indeed, as if the police had dragged along with it to Versailles all its Conservative friends." The cocottes had refound the scent of their protectors—the absconding men of family, religion and, above all, of property. In their stead, the real women of Paris showed again at the surface—heroic, noble and devoted, like the women of antiquity.

But this was only an interlude. Soon the police and its Conservative friends reoccupied Paris, after executing thirty thousand of the inhabitants. Soon the burglaries began again; soon the wealthy exiles reappeared on the boulevards; and for half a century their special city continued to grow.

Its population, however, had changed since the World War. The Russians still formed part of it, but they no longer had any ex-serfs to provide them with incomes—the Irish absentees had disappeared, after losing most of their estates—the British landlords, with heavier taxes to pay, were living at home—the Southern ex-slaveholders were dead and their descendants had joined the middle classes. Their places in the international set had been taken by the sons and daughters of Northern bankers, by Swedish match kings, by Spanish grandees—and also by strange new people, Chinese mandarins and war lords, Egyptian cotton growers, Indian maharanees, even a sprinkling of Negro kings from Senegal. Their places were also taken by a few French nobles, who had formerly despised these refugees, but were now beginning to feel akin to them, as refugees too, uprooted from the life of their own country. Indeed, all these people had this in common, that they lived at a great distance from their sources of revenue; that their money came to them, not smelling of blood, sweat and the soil, but in the shape of clean paper readily transformable into champagne and love. They were spending it faster and faster, but also more aimlessly. In everything they did there was now an air of uncertainty and strain. Something, the war, the Russian Revolution, had given them a sense that their order was crumbling and that they belonged to a dying world. Cartoonists used to depict them as skeletons dressed in banknotes.

This was the world and the city that Harry Crosby had chosen for home. He never quite belonged to it. He too was marked for death, but he was not yet a thing of bones and paper; he had too much sinew not to grow tired of his fellow townsmen. Toward the end, a note of fatigue and disgust with Paris began to creep into his diary; he was beginning to be irritated by the people always crowding about him. "Really the stupidity of the French is beyond imagination."—"And I hate the English Jesus how I hate the English so damn bourgeois and banal." —"I like New York much better than Paris." It was becoming evident that the home he had so joyously chosen, after destroying the traces of his boyhood, was not to be his home after all. Perhaps he could find a new home in New York. Or else, if that failed him—

He had meanwhile another problem to solve. In addition to a way of living and a home that had served him temporarily, he needed also a faith and a ritual. Poetry in itself was not enough: he wanted something beyond it, a transcendent symbol he could celebrate and adore.

The symbol he chose for himself was the Sun.

I don't know how he came to make this choice. He may have done so arbitrarily, during his boyhood; in any case he already regarded himself as a sun-worshiper before beginning his diary. He tried from the beginning to dignify his faith by finding historical parallels, and was delighted to learn that the Peruvians, the Persians, the Egyptians and many other ancient peoples had also worshiped the sun; he memorized the names of their sun-gods and adopted some of their rituals. In those religions, however, the sun had usually represented a principle of fertility: it was what caused the wheat and maize to grow and thus preserved and symbolized the life of the tribe or nation. Harry's sun-worship was something different, a wholly individual matter, a bloodless, dehumanized religion without community or fraternity or purpose. Yet he fanatically clung to it and, at least toward the end, believed in it sincerely.

It seems to have stood for many different things. Sometimes it was nature-worship—"I am a mystic and religion is not a question of sermons and churches but rather it is an understanding of the infinite through nature (Sun, Moon and Stars)." Sometimes it seemed to be light-worship. Sometimes it was plainly self-worship, Harry himself becoming a sun-symbol—"Today read in Schopenhauer that the center of gravity (for me the Sun) should fall entirely and absolutely within oneself." It was often body-worship—one of the rites that Harry invented for himself was sun-bathing, preferably on top of a tower, until his whole body was "sunnygolden" and until he "exploded into the Sun." Still oftener it was sex-worship—"My soul today is a young phal-

lus thrusting upwards to possess the young goddess of the Sun."
He gave sun-names to the women he loved, so that his union with
them symbolized a union with the sun itself.

His faith was also a refuge from ugliness and industrialism—
"I believe in the Sun because the Sun is the only thing in life that
does not disillusion."

But his transcendent symbol was something else besides, something that wasn't clear in his own mind but stands forth un-
mistakably to the reader of his diary. Because the Sun was at
the center of his life—because the center of his life was empty,
no living impulse being able to cross the moat of fire with which
he had surrounded himself, and because, ever since that day at
Verdun, death ruled as master in his inmost castle—because of
all this, and by a simple process of transference, the sun became
a cold abyss, a black sun, a gulf of death into which he would
some day hurl himself ecstatically, down, down, downwards,
falling "into the Red-Gold (night) of the Sun . . . SUNFIRE!"
His worship of the Sun became the expectation of, the strained
desire for, "a Sun-Death into Sun."

The truly extraordinary feature of Harry Crosby's life, the
quality that gave it logic and made it resemble a clear syllogism,
was the fashion in which all the different strands of it were woven
together into the single conception of a sun-death.

Take the first strand of all: take the war. Harry often mentions it in his diary; he dwells on it with a horrified fascination
that becomes almost love. Yet he never mentions the historical
causes or results of it, never seems to regard it as a struggle among
nations for survival and among industries for markets. To him
it was a blind, splendid catastrophe that meant only one thing,
death. It was kept fresh in his mind by symbols like his dead
friends, his nearly fatal adventure at Verdun, the Unknown Soldier, the military graveyards, always by corpses—and since these

deaths were fine and courageous, were good deaths, the war itself was good.

Here are a few of his reflections on it:

February 1, 1925.—Above all, we who have known war must never forget war. And that is why I have the picture of a soldier's corpse nailed to the door of my library.

November 22, 1925.—All day in the streets the hawkers hawk their wares . . . and at night in a glass of brandy a toast in honor of the day (the day of the barrage at Verdun, the day S was wounded).

There will always be war.

November 11, 1927.—Armistice Day day that for me is the most significant day of the year . . . before going to bed I smoked my pipe and drank two glasses of brandy, To Oliver Ames Junior (killed in action) to Aaron Davis Weld (killed in action).

One Fourth of July in Paris, he attended the unveiling of a statue to Alan Seeger and heard the reading of his "Rendezvous with Death":

At the end, to the triumphant sound of trumpets, troops at attention defiled past the grandstand: Foch, Pétain, Joffre, Mangin, Poincaré, Millerand and our uninspiring Ambassador. Very impressive, very significant, as all such things are to those who went to war. Stood with the small contingent of members of the Field Service, and afterwards we were invited to the Elysée Palace to meet Millerand and Mangin (how the poilus used to shake their fists at him and call him *le Boucher*).

This comment is, in Harry's own words, "very impressive, very significant." He had more or less consciously taken the side of Mangin the Butcher against the common soldiers whose lives were thrown away at Mangin's orders, whose bodies were melted down into the row of medals that Mangin wore on his left breast. He had taken the side of death against life; now he was preparing to act upon his choice. By committing suicide, he was rejoining his dead friends, his only true friends, and was fulfilling the destiny marked out for him at Verdun.

But just as his war service led him toward this end, so too did his study of the Symbolist poets and philosophers; they were still his guides. Out of his reading came the idea that the achievement of individuality was the purpose to seek above all others —the highest expression of the self was in the act of self-annihilation. Out of his reading came the idea that ecstasy was to be attained at any price—death was the last ecstasy. Out of his reading he learned to admire and seek madness—what could be crazier than killing oneself?—and learned that life itself might be transformed into a work of art rising to a splendid climax— "to die at the right time." His suicide would be the last debauch, the final extravagance, the boldest act of sex, the supreme gesture of defiance to the world he despised.

He had been seeking a home without really finding it. Death was his permanent home.

Even the religion of his boyhood resumed a place in his life when he learned that the birthday and high feast of Christianity was really the winter solstice, the birthday of the sun, and reflected that Jesus Christ, in a sense, had committed suicide. In the pursuit of death, all the strands united, aphelion and perihelion, boyhood and manhood, Boston and Paris, peace and war —all his conflicts were resolved. For the first time Harry Crosby became fully integrated, self-sufficient, complete.

During the summer of 1928 he spent a month at the Lido. All afternoon he would swim or lie basking in the sun among the almost naked pretty girls; at night he danced or drank champagne or read. His reading, like his dissipation, had now acquired a purpose; all of it pointed in one direction, thus:

July 2.—A reading about Van Gogh and the delirium of his vision . . . Van Gogh the example of triumphant individuality Van Gogh the painter of suns the painter of that Sun which consumed him and which was responsible for his final madness and suicide. A Sun-Death into Sun!

July 6.—Tonight in Nietzsche I read a significant passage: "Die at the right time." Die at the right time, so teacheth Zarathustra and again the direct 31–10–42. Clickety-click clickety-click the express train into Sun.

It must have been during the same exalted month that he wrote a prose poem, "Hail: Death!" which was published in the September 1928 issue of *transition:*

Take Cleopatra! Take the Saints and Martyrs! . . . Take Nietzsche: "Die at the right time," no matter where you are, in the depths of the coal pit, in the crowded streets of the city, among the dunes of the desert, in cocktail bars, or in the perfumed corridors of the Ritz, at the right time, when your entire life, when your soul and your body, your spirit and your senses are concentrated, are reduced to a pinpoint, the ultimate gold point, the point of finality, irrevocable as the sun, sun-point, then is the time, and not until then, and not after then (O horrors of anti-climax from which there is no recovering!) for us to penetrate into the cavern of the somber Slave-Girl of Death . . . in order to be reborn, in order to become what you wish to become, tree or flower or star or sun, or even dust and nothingness, for it is stronger to founder in the Black Sea of Nothingness, like a ship going down with flags, than to crawl like a Maldoror into the malodorous whorehouse of evil and old age.

In those days Harry Crosby seemed at the greatest possible distance from old age and decay, at the very perihelion of his youth. His physical condition was excellent, in spite of dissipation: he was all muscle and sinew and his skin was burned so red that Frenchmen took him for a Red Indian. He was taut with energy, burning with desire; he was swimming, dancing, drinking, making love, writing mad poems; and all the time he was laying plans for his final extinction. It was to take place on October 31, 1942—this date had acquired a symbolic meaning. With Caresse he was to fly an airplane over a forest and jump out. There was to be no funeral—"I do not want to be buried in the ground. I want to be cremated. . . . Take my ashes clean and white, ascend above New York at dawn and scatter them to the four winds."

All during the summer and autumn of 1928 these plans were taking shape. And during the same months Harry was enjoying himself with terrifying gusto:

September 4.—Read about the Synapothanomenos or band of those who wanted to die together formed by Anthony and Cleopatra after the battle of Actium and I should like to have influence strong enough to lead a band of followers into the Sun-Death.

November 7.—Perhaps in my soul I shall become great because I have Sun-Thoughts and this autumn I am very happy. It is very rare to be so very happy.

December 22.—I read in my notebook . . . that Aphelion in astronomy is the point of the orbit of a planet at which it is most distant from the Sun (the City of Dreadful Night); that the most simple Sun-Death is from an aeroplane over a forest (31–10–42) down down down down Bang! the body is dead— up up up up Bang!!!! the Soul explodes into the Bed of Sun (pull over us the gold sheets Dear).

One of his friends, a gifted poet, said that he could no longer bear to shake his hand. Harry had so definitely fixed the date of his death, had made up his mind so firmly, had died in anticipation so many times, that he was like Lazarus with the death-smell about him: shaking his hand was like shaking hands with a corpse—and yet what a lively, lustful, laughter-seeking corpse, with gold pieces in his pocket, hands always moving, teeth gleaming white and the glint of sun on his skin—a corpse already in winding-sheets, pleading for faster music as he screamed his triumphant dirge:

For the Seekers after Fire and the Seers and the Prophets and the Worshipers of the Sun, life ends not with a whimper, but with a Bang—a violent explosion mechanically perfect . . . while we, having set fire to the powderhouse of our souls, explode (suns within suns and cataracts of gold) into the frenzied fury of the Sun, into the madness of the Sun into the hot gold arms and hot gold eyes of the Goddess of the Sun!

3: The Revolution of the Word

Logically that was the end of Harry Crosby, his problems and his way of solving them. But there is still one question to be answered. He had determined to commit suicide at a certain time, in a certain way. Why did he kill himself thirteen years before his chosen date, in a borrowed New York apartment, in the arms of a young woman he did not meet until after his plans were already shaping themselves?

In part this question can either be answered from his diary, like the others, or else need never be answered. But also in part

—and this is the most interesting feature of it and the reason Harry Crosby becomes a symbol—it carries us outside his own story, that of a minor poet, into the history of an era about to end. A curious change took place in him. Just as his life had gradually narrowed down to himself, so now, in his last year, it began to widen, to touch upon the international world of literature, finance and high society, before once again contracting to "a pinpoint, the ultimate gold point, the point of finality, irrevocable as the sun, sun-point."

In November 1928 he made a voyage to America. "Gang-planks are thrown down," he noted in his diary, "and there is a great pushing and crowding and stepping on people's feet and there is a great sign No Smoking Allowed and I shout at Caresse and I go through the customs my pockets stuffed with opium pills flasks of absinthe and the little Hindu love books." Well stocked with contraband to protect him against the rigors of this semi-foreign and miraculous country, he stepped out into the streets of New York at the height of the financial boom, the building boom, the buy-on-easy-installments boom—"New York gold city of the Arabian Nights towering into the gold of the Sun."

But before enjoying the pleasures of the city, he had to make a duty-visit to Boston, which as always he found sunless and dreary. He attended the Yale game in New Haven; that was a distraction. In those years the big college football games served as almost the only mass demonstrations of the American upper bourgeoisie. The Harvard-Yale game of 1928 was the biggest of all, the hardest to get tickets for, the most befurred, extravagant, silver-flasked, orchid-dotted and racing-car-attended. Between the halves a gray squirrel somehow got loose on the field and was pursued by a drunken man in an enormous coonskin coat; I remember that the scared animal seemed more human than the eighty thousand people who shrieked while it was being caught. Harry Crosby mentioned the squirrel in his diary; then shortly he was in New York again.

"I love New York," he wrote, "a madhouse full of explosions with foghorns screaming out on the river and policemen with shrill whistles to regulate traffic and the iron thunder of the Elevated and green searchlights stabbing the night." Once again as in wartime he had the thirst for pleasure that comes as a foretaste of death; a danger self-imposed had produced on him the same emotional effect as the German shells. His diary begins to reveal a straining of all the senses toward a sustained and almost incoherent ecstasy, a mingling of "whisky sours, Twin Suns crashing, the feeling of just before snow, the winter lawns, the Red Heart rum, the little ears, the fingers and toes the underclothes the ivory and the rose the winter snows, the green searchlight like a finger touching the breast of the night." There were a few days when he seems to have found the genuine madness for which he had been seeking. One thing is certain, that he enjoyed himself too intensely and paid an unexpected price for his pleasures by becoming dependent on the world by which they were provided. No longer able to exist without them, he lost his self-sufficiency and began to grow demoralized.

On the boat returning to France he felt lonely for the young American woman whom he called the Fire Princess. He had for the first time the sense of anticlimax that he always feared. And on Christmas Eve he noted in his diary, "Paris is dead after the madness of New York."

He tried instinctively to fill his life again, with love and literature. His diary often refers to meetings with the Sorceress and the Lady of the Golden Horse and there was still the Fire Princess, who paid a visit to Paris. At the same time he was seeing more of Eugene Jolas, the editor of *transition*.[1] Harry contributed

[1] Jolas was the right editor for an international magazine of the arts.

more poems and prose to the magazine, helped it financially, too, and after the spring issue of 1929 he became one of the advisory editors.

Transition was the last and biggest of the little magazines published by the exiles. There had been many of them: *Gargoyle* (which was Greenwich Village in Montparnasse), *Broom* (at first art-for-art's sake, then machine-loving), *Seccession* (Dadaism tempered with pedantry), the *Transatlantic Review* (hardboiled and Midwestern, though an Englishman was the editor), *This Quarter* (intense and angry like its founder, Ernest Walsh, who was dying of consumption), *Tambour* (half French), the *Little Review* (which moved from Chicago to New York to Paris before it died), *Exiles* (Ezra Pound's more or less personal organ)—there must have been others, too, but those were the more important. Toward the end it was getting hard to tell them apart, except by their typography; they had much the same contributors.

Transition began as a repository for all the types of writing that had already appeared in the little magazines. Since it had more space—often it ran to three hundred pages after becoming a quarterly—even more types were represented, with good writing of most types and bad writing of all. Angry, sophisticated, high-spirited, tired, primitive, expressionist, objective, subjective, incoherent, flat, it included everything that seemed new; rhapsodies to the machine were printed side by side with poems of escape from the machine, while Functionalism, Surrealism and Gertrude Stein all nudged one another. But that was chiefly in the beginning. As the magazine continued, it began to work toward a policy of its own, one that would combine the editor's

---

He was born in New Jersey, but his family went back to its home in a French-speaking part of Lorraine that was then under the German flag, and Jolas attended German schools before joining his American relatives in Iowa. Later he lived in France and worked as a reporter for the Paris *Herald*. His revolution of the word was trilingual.

three principal admirations: for Rimbaud (the hallucination of
the senses), for Joyce (the disintegration of the English language) and for the Surrealists (the emphasis on dreams and on
the "autonomous" imagination).

Harry Crosby was present at meetings where this policy was
discussed. On April 3 he noted:

The Jolases appeared and we discussed the future of *transition*. A
policy to be based on *Une Saison en Enfer,* a policy of revolution, of
attack, of the beauty of the word for itself, of experiment in painting,
in photography, in writing, of a tremendous campaign against the
philistines, of explosions into a Beyond, and then we all four went
to Pruniers to eat oysters and drink Anjou.

The campaign was launched in the June issue, in the form of
a "Proclamation" signed by sixteen writers. It begins: "Tired of
the spectacle of short stories, novels, poems and plays still under
the hegemony of the banal word, monotonous syntax, static psychology, descriptive naturalism, and desirous of crystallizing a
viewpoint, we hereby declare that"—but the document is worth
quoting in full. It is funny; and it sets forth the doctrines that
writers were willing seriously to uphold in that year when even
the craziest little magazines were saner than the Stock Exchange.

There are twelve propositions:

1. The revolution in the English language is an accomplished fact.
2. The imagination in search of a fabulous world is autonomous
and unconfined.
3. Pure poetry is a lyrical absolute that seeks an a-priori reality
within ourselves alone.
4. Narrative is not mere anecdote, but the projection of a metamorphosis of reality.
5. The expression of these concepts can be achieved only through
the rhythmic "hallucination of the word."

6. The literary creator has the right to disintegrate the primal matter of words imposed on him by textbooks and dictionaries.

7. He has the right to use words of his own fashioning and to disregard existing grammatical and syntactical laws.

8. The "litany of words" is admitted as an independent unit.

9. We are not concerned with the propagation of sociological ideas, except to emancipate the creative elements from the present ideology.

10. Time is a tyranny to be abolished.

11. The writer expresses. He does not communicate.

12. The plain reader be damned.

(Damn braces! Bless relaxes . . . Blake)

I have since talked with several of the persons [2] who put their names to this portentous document. Some of them never really understood what it said; they had simply liked the bombastic tone of it. Hart Crane was ashamed of having signed it; he said he was drunk. Jolas believed it word for word, and so did Harry Crosby. In his literal-minded fashion, Harry set out to apply it: he damned the plain reader and wrote hallucinated poems that expressed himself and communicated nothing. But the tenth of the propositions impressed him more than the others. In the midst of dissipations now grown frantic and aimless, he kept repeating that time was a tyranny to be abolished.

That was the year the Crosbys entertained. They were living in an old mill on the estate of the Duc de la Rochefoucauld, just near enough to Paris so that they could never be sure who would drop in for an afternoon call prolonged till midnight—Douglas Fairbanks, the Polignacs, a man with dogs to sell, a double brace of assorted royalty or Hart Crane with a bottle of Cutty Sark and

[2] The signers were Kay Boyle, Whit Burnett, Hart Crane, Caresse Crosby, Harry Crosby, Martha Foley, Stuart Gilbert, A. L. Gillespie, Leigh Hoffman, Eugene Jolas, Elliot Paul, Douglas Rigby, Theo Rutra, Robert Sage, Harold J. Salemson, Laurence Vail.

a sheaf of poems under his arm—always there was a coming and going, a great laughing and shrieking:

February 3.—Mob for luncheon—poets and painters and pederasts and lesbians and divorcées and Christ knows who and there was a great signing of names on the wall at the foot of the stairs and a firing off of the cannon and bottle after bottle of red wine.

May 4.—En repos at the Moulin Caresse and I are a little like the shock troops in the war who were often en repos because they often attacked.

That was the year when anything was expected to happen, and did, and wasn't very exciting after all. It might be Hart Crane arrested for knocking down a policeman and kept a week in prison, where "the dirty skunks in the Santé wouldn't give him any paper to write poems on, the bastards"—Harry helped him get out and gave him passage money back to New York; or it might be a scandal casually repeated—"Today P appeared for a cocktail he told us of how Iudira made almost a million francs in Cannes at baccarat and he told us of a men's party he had given in London where the Negro orchestra and the waiters and the guests all raped each other"; or it might be simply "ping-pong and people arriving and more plunging in the pool and Max Ernst was here and Ortiz and the usual raft of royalty"; and then, after the shouting and the drinking, "everyone departed Parisward and C and I were left alone together. What a relief!" But they weren't often alone that year. Usually they rushed off with their guests, all in big motorcars, hurrying to the Château, to Paris, to the races, to Deauville for the bathing, driving at eighty-eight miles an hour on the straightaways, piling up into ditches in the fog, often all blind drunk including the chauffeurs.

It was a life that required more and more stimulants to make it livable. There was alcohol always; there was the acting on sudden impulses; there were drugs—"I mustn't take any more of those opium pills they play hell with one"; there was love taken as a drug—"In the evening gin fizzes color of green and silver and the Sorceress girlish like a young actress feline as a puma she is even more feline and amorous by night and now that we are together would that we might vanish together into sleep and . . ."; then, after the stimulants had produced a state of intolerable tension, there was the need for other drugs to assuage it, for "Passifloreine to make me less nervous."

Always, everywhere, there was jazz; everything that year was enveloped in the hard bright mist of it. There were black orchestras wailing in cafés and *boîtes de nuit,* radios carrying the music of the Savoy ballroom in London, new phonograph records from Harlem and Tin Pan Alley played over and over again, "Organ Grinder," "Empty Bed Blues," "Limehouse Blues," "Vagabond Lover," "Broadway Melody"—"After supper everybody went over to the party at the Château but I stayed and played Vagabond Lover on the graphophone and sat in front of the fire drinking and thinking of fire princesses and sorceresses until I got quite tight (second bottle of champagne) and danced and shouted and branded myself with burning coals from the fire (Fanatic) and at last fell asleep under the zebra skin in the corner by the cider barrel." In the morning there would be more jazz—"We play (taking turns at winding the graphophone) the Broadway Melody from before breakfast till after supper (over a hundred times in all)"; and when the records wore out there were new ones to take their places, new orchestras hot and sweet, jazz omnipresent and always carrying the same message of violent escape toward Mandalay, Michigan, Carolina in the morning, one's childhood, love, a new day. Everywhere was the atmosphere of a long debauch that had to end; the orchestras played too fast, the stakes were too high at the gambling tables, the players were so empty, so tired, secretly hoping to vanish together into sleep and . . . maybe wake on a very distant morning and hear nothing whatever, no shouting or crooning, find all things changed.

Everybody had money that year and was spending it. Harry had money too, but was living far beyond his comfortable income; he was committing what is regarded in Back Bay as the unforgivable sin of drawing against his capital. Already on January 11 he had written his father "to sell $4,000 of stock to make up for certain past extravagances in New York." Again on May 28 he noted, "sold $4,000 of stock enjoy life when you can." And on July 19, "after innumerable sherry cobblers we stopped at the post office and sent the following cable to the family, 'Please sell $10,000 worth of stock—we have decided to lead a mad and extravagant life.'" This time the family, instead of complying, sent him heartbroken cables. He answered in an eloquent letter that "for the poet there is love and there is death and infinity and for other things to assume such vital importance is out of the question and that is why I refuse to take the question of money seriously."

Yet he took the getting and spending of it seriously enough. Eternal and infinite things were being forgotten in the general demoralization of his age, of which Harry was a part, a unit scarcely distinguishable now from the others. Like his friends, he tried to recoup himself at baccarat. Like his friends, he gambled more desperately on the races, no longer able to confine himself to the system he used to follow, of betting a thousand francs on a chosen horse "to win," but instead plunging at random, following hunches, doubling and tripling his bets to make up for his losses and always falling farther behind. Like his friends, too, he visited fortune tellers to inquire about the future that had become more disturbing since he was no longer able to control even his own part in it. But everybody was a fortune teller that year; everybody knew of a stock that was sure to go up. "To the Bank," Harry wrote, "where I saw a racy girl in black to whom I talked (she turned out to be a sort of cousin) and we went to the Ritz for champagne cocktails and before leaving she gave me a tip on the stock exchange (I sent a wire to SVRC)."

Meanwhile it seemed to him that all the time he was growing stronger, was developing himself:

August 10.—*Il faut se développer* . . . and today I advance by destroying statistics. This just as I was getting into the car to go to Deauville I had a gin ginger ale and I ran back and went upstairs and tore up pages of statistics who in hell wants to keep track of the number of drinks he has drunk (it ruins drinking) or the number of cigarettes smoked or the number of cold baths taken or the number of sun-baths or the number of orchids sent or the number of times I have made love. Harra-Bourra statistics are destroyed and now Deauville for the beach for bacardis for baccarat and tonight I won two hundred dollars at cards.

August 11.—How fast the past year has gone the fastest I can remember like a flash of lightning not one vibration of a clock since a year ago and perhaps now I can destroy time as I have destroyed statistics.

Merely by yielding to the madness of his class and age, he produced in himself the illusion of new power. He was like a swimmer who, after battling the current, turns and swims with it in a magnificent burst of speed and vigor, each of his strokes being multiplied three times by the power of the stream, congratulating himself, moving faster, till at last the cataract. As he drew near the edge of it, he once more began thinking about death. But the phrase he had often quoted from Nietzsche, "Die at the right time," was giving way to another maxim. He now wrote:

"The first of October is the day I should like to die on, only not this year. But I must remember what Jolas said, 'that time is a tyranny to be abolished.'" With a knife or a pistol, anywhere. with anyone, he could instantly abolish time.

4: To Die at the Right Time

The rest of his story was told in the New York newspapers of December 11. "Henry Grew Crosby, 32 years old"—the *Times* began with an error, for Harry was really 31, but the rest of its facts were accurate—"of a socially prominent Boston family, and Mrs. Josephine Rotch Bigelow, 22 years old, the wife of Albert S. Bigelow, a postgraduate student at Harvard, were found dead about ten o'clock last night, each with a bullet wound in the head, in the apartment of Crosby's friend, Stanley Mortimer, Jr., a portrait painter, on the ninth floor of the Hotel des Artistes, 1 West 67th Street.

"The couple had died in what Dr. Charles Norris, Medical Examiner, described as a suicide compact (*I should like to have influence strong enough to lead a band of followers into the Sun-Death*). The police believe that Crosby, in whose hand they found a .25 Belgian automatic pistol, had shot Mrs. Bigelow and then turned the weapon on himself. There were no notes and the authorities were unable to obtain information pointing to a motive for the deaths."

According to the *Herald Tribune,* the two of them lay fully clothed in bed (*in the Bed of the Sun*). "Crosby's left arm encircled the woman's neck"—suddenly the Fire Princess had become simply the woman—"and was clasped in her left hand.

They lay facing each other, a blanket drawn up to their shoulders (*Pull over us the gold sheets Dear*)."

"There was a bullet hole in Mrs. Bigelow's left temple and another in Crosby's right temple (*having set fire to the powderhouse of our souls*). His right hand clutched a small-caliber automatic pistol of foreign manufacture (*life ends not with a whimper, but with a Bang—a violent explosion mechanically perfect*)."

The newspapers of the following day added a few more details to the story. But time went on for them if not for Harry, and on the third day his death was not mentioned at all, being crowded out by other news. Stocks had suddenly fallen an average of 4.42 points, the worst break since November 12. In Chicago Charles M. Schwab declared that American business had never before been "so firmly entrenched for prosperity as it is today." And the country, indeed, was still enjoying the aftermath of the boom; department stores were getting ready for their biggest Christmas. There was a civil war in China; there were halfhearted negotiations for reducing the German debt. And Harry Crosby? Back Bay was scandalized but unchanged by his career. E. E. Cummings, whom he so admired, wrote a funny and cryptic poem about the Fire Princess and Harry; he called them

> 2 boston
> Dolls;found
> with
> Holes in each other

's lullaby.

Jack Wheelwright,[3] another Back Bay rebel, wrote a longer

[3] John Brooks Wheelwright, born in 1897, was in the Harvard class of 1920. He published several books of poems that showed an extremely

poem about Harry Crosby and the Wise Men of Boston, setting
one against the others with equal ridicule. By way of tribute
there were a dozen pages in the next issue of *transition,* with
praise and regrets from Crane, MacLeish, Kay Boyle, Jolas and
Stuart Gilbert. That was all. For months and years he wasn't
mentioned any more except in the conversation of those who
had known him intimately. But time went on, more quickly
now, it seemed, and Harry was remembered again by others. His
death, which had seemed an act of isolated and crazy violence,
began to symbolize the decay from within and the suicide of a
whole order with which he had been identified.

Things had changed everywhere. The lost generation had
ceased to deserve its name; the members of it had either gone
under, like Crosby and Crane after him, or else had found their
places in the world. The postwar era had definitely ended and
people were saying that it had given way to another prewar era.
Paris was no longer the center of everything "modern" and aes-
thetically ambitious in American literature. The little exiled
magazines were dead: there was only *transition,* the sturdiest of
the lot, that still appeared sporadically.[4] The little magazines of
the new era were being published in Brooklyn, Beverly Hills,
Chicago, Davenport, Iowa, and Windsor, Vermont. Most of
them were full of class-conscious "proletarian" writing: that was
the new mode.

The exiles and refugees of art were all of them home again.

Though they had fled from machinery, they had continued

---

personal gift of expression; perhaps the best of them was *Rock and Shell*
(1933). He was a devout Episcopalian and also, in the last years of his
life, a member of the Socialist Workers Party. While crossing Massachusetts Avenue in Back Bay he was run down and killed by a drunken
driver on September 15, 1940—three months before Nathanael West was
killed in another accident.

[4] In 1950 it was again revived as *Transition Fifty,* a bilingual magazine
edited in Paris by Georges Duthuit.

to live on the profits of machine production, or else to live on the demand for luxuries of the people who received those profits, which amounted to the same thing. For, when the factory wheels stopped turning, and wages dwindled away, and dividends, after first being raised "to restore confidence," shrank in their turn, the whole tide of middle-class migration turned backward over the Atlantic. Those of brief culture and unsteady fortunes went first, then the richer ones, then the bank clerks and portrait painters and reporters for American newspapers abroad who had depended on the presence of expatriated wealth —then, after the banking crisis of 1933 and the depreciation of the dollar, the stream became a flood: Majorca, Bali, Capri and the Riviera were emptied of Americans. People reappeared in Manhattan who hadn't been there since the days of issues and arguments that everybody had forgotten; even Harold Stearns, the Young Intellectual of 1922, was back in New York.[5] The returning refugees began by talking about things out of the past—how America was lacking in real culture and cursed with puritanism, and how nice it was to sit at a sidewalk table sipping

[5] Stearns had come back for good in 1932. On an earlier visit to this country he had landed in Baltimore and had wired me to meet him at the Pennsylvania Station in New York. My wife didn't think that his return should go uncelebrated, considering the sensation caused by his departure, and she made a big badge for me, a paper sunflower with "Harold Stearns Welcoming Committee" printed across the face of it. The Pennsylvania Station was crowded with radicals meeting a delegation they had sent to Washington; there were all sorts of badges and nobody noticed mine. Stearns didn't notice it either, but then he was never very observant. In the subway—we weren't rich enough for taxis—two women stared at the badge and whispered to each other. After a while I unpinned it shamefacedly and slipped it into my pocket while Stearns went on talking about Paris.

In New York he became a reformed character. He wrote the story of his exile and his rediscovery of America (*The Street I Knew*, 1935) and later he edited a big symposium (*America Now*, 1938) as a companion volume to his famous *Civilization in the United States*. He died in 1943.

one's drink and letting the world glide by—but nobody had time to listen, and soon the exiles, too, were caught up in the new life, were adopting political doctrines and preparing to carry them into action, were perhaps marching in demonstrations of the unemployed.

They had silently abandoned the creed that had guided and sustained them on their long pilgrimage abroad. The religion of art was dead, not only in spirit and inner logic, but this time in practice also. Its saints were either being neglected, or else, like Joyce and Gertrude Stein, they were becoming popular authors, best-sellers in New York, no longer venerated by an esoteric cult. The new young men weren't planning to follow in their footsteps.

In spite of its faults and failures the religion of art had left behind it a rich heritage. It had greatly enlarged the technical resources available to all writers, even to those who were determined to be proletarians or social realists. Poetry would not again be the same as it was before Rimbaud, or fiction what it was before Proust and Joyce. For all artists the religion of art was better than having no religion at all. Even if they were not gifted enough to become saints or prophets of the religion, it furnished them with ideals of workmanship that were, in effect, moral ideals and that gave them a steady purpose in the midst of their dissipations.

On the other hand the religion of art had failed when it tried to become a system of ethics, a way of life. During the 1920s all the extreme courses of action it suggested had been tried once again, and all its paths had been retraced—the way of dream, the way of escape, the ways of adventure, contemplation and deliberate futility had all been followed toward the goal they promised of providing a personal refuge from bourgeois society, an individual paradise. But once more, and this time inescapably, it became evident that all those extreme courses were extreme only as ideals: in life there was always a sequel. The young man who tried to create a vacuum around himself would find in the end that he could not support it. He would find that the real extremes were not those of Axel's lonely castle, or Gauguin's Tahiti, or Van Gogh's fanatical trust in the Sun: they were inertia, demoralization, delusions of persecution and grandeur, alcohol, drugs or suicide. And he would find, too, if he was more observant and less stubborn than Harry Crosby, that even as a theory of writing and painting the religion of art inevitably led into blind alleys. It led to abstract paintings so purified of any human meaning that they were valuable only for their workmanship and appropriate only as decorations, as patches of color and design to brighten a modernique bar; it led to Valéry's conception of art as a leisure-class sport for the benefit of those too sedentary to play polo; it led to the disheartening spectacle of James Joyce spending three days in elaborating a single sentence containing words of Finnish derivation and ending with the word "finish" as a key to future scholars who might or might not be interested in unraveling his meaning—the author of *Ulysses* wasting himself on erudite puns and crossword puzzles. Along this path there was nothing more to be found. The search itself was ending, and a new conception of art was replacing the idea that it was something purposeless, useless, wholly individual and forever opposed to a stupid world. The artist and his art had once more become a part of the world, produced by and perhaps affecting it; they had returned toward their earlier and indispensable task of revealing its values and making it more human.

But the changes in aesthetic ideals and in manners of life were merely the symptoms of a vaster change. Behind the religion of art was the social system that made it possible—the system that encouraged false notions of success and a mistaken form of reaction against them; the system that uprooted artists and workers from their homes, that produced the Wall Street boom and financed the middle-class migration to Europe. Now the system itself was threshing about in convulsions like those of the dying. A financially bankrupt world had entered the age of putsches and purges, of revolutions and counterrevolutions. Harry Crosby, dead, had thus become a symbol of change. It was not so much that he had chosen the moment for suicide as rather that in his disorganized frenzy the moment had chosen him. In spite of himself he had died at the right time.

Epilogue: New Year's Eve

As I read over these chapters written almost twenty years ago, the story they tell seems to follow the old pattern of alienation and reintegration, or departure and return, that is repeated in scores of European myths and continually re-embodied in life. A generation of American writers went out into the world like the children in Grimm's fairy tales who ran away from a cruel stepmother. They wandered for years in search of treasure and then came back like the grown children to dig for it at home. But the story in life was not so simple and lacked the happy ending of fairy tales. Perhaps there was really a treasure and perhaps it had been buried all the time in their father's garden, but the exiles did not find it there. They found only what others were finding: work to do as best they could and families to support and educate. The adventure had ended and once more they were part of the common life.

For most of them the adventure had been divided into four stages. There was the first stage when young writers born at the turn of the century were detached from their native backgrounds and were led to think of themselves as exiles in fact, even when living at home. There was the second stage when they went abroad, many of them with the intention of spending the rest of their lives in Europe. The voyage had an unexpected effect on most of them: it taught them to admire their own country, if only for its picturesque qualities. But they still pre-

ferred to admire it from a distance, and many of the younger
exiles would have agreed with the opinion that Hawthorne
expressed to his publisher in 1858. "To confess the truth," he
said in a letter from Italy, "I had rather be a sojourner in any
other country than return to my own. The United States are
fit for many excellent purposes, but they are certainly not fit
to live in." Yet Hawthorne went home to Concord in 1860,
whether or not it was a fit place for him to live, and the new
generation of exiles came straggling back to New York.

They had entered a third stage of the adventure, one in which
the physical exile had ended while they were still exiles in
spirit. At home they continued to think of themselves as oppressed by the great colorless mass of American society, and
they tried to defend their own standards by living apart from
society, as if on private islands. They were, however, dependent
on American business for their generally modest livelihoods,
and they were willing to leave their islands when they were
invited to spend week-ends with rich friends. In those days
most young writers lived more simply than other college-bred
Americans, because they had less money; but they allowed
themselves to become involved by slow degrees in the frenzy
of the boom years, with the result that they were also involved
in the moral and economic collapse that followed. For some
of them, like Harry Crosby, that was the end of the story.

There was a fourth stage for others, and it was their real
homecoming. Since it took place during the depression it lies
beyond the present narrative, which ends with the 1920s, but
its nature can be suggested in general terms. During the years
when the exiles tried to stand apart from American society
they had pictured it as a unified mass that was moving in a
fixed direction and could not be turned aside by the efforts
of any individual. The picture had to be changed after the
Wall Street crash, for then the mass seemed to hesitate like a

cloud in a cross wind. Instead of being fixed, its direction proved to be the result of a struggle among social groups with different aims and of social forces working against one another. The exiles learned that the struggle would affect everyone's future, including their own. When they took part in it, on one side or another (but usually on the liberal side); when they tried to strengthen some of the forces and allied themselves with one or another of the groups, they ceased to be exiles. They had acquired friends and enemies and purposes in the midst of society, and thus, wherever they lived in America, they had found a home.

That is the pattern of the adventure as we look back at it after twenty years. I think the pattern is true to history so long as it is stated in general terms, but it is less true when applied to individual writers. Not all the persons mentioned in this narrative saw military service during the First World War and not all of them spent their postwar years in Europe. Kenneth Burke, for example, was rejected by the army doctors and worked in a shipyard. In 1922 he bought an abandoned farm in the New Jersey hills and he lives there today; he has never been east of Maine. William Faulkner came home to Oxford, Mississippi, after serving in the Royal Air Force. He was postmaster at Oxford for about two years, then lost the job and went to New Orleans, where he was hired to pilot a cabin cruiser through the bayous with illegal cargoes of alcohol. In the summer of 1925 he took a walking trip through France and Italy. It was his first visit to Europe and would be the last until he won the Nobel Prize in 1950.

Each life has its own pattern, within the pattern of the age, and every individual is an exception. Katherine Anne Porter worked for a newspaper in Denver before she went to Mexico City, where she lived and worked for most of the decade. At no time did she think of herself as being expatriated. Thomas

Wolfe was a shipyard worker, being too young for the army.
He spent two of his postwar years at Harvard, studying the
drama under George Pierce Baker, and then became an in-
structor at Washington Square College. After 1925 he traveled
widely in Europe, but he differed from the other exiles in preferring Germany to France. Before the Nazis took over he felt
more at home in Munich than he did in North Carolina. John
Dos Passos was the greatest traveler in a generation of ambulant
writers. When he appeared in Paris he was always on his way
to Spain or Russia or Istanbul or the Syrian desert. But his
chief point of exception was to be a radical in the 1920s, when
most of his friends were indifferent to politics, and to become
increasingly conservative in the following decade, when many
of his friends were becoming radical. Scott Fitzgerald is always
described as a representative figure of the 1920s, but the point
has to be made that he represented the new generation of
ambitious college men rising in the business world much more
than he did the writers. He earned more money than other
serious writers of his generation, lived far beyond their means
—as well as living beyond his own—and paid a bigger price
in remorse and suffering for his mistakes. Like the others, he
followed his own path through life, and yet when all the paths
are seen from a distance they seem to be interwoven into a
larger pattern of exile (if only in spirit) and return from exile,
of alienation and reintegration.[1]

[1] Ernest Hemingway lived in Cuba until Castro's revolution. But the
novel he published in 1940, *For Whom the Bell Tolls,* was a symbolic
return to society after a spiritual exile that had begun for him in 1918,
with the wound he received in Italy. I thought when revising the present
narrative in 1951 that the only permanent expatriate among the writers
mentioned was Kay Boyle. When she was eighteen years old, in 1921,
Miss Boyle had married a Frenchman in New York. They went to Paris
the following year, and—except during World War II—she would stay
in Europe for the next three decades. In 1953, however, she would return
to this country with her third husband, an Austrian baron.

The last stage of one adventure was, as always, the first stage of another. The new adventure that began with the depression has never been described with the sort of understanding that Fitzgerald showed when writing about the 1920s. He combined intimacy with distance; he seemed to be standing inside and outside the period at the same time; but nobody has displayed the same mixture of qualities when writing about the period that followed. The 1930s are becoming the great unknown era in American history. The public wants to forget them, the politicians distort them and they have not yet been re-created by novelists or historians; yet we cannot form a true picture of the present while trying to abolish the recent past.

The 1930s were the pentecostal years when it seemed that everyone had the gift of tongues and used it to prophesy the millennium. For some reason the economic system had broken down and almost everyone seemed to feel that it could be set in motion again by some entirely simple operation—it was like a motor that had died because the sparkplugs were dirty or because the battery terminals had shaken loose, or perhaps because the carburetor was flooded, in which last case we had only to wait for the gas to drain off and then step on the starter. That was President Hoover's feeling, but others insisted on positive measures, and thousands of mechanics came forward with hundreds of suggested operations—let the currency be changed or the banking system be remodeled, or let the closed factories be reopened by the government, for use not profit, and not only would the engine run again but it would carry us securely into the future.

Then, with the German crisis and the banking crisis in the early months of 1933, the intellectual atmosphere changed again. Thousands were convinced and hundreds of thousands were half-persuaded that no simple operation would save us; there had to be the complete renovation of society that Karl Marx had prophesied in 1848. Unemployment would be ended, war and fascism would vanish from the earth, but only after the revolution. Russia had pointed out the path that the rest of the world must follow into the future. . . . What came next would be a struggle to possess the future and mold it into a predetermined form; there would be a vast crusade that was inspired by generosity and public spirit, then slowly corrupted by individual pride and thirst for power and for influence over the future, always the future—until the army of the future fell apart into bitterly quarreling groups and lonely individuals, and until the Russians, who had helped to inspire the crusade, proved by their alliance with Hitler that they had no interest whatever in the fate of Western liberals. Some day the story will be told in full, but it should wait for calmer years; as long as the hurt bitterness remains it cannot be a true story.

When it is told we shall find that the members of what used to be called the lost generation played only a secondary part in it. Most of the intellectuals who joined the Communist Party during the 1930s, then left it while blaming others for their mistakes—the "generation on trial," as Alistair Cooke described them in his book on the Hiss case—belonged to a somewhat younger group; they were the brilliant college graduates of the years after 1925. That generation was more affected than its elders by the depression and by the lack of opportunities, after the crash, for success achieved by private initiative. Its members were more inclined to attach themselves to thriving institutions that could promise them a step-by-step rise to positions of affluence or honor—not necessarily the highest positions. In general, security was their ideal, rather than glory or independence, and many of them pictured a future in which everyone would be made secure by collective planning and social discipline; that explains the special appeal to them of the Russian experiment. Most of the writers mentioned in this narrative had a different mentality.[2] They had grown up in the confident age before the war and had started their careers in the 1920s, when it was easier to earn a living and "even when you were broke," Fitzgerald said, "you didn't worry about money because it was in such profusion around you." During the depression they continued to think of themselves as able to survive without salary checks, and most of them were refractory to social or political discipline. To use a phrase that was popular at the time, they were rebels rather than revolutionists.

They had always rebelled, if only by running away. First it was against the conventionality of their elders and the gentility of American letters; then it was against the high phrases that justified the slaughter of millions in the First World War; then it was against the philistinism and the scramble for money of the Harding years (although that rebellion took the form of flight). Having returned to this country they rebelled once more, against the illogic of the depression, and this time they found a host of allies; yet very few of the literary rebels were willing to march with others in disciplined ranks. Very few of them followed the current fashion by writing socially conscious poems or proletarian novels. They formed a persistent opposition, a minority never in power and never even united in its opinions, except for a short period during the Spanish civil war; that was the one issue on which they agreed. On other fronts their rebellion was not only individual and unpolitical, in the narrow sense of the word, but also essentially conservative. They didn't look forward, really, to a new collective society based on economic planning and the intelligent use of machines; they were skeptical and afraid of bigness; in their hearts they looked toward the past. Their social ideal, as opposed to their literary ideal, was the more self-dependent, less organized Amer-

[2] As junior editor of a liberal weekly I was more involved in the political movements of the time than were many of the others.

ica they had known in their boyhoods. Dos Passos was speaking for almost all of them when, in the last days of his uneasy alliance with the Communists, he described himself as "just an old-fashioned believer in liberty, equality and fraternity."

The exiles fled to Europe and then came back again. A decade was ending and they didn't come back to quite the same country, nor did they come back as the same men and women.

The country had changed in many ways, for better and worse, but the exiles were most impressed by the changed situation of American literature. In 1920 it had been a provincial literature, dependent on English standards even when it tried to defy them. Foreign countries regarded it as a sort of colonial currency that had to be assigned a value in pounds sterling before it could be accepted on the international exchange. By 1930 it had come to be valued for itself and studied like Spanish or German or Russian literature. There were now professors of American literature at the great European universities. American plays, lowbrow and highbrow, were being applauded in the European capitals. American books were being translated into every European language and they were being read with enthusiasm.

The exiles were still too young in 1930 to be responsible for the change; their effect on the international position of American writing would come in later years. So far as the change was produced by literary efforts, it was the work of an older generation. The literary scene had been dominated for ten years by a group of powerful writers that included Dreiser, Anderson, Mencken, Lewis, O'Neill, Willa Cather and Robert Frost. As a group they had fought against the prevailing convention of gentility or niceness and they had won the right to present each his own picture of life, in his own language. They had spoken with force enough to be heard outside their country, and one of them, Sinclair Lewis, would soon be the first American to win the Nobel Prize for literature. It would, however, be innocent to suppose that this award, with the recognition it implied for Lewis and his colleagues, was purely an honor paid to literary merit. There was also the fact that American literature had come to seem more important because America herself was more important in world affairs. In December 1930, when the Swedish Academy gave Lewis a prize that it hadn't offered to Mark Twain or Henry James, it wasn't really saying that it regarded Lewis as a greater writer; it was chiefly acknowledging that the United States was a more powerful country than it had been in 1910.

The representative quality of Lewis's work was emphasized in a welcoming address by the permanent secretary of the Swedish Academy. "Yes," he said, "Sinclair Lewis is an American. He writes the new language—American—as one of the representatives of a hundred and twenty million souls. He asks us to consider that this nation is not yet finished or melted down; that it is still in the turbulent years of adolescence. The new great American literature has started with national self-criticism. It is a sign of health."

Lewis answered as a spokesman for his generation of American writers. He attacked the genteel tradition that had prevailed in his younger days; he called the roll of his literary colleagues who might have received the prize, beginning with Dreiser and O'Neill; he complained of the artist's lot in American society and he ended by praising the writers of a younger generation —"most of them living now in Paris, most of them a little insane in the tradition of James Joyce, who, however insane they may be, have refused to be genteel and traditional and dull. I salute them," he continued, "with a joy in being not yet too far removed from their determination to give to the America that has mountains and endless prairies, enormous cities and far lost cabins, billions of money and tons of faith, to an America that is as strange as Russia and as complex as China, a literature worthy of her vastness."

Although the exiles were gratified by his praise of their work and liked his truculent generosity, they didn't agree with his statement of their aims. They had never felt the desire to give America "a literature worthy of her vastness." The phrase sounded too much like an invitation to make vast surveys of American geography and the American past. What the exiles wanted to portray was the lives and hearts of individual Americans. They thought that if they could once learn to do this task superlatively well, their work would suggest the larger picture without their making a pretentious effort to present the whole of it. They wanted their writing to be true—that was a word they used over and over—and they wanted its effect to be measured in depth, not in square miles of surface. Moreover, they had an ideal of perfection gained from their study of foreign writers and they wanted to apply the ideal at home. They didn't want to write family sagas or epics of the Northwest, huge as the Chicago Auditorium and with nothing inside but strangers seated on rows of folding chairs. They wanted to build smaller structures, each completely new but with the native quality of New England meeting houses or Pennsylvania barns, each put together with patient pride, each perfectly adapted to the life it sheltered.

The exiles had changed during their years in Europe and especially they had changed their notions of what American literature should be. They had gone abroad in almost total ignorance of everything written in this country before 1910— among the American classics they had read *Huckleberry Finn* and "The Legend of Sleepy Hollow" and perhaps *Moby Dick,* but that was about all. American literature wasn't taught in the colleges, except incidentally, and only the current American books were mentioned in literary discussions. The New England tradition had died of anemia. The few nineteenth-century authors who could be admired were French or English or Russian.

That continued to be the accepted opinion during their years in Europe. The exiles studied French authors: Flaubert, Proust and Gide, Rimbaud and Mallarmé. With more immediate interest they studied Joyce, who was in the tradition of Flaubert, and Eliot, who was in the tradition of the French Symbolist poets. They had more to learn from French than from English masters at the time, and moreover the French influence proved to be safer for young American writers because it was in a different language. If they had studied English authors they would have become at best disciples and at worst copyists. Studying French literature, on the other hand, they had the problem of reproducing its best qualities in another language, and it led them to a difficult and fruitful search for equivalents. The language in which they tried to re-create the French qualities was not literary English but colloquial American. That was among the unexpected effects of their exile: it was in Paris that some of them, notably Ernest Hemingway, worked on the problem of transforming Midwestern speech into a medium for serious fiction. Others worked on the problem of giving a legendary quality to Southern or Midwestern backgrounds. The result of all these labors was a new literature so different from its French models that when the American writers of the lost generation became popular reading in France, as they did before and after World War II, the French spoke of them as powerful, a little barbarous and completely original. The French critics had failed to recognize that these foreigners belonged in part to the tradition of Flaubert.

They had also rejoined an American tradition that was older than Flaubert and that was the most interesting effect of their years abroad. Ignorant of their own literature, starting over as it were from the beginning and using foreign models for their apprentice work, the exiles ended by producing a type of writing that was American in another fashion than anyone had expected. Although critics were slow to find parallels in the American past, it finally became evident that some qualities of the new writing had been encountered before. The careful workmanship, the calculation of effects even when the novelist seemed to be writing in a casual style, the interest in fine shades of behavior (including abnormal behavior), the hauntedness and the gift for telling a headlong story full of violent action—all these qualities had appeared many times in American literature, beginning with Charles Brockden Brown, our first serious novelist, and extending in different combinations through the work of Poe, Hawthorne, Melville, Henry James, Stephen Crane and many minor writers, so that they seemed to express a constant strain in the American character. Here was a tradition that had been broken for a time, but the new novelists had re-established it, and that was perhaps the most important result of their adventure.

One footnote to the adventure is that they were followed westward across the Atlantic by hundreds of European writers. First came the Germans opposed to Hitler (with a few anti-fascist Italians), then the Spanish republicans, then the Austrians, then Jewish writers of many nations, then, after the second war began, scores of Frenchmen and Belgians and Central Europeans who had lost their refuge in France. There was a time when New York was what Paris had been in 1920, the place where every writer wanted to be, the capital of the literary world. Then the war ended, the French and the Belgians went home and many of the radical writers were deported, while new refugees from the Iron Curtain countries arrived to take their places—but once more I am running ahead of the story proper. It has a last chapter still to be told.

The 1920s didn't end with the Wall Street crash or the death of Harry Crosby or the last day of December 1929. The moral atmosphere of the boom continued after the boom had ended and the whole year 1930 belongs to the preceding period.

It was a strange year in the end, but it began like any other. During the spring Wall Street recovered from its fright and many stocks climbed above their 1928 levels, although they slumped again in May and June. Unemployment was increasing rapidly, but that was still a matter of argument and statistics, not of direct personal experience for the middle classes. The big newspaper story was prohibition and the lawlessness growing out of it. After that came other issues like the tariff debate that lasted all spring, the naval conference in London that summer, the visit of Ramsay MacDonald to Mr. Hoover's Rapidan camp and the great drought in the upper South, extending from Maryland into Oklahoma. Newspapers were trying to stop the business decline by banishing it to their inside pages, but even in private conversations it was not yet the principal topic. "After a 3500-mile journey through the Middle West," Bruce Bliven reported in the *New Republic,* "I feel able to report with some confidence for the benefit of other parts of this gr-r-reat country what that important section is thinking about. It is thinking about Midget, alias Tom Thumb, alias Pewee, alias Tiny, golf."

While midget golf courses flourished in every vacant lot and even in empty showrooms vacated by stock-selling outfits, life for the writers of the country went on as usual. It went on as usual for the returned exiles too, since most of them by now had rejoined the American literary community and were following the same customs. In May and June there was the same exodus from the big cities toward all the countrysides where writers and painters gathered—Woodstock, the Cape, the Vineyard, Bucks County and upper Connecticut. All sum-

mer there were the same shipboard parties for rich friends making another trip to Europe—in fact there would be more American tourists in France that year than at any time during the
roaring twenties. In the fall there were the same reunions in
New York and the same round of drinking and dancing parties
and publishers' teas. Liquor was cheaper: in the "cordial shops"
to be found all over Manhattan four bottles of gin with a Gordon
label sold for five dollars, and grain alcohol, 190 proof, was six
or eight dollars a gallon. The punch was stronger at publishers'
teas, but otherwise they were a little less sumptuous, and less
frequent; books weren't selling well and advances against
royalties were harder to get. Nothing else seemed to have
changed.

Yet even in the literary world, which was separate from the
business and political worlds, there were signs that an age was
ending. The 1920s had on the whole been an era of good feeling
among writers. Now suddenly they began to quarrel, not merely
about personal questions but about the meaning of literature and
its relation to life.

In December 1929, a few weeks after the crash, there was
suddenly a fierce discussion about Humanism with a capital
letter—not the classical humanism of sixteenth-century scholars
or the religious humanism of the liberal clergy, but the philosophical and literary doctrines propounded by Professor Irving
Babbitt of Harvard and Professor Paul Elmer More of Princeton. The Humanists issued a symposium; the anti-Humanists
issued another; magazines and newspapers joined in the conflict, with a good deal of sniping on both sides and the thunder
of heavy guns. The battle over Humanism was different in several respects from the guerrilla warfare and banditry of the
1920s. It was on a larger scale, with writers of many groups and
two or three literary generations involved on both sides. The
issues were confused, as might have been expected, but it was

clear enough that they included not only personal and aesthetic
but also moral questions, such as the fashion in which writers
should live and their relationship to society. There were overtones of politics, rising from the fact that most of the Humanists
were conservative while all the radicals were anti-Humanist.
There was the suggestion that the 1920s were a definite period
in literature and life and that their principal efforts might have
been mistaken. Finally there was an unfamiliar note of acerbity
in the discussion. Allen Tate had written an essay against
Humanism in the fall issue of the *Hound and Horn*. In the
January 1930 issue of the *Bookman* one of the Humanists answered him, partly with logic and partly with invective. "Not
hastily or willingly," he accused Tate of "deliberate misrepre-
sentation," of "puerile inconsequence," of impudence that
"could no further go"; and he ended unsmilingly by calling him
"a mere talking mole! . . . A fellow so utterly nothing as he
knows not what he would be." Such language had seldom been
used in the late 1920s, but within two or three years it would
seem restrained, in the midst of fiercer epithets.

The *New Republic* printed a book review that started a violent
discussion: "Wilder: Prophet of the Genteel Christ," by Michael
Gold. It was an attack on Thornton Wilder for having been a
parlor Christian and for having escaped in his books from the
contemporary world. "Where are the modern streets of New
York, Chicago and New Orleans in these little novels?" Gold
asked. "Where are the cotton mills, and the murder of Ella May
and her songs? Where are the child slaves of the beet fields?
Where are the stockbroker suicides, the labor racketeers or the
passion and death of the coal miners?" Although Wilder had
offered himself as a spiritual teacher he had done nothing, Gold
said, to help the spirit trapped in American capitalism; instead
he had become the poet "of a small sophisticated class that has
recently arisen in America—our genteel bourgeoisie. . . . Tak-

ing them patiently by the hand, he leads them into castles, palaces and far-off Greek islands, where they may study the human heart when it is nourished by blue blood. This Emily Post of culture will never reproach them; or remind them of Pittsburgh and the breadlines."

This judgment in terms of social classes and this demand that novels should portray the social struggles of their times, with villainous bosses set against heroic workingmen, would be many times repeated in the critical writing of the next few years. Even in 1930 they were familiar doctrines to the readers of a few radical magazines; but they were strange to the liberal audience of the *New Republic*. Gold's review was the occasion for scores and then hundreds of letters to the editor, some carefully reasoned, some violent and almost hysterical. At first all the letters defended the novelist and attacked the reviewer. The burden of them was that reviewers should confine themselves to the style and pattern of a book, taking its subject matter for granted. Said one correspondent, "I have been taught, erroneously, no doubt, that the final test of any piece of writing is the manner in which the material is presented, not the material itself." Said another, roused to fury, "It is scurrilous, profane, dirty. . . . I heartily resent, as do many of my liberal friends, this attack on a man who we consider has done lovely things and who we believe is endowed with a very lovely nature." The effect of letters like these was the opposite of what their writers intended and soon most of the correspondents were half-agreeing with Gold. He had ridiculously overstated his case; he had failed to see that Wilder was a serious writer preoccupied with moral problems and that they were our own problems, even though Wilder's characters were disguised in Peruvian or Greek costumes; yet he had correctly diagnosed the weakness of Wilder's readers while missing the virtues of the author, and he had expressed a mood that was growing as the situation of the country became more desperate. Literature for the next few years would be asked to deal in one way or another with the problems of the day.

There were other signs of change in the literary world, although it would be hard to suggest them by quotations or reduce them to statistics. As I look back on the year 1930 it seems to me that there were never so many shifts in the personal relations of people one knew well or faintly or by reputation. Marriages that had endured all through the 1920s, though both partners had been indifferent to each other and in some cases notoriously unfaithful, now ended in sudden quarrels and separations. Old love affairs ended that had seemed as respectable as marriages. Friendships were broken off. People could no longer endure the little hypocrisies that had kept their relations stable; they had to set everything straight, like a man preparing for death. There seemed to be more drinking than before, in literary and in business circles; at least it was noisier and more public. It appeared to be a different sort of drinking, with more desperation in the mood behind it. People no longer drank to have a good time or as an excuse for doing silly and amusing things that they could talk about afterward; they drank from habit, or to get away from boredom, or because they had a physiological need for alcohol. There was as much horseplay and laughter as before, but it seemed strained and even hysterical. Every crowd or set had its young man who used to be so entertaining after the third cocktail but now you couldn't tell what he would do. "Just when somebody's taken him up and is making a big fuss over him," Fitzgerald wrote about one of the fictional heroes he identified with himself, "he pours the soup down his hostess's back, kisses the serving maid and passes out in the dog kennel. But he's done it too often. He's run through about everybody."

In New York the year was one of nervous breakdowns; the psychiatrists were busy when every other profession except that of social service was losing its clients. One friend who was being psychoanalyzed told me that the doctor's office was crowded with people he knew; it was like a publisher's tea. Many of the letters one received would be dated from sanitariums in Pennsylvania or Massachusetts. It was a year of suicides, not only among stockbrokers but also among wealthy dilettantes. It was a year when faces looked white and nervous; a year of insomnia and sleeping tablets. It was a year when classmates and former friends became involved in speakeasy brawls, divorces, defalcations and even murders; the underworld and the upper world were close to each other. Most of all it was a year when a new mood became perceptible, a mood of doubt and even defeat. People began to wonder whether it wasn't possible that not only their ideas but their whole lives had been set in the wrong direction.

By autumn the breadlines in more than one American city had spread from back streets into the business section. The Communists were demanding relief for the unemployed and the police were smashing their demonstrations; everywhere one heard stories of bystanders, perfectly nice people, who were kicked or clubbed because they weren't wearing hats and hence were mistaken for radicals. The National Apple Sellers' Association had thought of a new way to get rid of its surplus, by selling it to the unemployed on credit at wholesale prices. When the weather turned colder there were men without overcoats shivering on every street corner, not only selling apples but also, in effect, crying out to passers-by that they were penniless, willing to work and could find no jobs. The rich merchants had become disturbed; they were organizing charity drives and in a few cases were permitting the homeless to take shelter in their great empty warehouses.

Stocks were falling again, after having risen during the summer. This time their decline was "orderly," but that made the situation no less dangerous for the corporations that had borrowed money against them and the banks that held them as security. Caldwell and Company, of Nashville, went bankrupt on November 14. It was one of the largest investment houses in the South, with dozens of affiliates, and its failure caused the closing of banks in half a dozen states. Soon afterward Bankers Trust, of Philadelphia, closed its doors and those of its twenty-one branches. When the Bank of United States went under, on December 11, it was described by the *New York Times* as "the largest bank in the United States ever to suspend payments"; it had fifty-nine branches and more than four hundred thousand depositors. People began to fear that the whole structure of American finance would crash to the ground.

Meanwhile the round of parties continued, and those given to celebrate the New Year's Eve of 1930–31 were the biggest and noisiest of all. There were so many parties that people got invitations to six or eight of them and accepted all the invitations and went instead to parties to which they hadn't been asked. They traveled about the city in caravans of taxicabs, then irrupted into a strange apartment in a mass attack of rainbow silks and uniform white shirt fronts. For an hour, for an age (time is a tyranny to be abolished), every corner of the apartment was filled with screeches and guffaws. When the hostess ran out of glasses, drinks were passed round in paper cups that leaked on the table tops. "The market will turn up in April—first industrials, then rails," a man insisted to the lacquered woman he was holding by both her bare shoulders while he looked deep into her eyes. Somebody was locked in the bathroom and somebody else was hammering at the bathroom door. In the hall bedroom a girl with an innocent and compassionate air was explaining to her lover why she had left him.

"I truly love Harry," she said, "and it doesn't matter if he loves his wife better than me, I'm going to live with him until he sends for her." . . . "Maybe it's my job to make time with his wife," the deserted lover said. Back in the living room the punch bowl was empty except for cigarette stubs floating in a pint of pinkish liquid smelling of raw alcohol. The women had gone into a bedroom and were shrieking as they tried to pull their coats from under a girl who had passed out on the bed. "Does anyone know who brought her?" a sober woman asked. Suddenly the crowd was gone, trumpeting down the stairs, while the host and hostess were left behind to care for the girl and mop spilled drinks from the floor—or perhaps they forgot the stranger in their bedroom and, with the last departing guests, piled into taxicabs that joined the caravan. Curious things happened that night, quarrels of principle and declarations of faith that people heard in the confusion and remembered long afterward. I was most impressed by the story of a friend who told me that after four successive parties he found himself dancing in a subcellar joint in Harlem. The room was smoky and sweaty; all the lights were tinted green or red and, with smoke drifting across them, nothing had its proper shape or color; it was as if he were caught there and condemned to live in somebody's vision of Hell. When he came out on the street, he said, it was bathed in harsh winter sunlight, ugly and clear and somehow reassuring. An ash-colored woman was hunting for scraps in a garbage can.

That was the way a decade came to its end.

It was a better age for writers than I have made it seem—more serious, harder working, more soulful in its dissipations, and above all more fruitful. By choosing for emphasis some of its more picturesque episodes and characters I have given a partly distorted impression. By using books chiefly as texts I have done less than justice to many of the fine novels and poems that the age produced. It was an easy, quick, adventurous age, good to be young in; and yet on coming out of it one felt a sense of relief, as on coming out of a room too full of talk and people into the sunlight of the winter streets.

Clarksville, Tennessee, April 1933.

Sherman, Connecticut, March 1951.

Appendix: Years of Birth

This is a list of writers born in the fifteen years from 1891 to 1905, inclusive, grouped by their years of birth. There are no critical judgments intended either by the inclusions or by the omissions. I started by listing all the American writers in the given age group who were sufficiently prominent in 1942 to have their biographies included in that curious and useful book, *Twentieth Century Authors* (edited by Stanley J. Kunitz and Howard Haycraft). Then I added a few additional names, if I could find the years of birth in *Who's Who* or elsewhere: first, those of writers in the age group who had become prominent after 1942 (I must have missed some of them), and second, those of writers whose names were mentioned in my own narrative. Then, finding that the list had become too long and feeling that it was getting too far from literature proper, I omitted certain categories of authors: Western writers, mystery writers (except Dashiell Hammett, who had an effect on narrative technique; Raymond Chandler had one too, but was born before 1890), popular romancers, one-book authors (unless the book was famous), scholars and scientists (except those like Crane Brinton and Margaret Mead who also write for the public), children's authors and writers on public affairs (except those who are also novelists or critics). Even in its shortened form the list seems to me a pretty impressive record of literary activity.

1891

Herbert Asbury, popular historian
Margaret Culkin Banning, novelist
Lewis Gannett, critic
Maurice Hindus, novelist, reporter
Sidney Howard, playwright
Marquis James, biographer

Lloyd Lewis, biographer
Percy Marks, novelist
Henry Miller, novelist, essayist
Elliot Paul, novelist
Lyle Saxon, regional writer
Harold Stearns, essayist

1892

Djuna Barnes, novelist
John Peale Bishop, poet, critic
Bessie Breuer, novelist

Pearl Buck, novelist
James M. Cain, novelist
Robert P. Tristram Coffin, poet

1892 (cont'd)

Ward Greene, novelist
Will James, regional writer
Harold Lamb, historian
R. S. Lynd, sociologist
Archibald MacLeish, poet
Edna St. Vincent Millay, poet

Reinhold Niebuhr, theologian
Burton Rascoe, critic
Elmer Rice, playwright
James Stevens, regional writer
Ruth Suckow, novelist
Frank Sullivan, humorist

1893

S. N. Behrman, playwright
Morris Bishop, humorist
Maxwell Bodenheim, poet
Carl Carmer, regional writer
Elizabeth J. Coatsworth, poet
Russel Crouse, dramatist
S. Foster Damon, critic, poet
Donald Davidson, poet
Mathilde Eiker, novelist
Irving Fineman, novelist
Herbert Gorman, novelist
Ben Hecht, novelist, playwright
Joseph Wood Krutch, essayist

Anita Loos, humorist
William March (William Edward
  March Campbell), novelist
John P. Marquand, novelist
Lloyd Morris, critic, historian
Dorothy Parker, story writer, poet
Cole Porter, song writer
Evelyn Scott, novelist
Gilbert Seldes, critic
Thorne Smith, novelist
Hudson Strode, traveler, teacher
John W. Thomason, biographer, sol-
  dier

John V. A. Weaver, poet

1894

Brooks Atkinson, critic
John Bakeless, biographer
E. E. Cummings, poet
Clyde Brion Davis, novelist
Rachel Lyman Field, novelist
Esther Forbes, novelist
Michael Gold, novelist, columnist
Paul Green, playwright
Dashiell Hammett, novelist
Raymond Holden, poet
Rolfe Humphries, poet
Joseph Henry Jackson, critic
Eugene Jolas, poet, editor

Robert Nathan, novelist
Kenyon Nicholson, playwright
Jessica Nelson North, poet
Katherine Anne Porter, novelist
Phelps Putnam, poet
Samuel Rogers, novelist
George N. Shuster, critic, educator
Chard Powers Smith, novelist
Laurence Stallings, playwright
Donald Ogden Stewart, humorist
Genevieve Taggard, poet
James Thurber, humorist
Mark Van Doren, poet, critic

Thames Williamson, novelist

1895

Ben Lucien Burman, novelist
Babette Deutsch, poet
Vardis Fisher, novelist
Rose D. Franken, playwright
Caroline Gordon, novelist
Oscar Hammerstein, 2d, librettist
Robert Hillyer, poet

John Howard Lawson, playwright
Lin Yu-t'ang (China), essayist
Lewis Mumford, essayist
Leonard Nason, novelist
George R. Stewart, novelist
Hans Otto Storm, novelist
Nora Waln, novelist

Edmund Wilson, critic, man of letters

1896

Philip Barry, playwright
Roark Bradford, story writer
Louis Bromfield, novelist
Slater Brown, novelist
Kyle S. Crichton, humorist
H. L. Davis, novelist, poet
John Dos Passos, novelist, historian
Irwin Edman, essayist

F. Scott Fitzgerald, novelist
Ramon Guthrie, novelist, poet
Gorham B. Munson, critic
Marjorie Kinnan Rawlings, novelist
Isidor Schneider, poet, novelist
Robert E. Sherwood, dramatist
Grace Zaring Stone, novelist
Virgil Thomson, critic

1897

Herbert Agar, essayist
Joseph Auslander, poet
Louise Bogan, poet
Catherine Drinker Bowen, biographer
Kenneth Burke, essayist
Robert M. Coates, novelist
Bernard DeVoto, critic, novelist
William Faulkner, novelist
Joseph Freeman, novelist
Virgil Geddes, playwright
Josephine Herbst, novelist

Christopher La Farge, novelist, poet
Josephine Lawrence, novelist
Eugene Lohrke, novelist
Van Wyck Mason, novelist
Houston Peterson, critic
Dawn Powell, novelist
Henry F. Pringle, biographer
Lillian Smith, novelist
John Brooks Wheelwright, poet
M. R. Werner, biographer
Thornton Wilder, novelist, playwright

1898

Ludwig Bemelmans (Austria), novelist
Stephen Vincent Benét, poet, novelist
Thomas Boyd, novelist
Crane Brinton, historian
Malcolm Cowley, critic, poet

Eleanor Carroll Chilton, novelist
Henry Grew Crosby, poet
Horace Gregory, poet, critic
Harlan Hatcher, novelist, critic
Donald Culross Peattie, nature writer
Edward A. Weeks, Jr., critic, editor

1899

Léonie Adams, poet
Archie Binns, novelist
Whit Burnett, story writer, editor
W. R. Burnett, novelist
LeGrand Cannon, novelist
Bruce Catton, historian
Humphrey Cobb, novelist
Hart Crane, poet
James Gray, novelist, critic

Anne Green, novelist
Ernest Hemingway, novelist
Matthew Josephson, biographer
Janet Lewis, novelist, poet
Walter Millis, historian
Lynn Riggs, playwright
Vincent Sheean, personal historian
Phil Stong, novelist
Allen Tate, poet, critic

E. B. White, essayist, poet

1900

Newton Arvin, critic
Emjo Basshe, playwright
Myron Brinig, novelist
John Mason Brown, critic

V. F. Calverton, critic
Cyril Hume, novelist
Margaret Mitchell, novelist
Ernie Pyle, reporter

1901

John Gunther, reporter   Margaret Mead, anthropologist
Granville Hicks, critic   Laura Riding, poet
Oliver La Farge, novelist   Mari Sandoz, novelist, biographer
                    Glenway Wescott, novelist

1902

Nathan Asch, novelist   Corliss Lamont, essayist
Katharine Brush, novelist   Max Lerner, essayist
Kenneth Fearing, poet   Andrew Nelson Lytle, novelist
Wolcott Gibbs, critic, playwright   F. O. Matthiessen, critic
C. Hartley Grattan, essayist   Ogden Nash, poet
Sidney Hook, essayist   John Steinbeck, novelist
Langston Hughes, poet   Philip Wylie, novelist, essayist
                    Marya Zaturenska, poet

1903

Kay Boyle, novelist   Dudley Fitts, poet
Erskine Caldwell, novelist   Paul Horgan, novelist
John Chamberlain, critic   Zora Neale Hurston, novelist
Paul Corey, novelist   Younghill Kang (Korea), novelist
James Gould Cozzens, novelist   Alexander Laing, novelist
Countee Cullen, poet   Irving Stone, biographer, novelist
Walter D. Edmonds, novelist   Leane Zugsmith, novelist

1904

Hamilton Basso, novelist   Moss Hart, playwright
Richard P. Blackmur, critic, poet   Bravig Imbs, novelist
Gladys Hasty Carroll, novelist   MacKinlay Kantor, novelist
Clifford Dowdey, novelist   Louis Kronenberger, critic
Clifton Fadiman, critic   Vincent McHugh, novelist
James T. Farrell, novelist   S. J. Perelman, humorist
Francis Fergusson, critic   Charles Allen Smart, novelist
Albert Halper, novelist   Nathanael West, novelist

1905

David Cornel De Jong, novelist   Meyer Levin, novelist
Viña Delmar, novelist   Phyllis McGinley, poet
Leonard Ehrlich, novelist   John O'Hara, novelist
Charles G. Finney, novelist   Lionel Trilling, critic, novelist
Lillian Hellman, playwright   Dalton Trumbo, novelist
                    Robert Penn Warren, novelist, poet

The list of 236 names includes those of writers in many fields from
the frivolous to the solemn and from musical comedy (Cole Porter,

Oscar Hammerstein, 2d) to prophecy (Lewis Mumford), philosophy (Kenneth Burke), and theology (Reinhold Niebuhr). But the 107 writers who are primarily novelists outnumber all the other categories, and among them are most of the very familiar names. The emphasis on fiction seems even stronger when we observe that many other writers in the list—most of the poets (36) and a good proportion of the critics (27), the essayists (12), and the biographers (9)—have each written one or two novels. Fiction was by far the most popular medium in the years when these writers came forward, and many an idea that might have been embodied in an essay, a drama, a long poem, or even a short one, was inflated into a novel. The situation changed in later years. A list of writers born after 1905 would include many more critics proportionately, and I used to hear it argued that criticism was the central medium of the 1950s, just as the drama was central in Elizabethan England.

There are comparatively few women in the list: only 44 by my count as against 187 men. Some of the women are greatly talented, but only one of them—Katherine Anne Porter—has had as much praise or critical attention as half a dozen men of the same age have each received. I think we should find a different situation if we listed the American writers born between 1860 and 1890 or those born after 1905; both groups, but especially the second, would contain a higher proportion of women. The lesson would seem to be that women born at the turn of the century not only had less chance than men to develop their talents—a familiar complaint—but also that they were less challenged by the events described in this book. Not many of them served in the Great War, which was fought without the help of Wacs or Waves. After the war, not so many women as men had the opportunity of living in France as exiles of the arts.

Year of birth has more than its usual importance in the case of American writers born between 1891 and 1905. They grew up at a time when the literary atmosphere of the country was changing rapidly, with the result that each age group was likely to form its own ideals of what a good novel or poem should be. As examples of the difference between age groups, compare the work of Scott Fitzgerald, William Faulkner or Ernest Hemingway, all born between 1896 and 1899, with that of Pearl Buck (1892) or John P. Marquand (1893); or again compare it with the work of younger men like John Steinbeck (1902) or James T. Farrell (1904). The lost generation, so called, was composed of writers most of whom were born between 1894 and 1900, though it also included a few slightly older and

slightly younger writers who lived for a time in Europe. The story of
exile and return doesn't apply to some gifted authors of the same age
who never accepted the European influence and, in a sense, never left
home.

Persons and Books: A Brief Index

FOR THE BEST IN PAPERBACKS, LOOK FOR THE

In every corner of the world, on every subject under the sun, Penguin represents quality and variety—the very best in publishing today.

For complete information about books available from Penguin—including Pelicans, Puffins, Peregrines, and Penguin Classics—and how to order them, write to us at the appropriate address below. Please note that for copyright reasons the selection of books varies from country to country.

In the United Kingdom: For a complete list of books available from Penguin in the U.K., please write to *Dept E.P., Penguin Books Ltd, Harmondsworth, Middlesex, UB7 0DA.*

In the United States: For a complete list of books available from Penguin in the U.S., please write to *Consumer Sales, Penguin USA, P.O. Box 999— Dept. 17109, Bergenfield, New Jersey 07621-0120.* VISA and MasterCard holders call 1-800-253-6476 to order all Penguin titles.

In Canada: For a complete list of books available from Penguin in Canada, please write to *Penguin Books Canada Ltd, 10 Alcorn Avenue, Suite 300, Toronto, Ontario, Canada M4V 3B2.*

In Australia: For a complete list of books available from Penguin in Australia, please write to the *Marketing Department, Penguin Books Ltd, P.O. Box 257, Ringwood, Victoria 3134.*

In New Zealand: For a complete list of books available from Penguin in New Zealand, please write to the *Marketing Department, Penguin Books (NZ) Ltd, Private Bag, Takapuna, Auckland 9.*

In India: For a complete list of books available from Penguin, please write to *Penguin Overseas Ltd, 706 Eros Apartments, 56 Nehru Place, New Delhi, 110019.*

In Holland: For a complete list of books available from Penguin in Holland, please write to *Penguin Books Nederland B.V., Postbus 195, NL-1380AD Weesp, Netherlands.*

In Germany: For a complete list of books available from Penguin, please write to *Penguin Books Ltd, Friedrichstrasse 10-12, D-6000 Frankfurt Main I, Federal Republic of Germany.*

In Spain: For a complete list of books available from Penguin in Spain, please write to *Longman, Penguin España, Calle San Nicolas 15, E-28013 Madrid, Spain.*

In Japan: For a complete list of books available from Penguin in Japan, please write to *Longman Penguin Japan Co Ltd, Yamaguchi Building, 2-12-9 Kanda Jimbocho, Chiyoda-Ku, Tokyo 101, Japan.*

FOR THE BEST IN LITERARY CRITICISM, LOOK FOR THE

☐ **THE MORONIC INFERNO**
And Other Visits to America
Martin Amis

With mixed feelings of wonder and trepidation, British writer Martin Amis examines America in an insightful, thoroughly stimulating collection of pieces.

"As surefooted in its march across cultural boundaries as it is enviably, infuriatingly fluent"—*The Boston Globe*
208 pages   ISBN: 0-14-009647-7

☐ **THE WRITER'S QUOTATION BOOK** (Revised Edition)
A Literary Companion
Edited by James Charlton

Updated to include more than 400 witticisms, confessions, opinions, and observations, this charming compendium covers every aspect of books and the writing life.

"Full of sparkle and wit"—*Cleveland Plain Dealer*
108 pages   ISBN: 0-14-008970-5

☐ **WRITERS AT WORK**
The *Paris Review* Interviews: Seventh Series
Edited by George Plimpton

As John Updike writes in the introduction to this volume, these interviews of Milan Kundera, John Barth, Eugene Ionesco, and ten others, are "testimonials to the intrinsic worth and beauty of the writers' activity."

"Even 300 years from now these conversations will be invaluable to students of 20th-century literature."—*Time*
332 pages   ISBN: 0-14-008500-9

FOR THE BEST LITERATURE, LOOK FOR THE

☐ THE BOOK AND THE BROTHERHOOD
Iris Murdoch

Many years ago Gerard Hernshaw and his friends banded together to finance a political and philosophical book by a monomaniacal Marxist genius. Now opinions have changed, and support for the book comes at the price of moral indignation; the resulting disagreements lead to passion, hatred, a duel, murder, and a suicide pact.　　　　　　　*602 pages*　　*ISBN: 0-14-010470-4*

☐ GRAVITY'S RAINBOW
Thomas Pynchon

Thomas Pynchon's classic antihero is Tyrone Slothrop, an American lieutenant in London whose body anticipates German rocket launchings. Surely one of the most important works of fiction produced in the twentieth century, *Gravity's Rainbow* is a complex and awesome novel in the great tradition of James Joyce's *Ulysses*.　　　　　　　*768 pages*　　*ISBN: 0-14-010661-8*

☐ FIFTH BUSINESS
Robertson Davies

The first novel in the celebrated "Deptford Trilogy," which also includes *The Manticore* and *World of Wonders*, *Fifth Business* stands alone as the story of a rational man who discovers that the marvelous is only another aspect of the real.　　　　　　　*266 pages*　　*ISBN: 0-14-004387-X*

☐ WHITE NOISE
Don DeLillo

Jack Gladney, a professor of Hitler Studies in Middle America, and his fourth wife, Babette, navigate the usual rocky passages of family life in the television age. Then, their lives are threatened by an "airborne toxic event"—a more urgent and menacing version of the "white noise" of transmissions that typically engulfs them.　　　　　　　*326 pages*　　*ISBN: 0-14-007702-2*

You can find all these books at your local bookstore, or use this handy coupon for ordering:

Penguin Books By Mail
Dept. BA Box 999
Bergenfield, NJ 07621-0999

Please send me the above title(s). I am enclosing _____ (please add sales tax if appropriate and $1.50 to cover postage and handling). Send check or money order—no CODs. Please allow four weeks for shipping. We cannot ship to post office boxes or addresses outside the USA. *Prices subject to change without notice.*

Ms./Mrs./Mr. _____

Address _____

City/State _____ Zip _____

☐ **A SPORT OF NATURE**
Nadine Gordimer

Hillela, Nadine Gordimer's "sport of nature," is seductive and intuitively gifted at life. Casting herself adrift from her family at seventeen, she lives among political exiles on an East African beach, marries a black revolutionary, and ultimately plays a heroic role in the overthrow of apartheid.

354 pages ISBN: 0-14-008470-3

☐ **THE COUNTERLIFE**
Philip Roth

By far Philip Roth's most radical work of fiction, *The Counterlife* is a book of conflicting perspectives and points of view about people living out dreams of renewal and escape. Illuminating these lives is the skeptical, enveloping intelligence of the novelist Nathan Zuckerman, who calculates the price and examines the results of his characters' struggles for a change of personal fortune.

372 pages ISBN: 0-14-009769-4

☐ **THE MONKEY'S WRENCH**
Primo Levi

Through the mesmerizing tales told by two characters—one, a construction worker/philosopher who has built towers and bridges in India and Alaska; the other, a writer/chemist, rigger of words and molecules—Primo Levi celebrates the joys of work and the art of storytelling.

174 pages ISBN: 0-14-010357-0

☐ **IRONWEED**
William Kennedy

"Riding up the winding road of Saint Agnes Cemetery in the back of the rattling old truck, Francis Phelan became aware that the dead, even more than the living, settled down in neighborhoods." So begins William Kennedy's Pulitzer-Prize winning novel about an ex-ballplayer, part-time gravedigger, and full-time drunk, whose return to the haunts of his youth arouses the ghosts of his past and present. 228 pages ISBN: 0-14-007020-6

☐ **THE COMEDIANS**
Graham Greene

Set in Haiti under Duvalier's dictatorship, *The Comedians* is a story about the committed and the uncommitted. Actors with no control over their destiny, they play their parts in the foreground; experience love affairs rather than love; have enthusiasms but not faith; and if they die, they die like Mr. Jones, by accident.

288 pages ISBN: 0-14-002766-1